A Field Guide for Managers

Bringing Out the Best in People

A comprehensive collection of usable, practical exercises, meeting formats, tools and techniques.

By Deni Lyall

Published by Motivational Press, Inc.
1777 Aurora Road
Melbourne, Florida, 32935
www.MotivationalPress.com

Copyright 2018 © by Deni Lyall

All Rights Reserved

No part of this book may be reproduced or transmitted in any form by any means: graphic, electronic, or mechanical, including photocopying, recording, taping or by any information storage or retrieval system without permission, in writing, from the authors, except for the inclusion of brief quotations in a review, article, book, or academic paper. The authors and publisher of this book and the associated materials have used their best efforts in preparing this material. The authors and publisher make no representations or warranties with respect to accuracy, applicability, fitness or completeness of the contents of this material. They disclaim any warranties expressed or implied, merchantability, or fitness for any particular purpose. The authors and publisher shall in no event be held liable for any loss or other damages, including but not limited to special, incidental, consequential, or other damages. If you have any questions or concerns, the advice of a competent professional should be sought.

Manufactured in the United States of America.

ISBN: 978-1-62865-451-6

Contents

About This Book.....5
Acknowledgements.....7

MINDSETS THAT ENGENDER TRUST AND OPENNESS.....9
Getting Past Your Judgment When it is Hindering You.....10
1. Understanding Their Perspective.....11
2. What is Driving Their Behaviour?.....24
3. People and Their Differences.....28

Aligning Your Team.....38
4. Creating Meaningful Work and Sense of Community.....39
5. What Makes You and Your Team Members Proud?.....44
6. What is the Added Value Your Team Delivers?.....47
7. A Mindset of Accountability.....49

Inspiring People.....54
8. Making People Feel Stronger.....55
9. How You Train People Through Your Actions.....58
10. Handling Negativity.....64

CAPABILITIES FOR CONNECTING WITH PEOPLE.....68
Questioning for Robustness.....69
11. Questions That Invite Others to Contribute.....71
12. Questions to Help Overcome Unhelpful Perceptions and Thinking.....77
13. Questions That Create a Step Change in Thinking.....90

Listening Productively.....98
14. Holding Eye Contact and Silences.....99
15. Listening With Your Eyes, Ears and Intuition.....102
16. Listening That Invites Others to Contribute.....107

Language That is Influential.....112
17. Productive Language.....113
18. But, And, Although and Others.....117
19. Reframing Perceptions.....120
20. Using Analogies and Stories.....124

Feedback That Develops People.....127
21. Giving Praise.....129
22. Reinforcing What You Want More Of.....131
23. Developing Through Feedback.....134

Maintaining Your Composure.....137
24. Maintaining a Positive Outlook When Life Knocks You.....138
25. Detaching to Get Things in Perspective.....146
26. Being Your Own Best Friend.....149

Building Enduring Relationships..152
27. Building Rapport 153
28. Looking at the Situation From Different Perspectives 164
29. Designing a Conversation to Influence 167
30. Giving Someone the Benefit of the Doubt 172

APPLICATIONS TO ENGAGE PEOPLE 176
My Part as a Manager 178
31. Adding Value as a Leader 179
32. Time for Your People 185
33. Delegating and Holding Others Accountable 189
34. Communicating to Your Team 198
Participative Meetings to Create Ownership and Motivation 201
35. Basic Meeting Outcomes, Structure and Tips 202
36. Monthly Team Meetings 210
37. Basic Kick-Off Meetings 217
38. Basic Review Meetings 221
Building Teams 224
39. The Yearly People Cycle 226
40. Team Deliverables for the Year 234
41. How Well are We Working Together as a Team? 252
42. Implementing a Team Appraisal Approach 260
Developing Individuals 265
43. Inductions That Build a Good Foundation for Work 266
44. Personal Development Plans (PDP) That Add Value 271
45. Having Difficult Conversations 287
46. Taking Individuals Through Change 299
Getting Your Team to Improve its Own Work 308
47. Making it Easy to Understand What Work is or is not Being Completed   309
48. Little and Often Improvements 318
Connecting With Others to Enable Your Team's Work to Happen 324
49. Developing Appropriate Inter-Team Relationships 325
50. Analysing Required Business Relationships 328
51. Internal Networking to Improve Your Team's Work 333
52. External Networking to Improve Your Team's Work 338

References..345
Index 346

About This Book

This book is predominately for people managing others either as a line manager, a team leader or a project manager. HR and L&D people may find that it is a useful book to work through with Line Managers to help develop the manager's abilities in leading people. If you need to engage people in activities, then there will be useful elements for you as well.

This book is about engaging with capable people so that they will chose to participate to the full extent of their ability, to deliver something that is mutually important to both them and the organisation. They will do this for managers and leaders who create and maintain an environment that enables this to happen. Overall, this book is about bringing out the best in people through the attitudes and intentions you adopt together with the skills and abilities you practice by using tools and techniques, which facilitate involving people fully within their work. The improved business results will follow.

This book has three parts

Part I 'Mindsets That Engender Trust and Openness' is about developing a mindset that allows the application of the skills and tools to be authentic and truly enable the results you wish for. People invariably 'understand or get' your intention and Part I will help you to develop an intention that engenders trust and openness. In turn, this will help increase the commitment of others to deliver the required outcome and results.

Part II 'Capabilities for Connecting With People' contains various skills, which require practice, so that you find your own style and competency with them. My son has just received his AS results and is very pleased with them. He is a capable young man and the valuable lesson he learned today is that effort (practice and application) gets results: It builds on what you are capable of and gives you the best chance to shine through. Parts II and III rely on this principle.

Part III 'Applications to Engage People' contains various pragmatic and effective tools and techniques, which when coupled with Parts I and II, give you the ability to deliver a step change in participation, engagement and outcomes from those commonly achieved in many businesses at the moment. Part III is about managing people as people rather than another as set of tasks to be worked through.

Parts I, II and III together enable you and the people you work with to feel proud about, and satisfied by, the work that they, and you, do and the results achieved. Everyone benefits - they do, you do and the organisation does. However, there is no 'magic pill' or short cut to achieving these outcomes. Practice is the way to build up capability. In fact, Neuroscience is demonstrating this to us with more and more clarity: Brain plasticity is amazing although the brain prefers to do as it has always done, it's simply easier and takes less energy. Therefore, a concerted effort and an enthusiasm to change is required along with practice. I have found that the material in this book delivers both time savings and the satisfaction of doing meaningful work that really gets results.

Using this book

My intention is to give you an informative read and practical methods that you can take, experiment with and make your own. I have designed the book to help address a need you may have. So when you think "How do I ...", go to the 'Contents in Detail' pages and find the chapter(s) which will help you. You can also use this book to develop your leadership skills by working through the chapters, one by one, across a two year period.

I feel that when you practice and experience the results you can get, that you will develop a more engaging and participative style of managing people. Once into your stride, it is a less stressful way to manage people, which brings out the best in them and where they will appreciate your trust in them. In this way it becomes self-reinforcing: You trust them, so they trust you which means that you trust them more. The outcome of this is that everyone can now focus more energy on the work so performance naturally improves as well. And so the cycle continues.

It helps to have a partner on this journey with you, as you need you to practice, reflect on what went well and what you need to do differently next time. If there are two or three of you experimenting with this material, then you can learn from each other as well as give each other encouragement and support.

The chapters vary in length although they all include exercises to help you become competent in the topic as my focus is on application and competency. The variation in length is due to what I have found to be the pertinent information and exercises required through using and training this material over the last 20 years.

The book 'Make It Stick' says that enduring learning comes from struggling to apply knowledge to your own real applications and persevering until you can do it. Here I hope to have given you enough information and structure to do that, so enjoy the journey and the results.

Acknowledgements

The biggest acknowledgement that I must give is to Alan Murray, as without his passion for asking me how to handle people issues I would never have had the belief to write this book. His encouragement and enthusiasm for getting me to put down my ideas on paper has been much needed at times and I thank him for that support. Also my husband, Mark, has been a great supporter and helped me maintain momentum by asking, at least weekly, how the book was coming along.

Also I want to acknowledge the generous help from Melinda Thurley in proof-reading the book for me and giving valuable suggestions in how things might be better understood. Kate Davies, Amanda Bouch and Caroline Talbott have all helped me with publishers, writing issues and keeping my confidence high when it dipped: Thank you. The enthusiasm for this book from so many of my colleagues, participants and coachees has been heart-warming and motivating.

The book is a distillation of twenty-five years of diverse reading, delivering training sessions and thought-provoking conversations. Many colleagues across the years have helped developed my thinking and understanding on many of these topics. In particular, Sari Robinson helped with chapters 2 and 9 and Alan Murray with Chapter 50. Colleagues such as those above as well as Rob Jackson, Gary Evans, Roger Putt, Robin Coulson and many more have helped directly and indirectly. Chapters 1, 12, 19, 24, 26, 27, 28, and 33 have been drawn from the field of Neuro-Linguistic programming (NLP) and Chapter 13 is based upon an article originally published in the Training Journal in June 2003.

Also I want to thank my teams for helping me to learn about being a manager, and the many participants and coachees from whom I have learned much about what is valuable to line managers.

This book is dedicated to all the managers I have met who were told that they must empower and motivate their people and yet were never told, or shown, how to do that.

This book is for you, so you can empower and motivate your people, and reap the benefits of doing so.

Mindsets That Engender Trust and Openness

Many years ago I heard a short story in a training workshop and I have used it a lot in my coaching and leadership workshops since then. It goes like this: A Lord back in the 14th century was riding his horse along a road when he came upon a number of workman building a cathedral. First he came upon three bricklayers. He went up to the first bricklayer and asked him what he was doing. 'Well' said the brick layer, 'I am laying bricks because that is what I do, I am a bricklayer'. 'Well done. Carry on' said the Lord and he went to the second brick layer and asked him what he was doing. 'Well' said the second bricklayer, 'I am building a wall because that is what I do, I am a wall builder'. 'Very good' said the Lord, 'Carry on' and he went on to the third bricklayer and asked him was he was doing. 'Well' said the third bricklayer, 'I am building a cathedral because that is what I do. I am a cathedral builder.'

I wonder what it would be like if we and our people had the mindset of the third bricklayer and we felt connected to the overall work that we were doing rather than just the element that we were working on: If we felt connected to meaningful work and were there to enable that to happen. To help our people to have the mindset of the third bricklayer two things are useful, firstly that we have that mindset ourselves and secondly that we have a belief that our people can have that attitude as well. Part I gives some simple and pragmatic ways in which to do those.

Overall I think it is about:

- **Getting Past Your Judgment When it is Hindering You**
- **Aligning Your Team**
- **Inspiring People**

Getting Past Your Judgment When it is Hindering You

Managing the tensions between work demands, environmental demands and the differences between people, plays a key part in anyone's life: Even more so in the role of a manager. Therefore, we are going to spend a bit of time exploring some ways that will be helpful in looking at these diverse and seemingly conflicting tensions.

Sometimes your judgment of others, where you are evaluating their behaviour against your own perceived values of right and wrong, can lead to people becoming defensive which invariably impacts on morale and performance. Being curious, that is finding out the reason why they have behaved as they have, rather than judging them is a good way to overcome your judgement. This builds a greater level of understanding and leads to a more open, accepting, trusting relationship that allows you to move past judgement and focus on outcomes. Once people feel valued and understood they tend to step up their performance and commitment.

Chapter 1 "Understanding Their Perspective" looks behind the person's behaviour and explore some possible reasons that may explain the behaviour being seen by you. We are not looking to agree or disagree with the behaviour, just to be able to put forward a likely rationale for it happening. Firstly, we will explore how our own judgment and beliefs of others can hinder us. Then we will look at some useful questions to create doubt in our judgment such that we enable a better relationship to be established.

Chapter 2 "What is Driving Their Behaviour" thinks about what could be true for that person at this moment and how that is affecting the decisions they make and how they behave.

Chapter 3 "People and Their Differences" looks at three personality models to enable you to interpret people's behaviour in a different light that, hopefully, will enable you to be more generous in your thinking towards how people behave in different situations. As we will discover, people's present behaviour is profoundly affected by their past experiences.

1. Understanding Their Perspective

What are the benefits of doing this?

If you find that you judge people and this is causing problems, then this topic will give you a method of being able to challenge your judgment and become more curious about the person. This will allow you to move past the judgement and get the best out of the person rather than getting stuck on judging them. Conversations where people feel judged can quickly become polarised and are then about who is right or wrong: It becomes about defending yourself or your position with the real purpose of the conversation often being forgotten. Judgment usually makes people feel personally evaluated and therefore they tend to perform less well. The focus is on the behaviour: Was it was right or wrong? Would I have done it or not? This rightness or wrongness may then get transferred to the person - whether they are right or wrong, good or bad. We can get caught up in the behaviour and forget to think about what could be driving that behaviour. Often, finding that out is quite surprising and helpful.

Long term, overly judging people is not good for developing trusting relationships as people tend to hold back on aspects that they feel 'unsafe' in sharing with you. Therefore, your idea of what is really happening can become limited without you knowing it and you find out things when it is too late. If you want people to feel safe enough to come and tell you the real issues and what they really think then this chapter will help you to become more curious and approachable.

The benefits of being curious with people are that they will open up quicker and get to the real issues that are often left hidden and unsaid. This creates valuable and trusting relationships where the focus is getting the work done rather than avoiding criticism and judgment.

Possible pitfalls and concerns to consider

- For some managers, letting go of an opinion can be difficult. In this chapter we are looking for believable alternative explanations for the person's behaviour or views. You do not have to agree with them although they do need to be plausible rather than trite. What might explain what is happening, is a good question to think about.
- I may be right in my judgment: Yes, this is perfectly ok as long as a judgment does not become embedded and mean that you are less than generous towards a person.

The wording can become colourful rather than rational, so a poor performer can become 'useless' or 'stupid'. It starts to become a label for 'who the person is' rather than their behaviour and people react badly to this type of labelling. So I am asking you to look beyond these statements and explore how this has come about, as poor performance can happen for many different reasons.

- Whilst being curious, managers can be worried about being seen as 'weak' or being taken advantage of. For me this depends on what happens afterwards. Usually you will have much more information available to make a reasonable assessment of the person and the situation. This leads to a more practical and effective way forwards. Using questions that invite participation creates a more meaningful outcome for everyone.

Other relevant chapters
- Chapter 2   What is Driving Their Behaviour?
- Chapter 3   People and Their Differences
- Chapter 46   Taking Individuals Through Change

How

Covers

    Six lenses to look through

    Using the lenses collectively to help you appreciate people's perspectives

    Applying the six lenses to your situation

Our beliefs shape and influence our thoughts and therefore our behaviour in many ways. The early studies within NLP (Neuro-Linguistic Programming) were undertaken with people who showed excellence in being able to get through to people in seemingly impossible cases. Further work was undertaken with people who showed excellence in engaging with others rather than creating defensive reactions. This work led to the 'NLP Presuppositions'. They are called 'Presuppositions' because we are going to 'presuppose that they are true' for the moment and see how that affects our thinking and therefore our behaviour. I am not asking you to believe in them, just to 'try them on' to help you drop some unhelpful judgments about people. Judgments that are getting in the way of you bringing out the best in people or are entrenching, or polarizing, the situation. In this way I am going to use six of them as six lenses to look through to help you think about the situation differently.

To start to influence others it is worth reflecting upon ourselves, especially around our beliefs and attitudes. It is interesting to see how much people hold onto their beliefs and yet how quickly these can be changed. Let me give you an example of that. Back in 2001 I heard about a large training programme that had been developed and then overnight, unexpectedly cancelled. The programme was about dealing with aggressive behaviour from passengers at airport check-in desks: This was mainly due to the time it took to do security checks. Just before the programme was due to be launched in October 2001 it got cancelled as it was no longer required. The problem had dramatically reduced almost overnight due to '9/11' - the 'Twin Tower attacks' in America. Suddenly everyone realised how important the security checks were so they were more tolerant of waiting in the queue for them to be completed properly: A shame it took such an incident for this to change.

> **Exercise:**
> 1. Think about someone you like and how you behave with them.
> 2. Now think of someone you struggle with and notice in what ways you behave differently with them.
> 3. What would be the difference if you behaved with the second person as you do with the first person?
>   i. And what would enable you to do that?

Here is a simple exercise that starts to highlight the different way we respond to people.

Therefore, let's start by looking at a way of reducing unhelpful judgements so that you can bring out the best in people rather than causing them to become defensive and risk adverse.

Remember this is not about how valid the six lenses (presuppositions) are; it is about 'if they were true, how do you now view the person or the situation?' In essence it is about putting doubt into your own thinking about how you've judged the other person. It is also about thinking about how to engage and connect with people so that you and they achieve more. It's about being more generous to them and then you'll respond differently and almost certainly they will too.

However, this is also about getting behind people's behaviour and understanding what is driving it. This doesn't mean to say that you agree with either the behaviour or the driver. It doesn't mean to say that you would do the same thing or that you respect or trust the person. But it does mean that you can put the jigsaw pieces together such that you have a consistent and predictable picture of why someone is choosing to do what they are doing given their experiences, values, beliefs and capabilities in this situation. From this understanding you are better placed to influence them and connect with them to build trust or to minimise the impact on you, and therefore move forwards in a constructive way.

Over the years, I have found the following six lenses (Presuppositions) to be valuable in connecting with people.

Six lenses to look through

"There is no failure only feedback."

The thought behind this presupposition is that you may get an outcome you didn't intend but that does not mean that it is a failure. 'Failure' is quite a big statement and there are lots of shades in between success and failure. Often people who view their mistakes as failures can feel angry, frustrated, upset or humiliated. These feelings are a signal that you are viewing the outcome negatively and it feels as if the outcome has determined who you are.

If we dwell only on what went wrong, then it is very easy to get entrenched in negative thinking which can move from blaming ourselves to blaming others. In "Authentic Happiness", Martin Seligman talks about how it is only when we look for learning, and how the event could have a useful meaning, that we move forward. Therefore, the second part of this presupposition, 'only feedback' gets us to do this. It assumes that whilst these are mistakes that we can learn from them that they are a natural part of the learning cycle, even if we would have preferred that they hadn't happened.

We learn a lot through mistakes and indeed many discoveries or inventions have occurred through mistakes. So when something does not go the way that you intended, instead of positioning it as a 'failure' think about it as 'an outcome I didn't intend'. Secondly, think about what you have learned from this outcome happening. Finally think about what you would have done differently and what you are going to do now because of the outcome you have got. This puts reasoning into your thinking and invariably your emotions will calm down.

"The map is not the territory. Respect the other person's view of the world "

The thought behind this presupposition is that our view of the world is just that, one view of the world built up from our values, beliefs, experiences and role models. Therefore, each person's view of the world will be slightly different and no one person's view is 'right'; it is just different and as valid as the next person's. In many cases people's views do coincide or overlap and that can give the illusion that our view is the 'right view'.

This presupposition is also asking you to accept your own view and the other person's view with equal weighting, value and scepticism. If you catch yourself not respecting the other person's view of the world, think about how you would feel if someone didn't respect your view of the world.

"Every behaviour has a positive intent"

The thought behind this presupposition is that there is a useful reason behind every action. We are still heavily driven by our survival instinct although in these modern times that is expressed in many different ways. The positive intent, of course, may only be useful to the other person and not to you: In one way or another it will always be useful to the other person. They may be "stuck between a rock and a hard place". So it may be about selecting the path of least resistance, or the least negative outcome and that will have a different meaning for different people. Sometimes we have misinterpreted the other person's intention and they may be very genuine in what they are doing. However, we are colouring what they are doing with our own view of the world and interpreting their behaviour with why we might behave that way.

According to psychology, these patterns of behaviour are mostly created and firmed up by the time we are around 21 years old although it does not mean that they are cannot be changed. Therefore, the behaviour you are experiencing could have been developed as a coping strategy when they were much younger and they have not had either a reason or the ability to change it.

This presupposition is asking you to think about what values, beliefs and experiences would 'create' someone who felt that this behaviour was useful in this situation. For example, someone who is quick to verbally attack others may have been brought up in a neighbourhood where aggression was rewarded and respected. In this case they may never have connected these two events and are just 'reacting' to the situation as they have always done. If you had been brought up in the same environment, then you would probably behave in the same way. So keep thinking until you can create a mindset that can see the behaviour as having a positive intent.

"Everyone makes the best choice available to them at the time they make it."

How do you make decisions? Do you think, "Option A is a good choice and option B is a bad choice, so I'll do option B"? Probably not. You probably go for option A. Well this is true of other people too. Again the choice may be between two bad outcomes and is about selecting the least bad option.

For example: If I leave early tonight I will let the team down by not completing the presentation deck for the client meeting tomorrow but if I stay late I will let my wife down by not taking her to visit her ill friend.

This presupposition reinforces 'Every behaviour has a positive intent' and gets you to really think hard about what that might be. It also reinforces 'People are much more than their behaviour' in that, if they had other choices then they would make better decisions at that time. Therefore, this presupposition looks to give us hope that just as we could improve what we do, so can others: They are not a 'lost cause' but rather 'someone who is worth investing in'.

"People are much more than their behaviour "

The thought behind this presupposition is that people are limited by their awareness, skills and knowledge. So that once they are more aware, or with new alternative options, they can choose to behave differently. Remember also that the environment or situation may be causing stress-related reactions that might not be their natural behaviour.

We have already discussed this topic when we talked about judgment and how the behaviour becomes the person: "This is an untidy person" rather than "the person is being untidy". Or one incident of driving dangerously does not necessarily make someone a dangerous driver. So this presupposition is inviting you to think about what the person needs to know, to believe or to understand, in order to have the ability to choose to do things differently. Think about where you get outcomes that aren't quite working for you, and think about what you would need to understand or be able to do to get a better outcome.

"The meaning of communication is in the response you get"

The thought behind this presupposition is that, when communicating, both parties are responding to the interaction between them. Therefore, their response is partly due to how and what you communicated to them. A colleague of mine gave this insight about this presupposition: " When I first read this one I interpreted it as 'I think I have communicated something and the person does something else'. In the past I would have judged them for that but now I ask myself what made them do that? Was it that I have not explained what I needed very well or what another genuine reason could it be? Whatever it is I get to understand them better and know how to deal with them in future."

This presupposition returns to the questions asked in the exercise at the beginning, about the two people; one you like and one you don't like. There will be subtle differences in what you say, how you say it, the way you behave and respond to them. All these signals will be picked up. If we are feeling threatened then sometimes we respond by being timid, sometimes by being defensive and sometimes by being aggressive: People will respond differently to each of these depending on who they are. Do they respond with compassion to someone who is timid or by dominating them? Do they respond defensively to someone who is aggressive or become aggressive themselves? So think about how you are responding to the behaviour you are experiencing and whether you are causing the behaviour that you wanted to prevent.

Using the lenses collectively to help you appreciate people's perspectives

Now we will look at a scenario and use the presuppositions to ask questions that help us put doubt into our judgement of the other person and so improve our working relationship with them. It may just be that we can handle their reaction better than before as we may not want to build a trusting relationship with everyone. I can think of a number of people who I have an understanding of why they behave as they do but I do not wish to have a trusting relationship with them. However, we do have a working business relationship where we get valuable work completed together in a business-like way.

Scenario:

You have just completed a report for a senior manager for whom you have not written a report for previously. After the initial brief conversation, you completed the report and gave them a copy. A week later you go into their office to see if they would like to meet to discuss the report. On their desk in front of them is your report. You can see that there are quite a lot of notes, in red ink, all over it. Then they say that they are glad you came by as they want to speak to you about all the mistakes in the report and the many corrections they have had to make.

> How would you feel about this, if it happened to you?

Firstly, to handle your reaction and maintain your balance, use **"There is no failure only feedback"**.

> The scenario above probably isn't the outcome you would have wanted.
> What can you learn from that outcome?
>
> What have you learned about yourself?
>
> What have you learned about others?
>
> What do you wish you had done differently to get a different outcome, given that you needed to write the report for that manager?

Next let's remember **"The map is not the territory: Respect the other person's view of the world"**.

Whilst you are thinking about the other questions, just hold this belief in the background as if it were true. This will help keep you focussed on exploring your thinking and their thinking rather than only coming up with negative reasons for their behaviour.

Now let us turn our attention towards the manager and the situation using **"Every behaviour has a positive intent"**.

> What do you think the manager was trying to achieve by doing this?
>
> What different positive intentions could they have had for themselves?
>
> What different positive intentions could they have had for you?
>
> What different positive intentions could they have had for others?

Now think about **"Everyone makes the best choice available to them at the time they make it"**.

> What made them think that that was a useful thing to do?
>
> What experiences, role models, values and beliefs would support that behaviour as the best choice to have made in this situation?

Next let's explore what they could have done differently in the context of **"People are much more than their behaviour "**.

> What does this person need to know or be able to do, so that they have a different choice available to them? (One that is more constructive for both people.)
>
> How could you help them achieve this?

Finally, it is worth thinking about how you communicated to them before and after you gave them the report using **"The meaning of communication is in the response you get"**.

> How could you have created or exacerbated the situation?
>
> What would you do differently next time?

Thoughts on the scenario

How would you feel about this, if it happened to you?

- Angry towards them: You may even react angrily towards them and ruin the relationship - or you end up being the problem rather than being the 'victim' or innocent person.
- Intimidated by them: Wished you had not done it; will probably be more cautious next time if you even do it again.
- Worthless/ Upset that you'd got it wrong: Makes you nervous and question your ability; feels unsafe to try new things as this was quite a knock back.
- Ok, with some pity that he feels this is ok to do (This is a more balanced response)
- Ok, as he is entitled to his opinion (This is a more balanced response)
- Ok, although he seems to have taken it quite seriously (This is a more balanced response)

What can I learn from this? What would I do differently next time?
- I wish I had asked for more information and got more clarity on his expectations
- May have been useful to talk to someone who had written a report for him before
- I should have asked someone else to review the report beforehand
- I rushed it as I knew I was short on time – just trying to be too helpful
- Didn't ask for help when I knew I should have – maybe I am not good at asking for help
- Maybe it says more about him than me?
- Glad he found all those mistakes otherwise I would have looked stupid to his boss.
- Wish I'd asked him first as he seems to know a lot and I wouldn't be here feeling stupid, so I'm a bit annoyed with myself.

"The map is not the territory: Respect the other person's view of the world".
- Some people value being competent above being liked
- Some people like to have impact (red pen) and expect others to step up to the job
- Some people value friendship and therefore ask friends to do work for them that they aren't very competent to do.

What do you think the manager was trying to achieve by doing this?
- Having very little time, it was quicker just to tell you what was wrong so you could correct it and get it completed sooner.
- Being helpful - if you know what you got wrong then you'll learn to be better next time.
- I am the manager, I need to ensure that people know who is in charge and I set the standard.
- I had a bad meeting with my boss so I wanted to take it out on someone else so I felt better about myself
- I enjoy making people feel small if I can: it amuses me

What made him think that that was a useful thing to do?
- This is what happened at school and then my first manager did this to me; Isn't this

what line management is about?
- I learn best by focussing on what I got wrong - that has always helped me to be successful with my work.
- When I grew up in my street, if you didn't show you were strong by being aggressive you got picked on.
- I think that negative feedback is useful and positive feedback weakens people
- Maybe he has poor interpersonal skills as he is only focused on the task and doesn't understand people's needs.

What does this person need to know or be able to do, so that they have a different choice available to them? (One that is more constructive for both people)
- If their intention was to help you learn then how could they have done this differently? Could you explain to them that it would also be useful to understand what you had done well?
- Does he understand the impact he is having? – a lot of people don't and are mortified when they eventually do.
- Maybe he can't handle praise himself or was embarrassed by it
- Maybe he thinks that this is the way to get things done and to get respect. Knowing that most people now accept that this thinking is outdated may be helpful to him.

How could you have created or exacerbated the situation?

When you gave the report to him, maybe you said:
- "Tell me what's wrong with it"
- "I'd really value your frank feedback"
- "I'm not sure that it's any good but see what you think"
- "I didn't really have enough time to do this so you'll probably find a lot of mistakes in it".

These can all happen when you are nervous: You tend to position it low so that you're not disappointed if the outcome is bad and some people take that as an invitation to criticise.

What would you do differently next time?
- "Here is the report"

- "Here is the report. When can we sit down and review it together?"
- "Here is the report. If there any issues I'd rather know sooner and then I can update the rest of the report, saving you time."
- "Here is the report. As I have not done one before it would be useful to know what was good about it and what I need to amend."
- Applying the six lens to your situation

Applying the six lenses to your situation

Here are the six presuppositions and their questions for you to use with your own scenarios. Take a situation where it didn't go as you wanted or one that is not going very well. For the situation, write down answers to each of the following questions:

There is no failure only feedback.
- What can you learn from that outcome/ this situation?
- What have you learned about yourself?
- About others?
- What do you wish you had done differently to get a different outcome?

The map is not the territory. Respect the other person's view of the world
- How may their view of the world differ to mine?

Every behaviour has a positive intent
- What do you think they were/are trying to achieve by doing this?
- What different positive intentions could they have for themselves?
    For you?
    For others?

Everyone makes the best choice available to them at the time they make it.
- What made them think that that was/ is a useful thing to do?
- What experiences, role models, values and beliefs would support that behaviour as the best choice to have made in this situation?

People are much more than their behaviour

- What does this person need to know or be able to do, so that they have different choices available to them? (One that is more constructive for both people)
- How could you help them achieve this?

The meaning of communication is in the response you get

- How could you have created or exacerbated the situation?
- What would you do differently next time/ can you do differently from now on?

2. What is Driving Their Behaviour?

What are the benefits of doing this?

If you are struggling to influence key people to get things done, then this is a very simple template of questions that helps you explore what maybe driving the behaviours you are experiencing. It works best if you have an attitude of curiosity as previously discussed. Exploring or knowing what is driving the other person enables you to create compelling cases to influence them and understand their behaviour. It will help you to understand what business cases, decisions and suggestions will and won't work for that person.

If you have an important or sensitive meeting to prepare for then this series of questions will also help you thoroughly prepare for it. They will give you a different perspective and thoughts on how to handle the situation. Usually it creates a better outcome for all.

These questions are useful relationship building questions: The more you can answer these questions, and know that you are correct, the more likely you are to have a good relationship with that person. In life and business, relationships really help to get things done quicker.

This template can help you plan for and overcome obstacles to getting your work done.

Possible pitfalls and concerns to consider

- You need to "stand in the other person's shoes" and think about what is true for them, rather than what you would do if you were them in that situation.
- It is very easy to answer these questions superficially but it is really worth answering them genuinely, as if you were that person: what might cause them to do that?
- This exercise may highlight how little you can answer these questions and know that your answers are true or likely to be true. In this case put together a plan on how you are going to build a better relationship with that person so that you know the true answers to the questions: If it is an important relationship to have then it is worth the effort long term

Other relevant chapters

- Chapter 1   Understanding Their Perspective
- Chapter 3   People and Their Differences
- Chapter 29 Designing a Conversation to Influence

How

Covers

1. Using the template
2. Using the information
3. Improving the quality of your information

1. Using the template

Before you go to a meeting where you are looking to gain support from a person, make a copy of the questions below so that you can put down your thoughts for each question. This can also act as a reference document for use in the future. One to one meetings work best for gaining an insight to these questions as a person's behaviour may change in a group situation. If a large number of people are present at the meeting, then it is beneficial to meet with the main influencers beforehand to gain their views and support before the meeting.

In this exercise I am asking you to think as if you were the other person rather than you thinking about how you would respond yourself.

Now write your answers to the questions below:

Outcome Focus How true do you think this is? 0--------5----------10	**What outcome(s) may they want?**
Drivers How true do you think this is? 0--------5----------10	**Who / What could be driving them?**
Priorities How true do you think this is? 0--------5----------10	**What priorities and consequences are they facing?**
Values & Beliefs How true do you think this is? 0--------5----------10	**What values and beliefs do they hold?** What is important to them and how may they view the world?

Expectations How true do you think this is? 0--------5----------10	What expectations may they have?
Assumptions How true do you think this is? 0--------5----------10	What assumptions may they be making?

2. Using the information

If your information is good enough then you can use it for the following situations

a. Understanding and responding to behaviour: Looking at the answers, what could be three valid reasons for the behaviour you are experiencing? How will you now handle that?

b. Preparing for a meeting: Looking at the answers, what preparation do you need to do to have the best possible chance of achieving the outcomes you'd like?

c. Creating a business case/ proposal: Looking at the answers, what needs to be in the business case/ proposal for that person to agree with it? What pre-work needs to be done with them or issues resolved?

d. Influencing key people: Looking at the answers, what is important for that person and how does what you are advocating link into that? What objections/ concerns are they likely to have and how do you address those?

3. Improving the quality of your information

Looking at the rating for each set of answers, create a plan for increasing each score out of 10. Having the conversation with the person and asking them is often the simplest way.

Outcome Focus	a. What actions could you take to improve the 0---10 rating?
How true do you think this is? 0--------5----------10	b. What action(s) will you do? By when?
Drivers	a. What actions could you take to improve the 0---10 rating?
How true do you think this is? 0--------5----------10	b. What action(s) will you do? By when?
Priorities	a. What actions could you take to improve the 0---10 rating?
How true do you think this is? 0--------5----------10	b. What action(s) will you do? By when?

Values & Beliefs How true do you think this is? 0--------5----------10	a. What actions could you take to improve the 0---10 rating? b. What action(s) will you do?　　　　　　By when?
Expectations How true do you think this is? 0--------5----------10	a. What actions could you take to improve the 0---10 rating? b. What action(s) will you do?　　　　　　By when?
Assumptions How true do you think this is? 0--------5----------10	a. What actions could you take to improve the 0---10 rating? b. What action(s) will you do?　　　　　　By when?

3. People and Their Differences

What are the benefits of doing this?

People are amazingly varied in what they value, respond to and what drives their behaviour: often much more than you expect. If you manage and interact with people a lot it is worthwhile having one or two basic frameworks from which to understand what may be happening for them and how you can influence that: becoming frustrated and thinking "why don't they just do ..., as that's what I would do" often leads to people feeling judged or not being allowed to think or explore for themselves.

At worst, you may be allowing your frustrations to show by becoming overly-directive and annoyed with others. Having a few frameworks gives you the ability to see how and why people think and act differently. They are also useful in maintaining your curiosity towards them and thinking about how you can successfully influence them. Not only will this enable you to build effective relationships, it will also improve the team's performance, morale and their tolerance of people's diversity.

Possible pitfalls and concerns to consider

- When talking about different personality models it can be very easy to pigeon-hole someone into 'that is who they are'. People are much more diverse and adaptable than simple models can cover and it is wise to remain open to who you have in front of you rather than putting them into a box. These models are constructive as an initial premise when dealing with people, as we tend to like frameworks to work from.

- There are numerous models available. Very few are 'better' than others and together they help us think about the differences and similarities in people. This is valuable as it gives people and teams a common framework to use when talking about differences in why and how they do things.

- Although there are training courses on personality models, there are also a number of good books and websites worth reading. You don't need to be able to precisely and deeply analyse each person as some general thoughts and themes are often enough: it is more about stretching your own understanding. Then you can decide if you want to study the topic in more detail.

Other relevant chapters
- Chapter 1   Understanding Their Perspective
- Chapter 2   What is Driving Their Behaviour?
- Chapter 15   Listening With Your Eyes, Ears and Intuition

How
Covers three different models
>Personality Adaptations
>Social Motives
>Metaprogrammes

From the reading I have done and the training that I have attended there is general agreement that young children have the ability to do many things. What is developed or not, is shaped during early childhood and firmed up during your latter teenage years. Therefore, by around the time someone is in their early twenties the patterns are largely set. They are then used, repeated and consolidated unless there is a compelling reason for that person to spend time uncovering those patterns, creating more suitable ones and embedding them. Overall the brain appears to dislike change because it takes up a lot of energy and it has perfected existing habits to enable it to be as efficient as possible. On the other hand, there is a growing body of neuroscience research that convincingly demonstrates that the brain is also very plastic and so able to make substantial changes. Although it requires concerted effort by the person until the new habit is firmly embedded but change is possible.

I think that these are useful contexts for any 'People Models' as they help us to understand people's behaviour rather than labelling them and to look for ways that a person can expand their current boundaries rather than putting people into fixed boxes. Here is a brief overview of them.

Personality Adaptations
Joines and Stewart's based their work on the premise that people have developed up to six ways to operate in the world, called personality adaptations. These ways of operating are unconsciously set up during childhood and then continue as unconscious drivers throughout our lives unless we actively raise our awareness of them and work to change them. Although people are complex, they tend to have a primary adaptation and often

a secondary one. I have found understanding these adaptations useful in helping me consider what is driving a person's thinking and therefore their behaviour. Therefore, I can take that aspect into account rather than confront their behaviour directly and exacerbate the problem. Joines and Stewart's book, Personality Adaptations, can give you more detail if you would like more.

Enthusiastic- Overreactor: (Please Others)

For Enthusiastic-Overreactors, life is about pleasing others. They focus their attention on attempting to address the needs of others and putting those before their own needs. They are very caring people who are generous and like being in a team. They are very sensitive to the moods of others and can become upset themselves if someone else is unhappy. On one hand they are cheerful and spontaneous and on the other hand they can easily become quite emotional. They can also allow their emotions to drive their actions although if they could stop and think clearly, they would understand that those reactions were not necessarily appropriate. It would be useful for them to realise that they cannot please everyone and that 'it is alright not to have to do that'. They should also learn to balance their own needs with the needs of others. From a manager's point of view, it is helpful to know that they often associate getting attention with how much they are liked. Therefore, a lack of attention may affect them quite badly as they will assume that they are not liked.

Playful-Resistor: (Try Hard)

For Playful-Resistors, life is a struggle where people are constantly trying, or perceived as trying, to control them to be someone they don't want to be. Therefore, they are seen as rebels and will become quite stubborn if controlled. They are quite loyal and tenacious employees who like to think for themselves and do things their own way. They are quite argumentative and tend not to get involved unless they are asked to do so. It would be helpful for them to learn that life is not so 'black and white' nor only 'right or wrong' but that they are many options in a situation. Often they are uncomfortable about expressing themselves clearly and learning that they can say no would be helpful rather than becoming passive and resentful. They often get caught up in unnecessary power struggles instead of finding a way forwards. As a manager, if you can ignore their struggles just focus on getting them working on the task in hand then they become more engaging to be with.

Creative-Daydreamer: (Be Strong)

For Creative-Daydreamers, life is about not being a problem to anyone else, therefore they keep their feelings under control and take care of themselves. They are quiet, stoic and pleasant people who don't create waves and are both supportive and respectful of others. They are low maintenance and hardworking although they like to be left to get on with things by themselves. They express very few emotions and are deep thinkers. If they feel threatened they are most likely to withdraw. If they become overwhelmed then they become confused, anxious or worried and stop thinking clearly. It would be useful for them to learn that they can get others to take their needs into account; they need to learn self-advocacy. As a line manager it is helpful to know that although quiet and detached, if you ask them to be involved or ask for their input then they willing give it.

Responsible-Workaholic: (Be Perfect)

For Responsible-Workaholics, life is about being perfect in one's self and everything they do, which is driven by a fear of being out of control and not knowing how to handle that. These people are perfectionists who tend to be organised and structured. They like order, lists and detailed plans. They are very productive and dependable although they can be overly conscientious and become exhausted through over working. Also, they can be quite tense and anxious as with an eye for detail they are good at spotting their own and others mistakes. This means that they are critical of themselves and of others, which can be quite demotivating for both. They are good thinkers and show little or no emotion. As they want to be perfect and fear being out of control, delegating and leading others can be even more stressful. It would be useful for them to learn that it's alright to make mistakes and to learn how to handle their feelings of anxiety.

Brilliant- Skeptic: (Be Perfect & Be Strong)

For Brilliant-Skeptics, life is about not feeling safe around others as you are never certain what they will do. Therefore, they are cautious and vigilant people who are attuned to other people's non-verbal communication. They are observant and quick thinkers who are often very knowledgeable. They like to keep on top of things so they are good workers although they can get rather paranoid and misread other people's actions. This can lead to them being quite critical or suspicious about the intentions of others. They are also careful and predictable, preferring certainty rather than surprises or spontaneity. Their main issue is around not being able to feel that they can trust others. It would be useful if they could learn to feel safer and to check out their suspicious assumptions rather than just assuming that they are true. As a line manager it is helpful to know that for them criticism is associated with shame and that they need to feel supported and safe.

Charming-Manipulator: (Please Others & Be Strong)

For Charming-Manipulators, life is a game of out manoeuvring others to get what they want because for them it's a 'winner takes all' world. They are energetic, charismatic, articulate and engaging people. They are fast thinkers so that they can stay one step ahead of everyone else and maintain the upper hand on them. They like stimulating environments and work where they will make things happen otherwise they will get bored and move on. They are quite manipulative, selfish and very competitive with others. They like being in the spotlight and will sometimes create a drama to get attention. It would be useful for them to learn that instead of playing power games to get what they want; they can just ask for it. As a line manager it is helpful to understand that these people are concerned with being vulnerable and they are worried about being rejected. It would be good if they can learn to take other people into account and work cooperatively with them.

Social Motives

David McClelland spent his life working on research that convincingly demonstrates that our thoughts, or motives, steer our behaviour and therefore shape the outcomes that we get over time. Even though day to day we will be affected by what is happening round us, over time people tend to have consistent patterns of thinking and related behaviour. While there are many different behaviours by which these motives show up, it is the underlying trend that these people have in common.

McClelland discovered that for the majority of people only three motives, the same three, are dominant in our thinking although we are each a unique blend of those. The three became known as The Social Motives. He also advocated that although these motives are pre-conscious and that we are generally unaware of them, if we make them conscious then we can develop different motive thinking if we want to. Therefore, he believes that we are not fixed and that change is possible, which is backed up by today's neuroscience research.

McClelland's book "Power: The Inner Experience" covers all the motives far better than I could give justice to them and if you are interested in finding out more, then this and other books on motives are worth looking at.

Briefly the three motives, or thinking patterns, are:

Achievement

This person is focussed on task: how well am I doing it or how can I improve what is being done? In many cases it is about getting the job done well, efficiently and effectively regardless of how people feel about having to do it and sometimes regardless of what difference it makes in the world.

Typical roles that Achievement people are successful in are engineering and scientific roles or 'singleton' type roles with a focus on doing it themselves rather than influencing others. They struggle in roles that require good relationship building or influencing skills. As team leaders or managers, they can be quite domineering as they prefer you to do it the way they say as they feel it is quicker that way. In their minds they have already worked out the most efficient way of doing it.

Affiliation

This person wishes to be personally liked by others and likes to build friendships, although just for friendships sake and for no other reason. To them, work is a lot about being with their colleagues and getting to know their colleagues well. Therefore, they will be concerned about how others are feeling and whether they are happy or not. They tend to be good listeners, so often they know a lot about how the team is feeling, although they can also be overly protective of the team's harmony as well.

Affiliation people tend to have good interpersonal skills and struggle with conflict situations because of their concern that you may not like them afterwards and therefore tend not to be very good managers. Managers need to make tough decisions and Affiliation people find it difficult to be that honest when face to face with someone. Also, it means that they tend to take most feedback personally regardless of the other person's intention.

Power

This person is concerned with influencing or being influenced. They are often popular and engaging with very high interpersonal skills because if they are going to be good at influencing people they need to be very emotionally intelligent. For Power people getting the job done perfectly is not their primary driver. Of course, Power thinking can also have a manipulative side to it where people are seen as a means to getting what that person wants for themselves.

What McClelland also found in his research is that the Power Motive is more complex: Some Power people just want direction and support from others in leadership positions; others would prefer to remain more self-centric, happy to give an opinion but less concerned with other people; others we would view as the 'typical boss' as they wish to get others to do what they feel is needed or best for themselves; and finally some Power people want to focus on collectively making a real difference through everybody pulling their weight.

Metaprogrammes

Metaprogrammes come from NLP (Neuro-Linguistic-Programming) and are a set of language traits that can be observed in people to help indicate they are motivated and how they go about doing things. Metaprogrammes can be very useful in understanding what is driving the other person and also how to say things in a way that works more easily for that person. I have found the four Metaprogrammes below particularly useful when managing, coaching or facilitating people, although there are more of them.

Each metaprogramme is a continuum from one end of the scale to the other and people rarely sit at either end. Metaprogrammes are thought to be independent of each other so take each one separately. When I am with a person in a particular situation I usually find that only one metaprogramme is important, so I focus on that one as it is a lot easier.

The metaprogramme can be primarily identified by what the person is saying: the words they choose to use, and how they choose to construct what they say. Therefore, listening to the person talking is the simplest way to gain an idea of what their Metaprogrammes could be. This is useful as they will not be aware of what you are doing and are therefore less likely to be modifying what they are saying. However, if you are only with them for a short time, you need to be careful as you may not be totally correct from the small amount you get. As with the other two topics on People Models, use these as a framework and keep an open mind about the person.

Away from – Towards: Are you motivated to achieve goals or solving /avoiding problems? Ask the person "What's important to you about (work)?" and listen to their answer. Do they talk about: -

1. Achieving things, gaining experience, getting what they want, having a goal to aim for. (You might say an 'optimistic view'; a 'half full' person)
2. Or is it about not wanting to ….; needing to ….; avoiding ……; getting rid of something; concerned with avoiding problems. (You might say a 'pessimistic view'; a 'half empty' person)

Towards People work towards achieving goals, focus on managing priorities, are excited and energised by their goals. Sometimes they have trouble in identifying problems or risks. To motivate these people, talk about the advantages, what will be achieved and the benefits gained.

Away from People focus on what they are trying to avoid or don't want. They focus on problem spotting and troubleshooting. They are motivated by crises, deadlines and threats and they are good at making plans robust. They tend not to be good at managing priorities and often get side-tracked by minor crises. To motivate these people, talk about preventing problems, avoiding things, "won't have to …" and getting rid of.

Internally – Externally Referenced: Do you have internal standards or beliefs that support what you do or do you need external input to tell you how things are going?

Ask the person "How do you know that you have done a good job?" and listen to their answer. Do they talk about: -

1. Because they know inside themselves: "I know it is a good job" or "I know I could have done better even though they liked it."
2. Because others tell them so or they get feedback that tells them: sales figures; "He liked it so it must have been good."

Internally referenced people rate how well something went by how they felt about it. If they feel it was good, then it was good. If they feel it was bad, then it was bad. Even if the feedback suggests otherwise they will argue with it or rationalise it away and do nothing. They tend to take feedback into consideration if it comes from someone they respect. These people provide their own motivation and need little management or praise. They often question other people and can be difficult to manage as instructions may be just another suggestion to them. Also if it doesn't fit with their thinking then they are likely to be resistant to doing it. They are good at doing roles that require independence and less interaction with others. To motivate them use suggestions, considering things, "what do you think", "it's up to you". Avoid phrases like "you should" or "you need to" wherever possible.

Externally referenced people do not know how well things are going without external feedback. They respond very well to (all) feedback and are therefore preferable in customer facing roles: "The customer is always right". If they are very externally focussed, then they may respond to everyone's request for to do something and will drop everything to go and do it. This can be a great distraction. These people need a lot of regular feedback, verbally or through metrics. These people can have problems with handling conflict or needing to prioritise different people's work requests. To motivate them talk about other people's reactions to their work or the external measures.

Options – Procedures (Possibilities – Necessities): Do you like finding new ways of doing things or do you prefer to follow set procedures and what needs to be done.

Ask the person "Why did you choose your current job?" and listen to their answer. Do they talk about: -

1. If they answer 'why' they will give values, such as it is fun, it's challenging, I'm not poor any more. The people prefer options and possibilities.
2. Or the person may change the question and answer 'how they got the job' such as 'well, my last job ended and this was what they offered me' or they may say that they 'had to take it'. These people prefer following procedures and doing what needs to be done. They tend to talk about how to do things rather than why. They often use words like 'have to' or 'need to'.

Options/ Possibilities people prefer finding new ways of doing things; they are interested in 'why'. They will be good at designing new procedures but less good at following them, as they will already be designing a new improved version. Motivate them by talking about options, alternatives, possibilities and new ways.

Procedures/ Necessities people prefer a right way of doing things and will do it over and over again. They are interested in 'how'. Once started they like to finish and they are not keen on bending the rules. They tend to be lost without a procedure to follow. Motivate them by talking about the right way of doing something, proven methodology; it's reliable, what needs to be done or should be done, Step 1 is … Step 2 is …, First … Second …., use facts.

Change – Stability: Do you like change and variety or stability and progress?

Ask the person "How does this (job) compare to (your last one)?" and listen to their answer. Do they talk about:-

1. The differences between them– how different they were.
2. Or is it about things that are the same – how similar they are.

People, who only look for differences love and prefer lots of variety and change. They tend to get bored if there is not enough change so ensure there is lots of variety for them. Motivate them with words like totally new, revolutionary, dramatically different, totally revamp.

People who mainly look for differences and notice some similarities also like change and variety. They often change roles every 18 months – 2years. Motivate them with words like significant upgrade, step up, really different. These people are often good at improving things as they focus on what needs changing.

People who mainly notice similarities and also see some differences prefer more stability. They may change roles about every 3-5 years. They prefer to build on what already exists. They tend to accept change if it is not too dramatic and when it is done incrementally. Motivate them with words like better than, upgrade, progress, improve on what we have, take it forward a step, similar with improvements. It is thought that around 50% of people prefer this option so if you are talking to a group of people this is a good style to incorporate.

People who only notice similarities like stability and this is what they focus on. They may have a role for 25 years and like maintaining what exists. They can find change very, very difficult and may not adapt to it. To motivate these people use words like same as before, in common with, like before, identical, 98% the same with minor alterations.

Aligning Your Team

Despite how some people come across, I feel that most people come to work to do something that is; meaningful, is something that they are proud of, and is part of a community. Although this may mean different things to different people. If these things are in place, then people really commit to the work and take their accountabilities seriously: They get on with it rather than you having to push all the time. This means the work gets completed sooner and people feel valued. If people are doing their job in isolation it can become very easy to become detached and this may result in a slight dip in commitment, not that they do anything bad, they just hold back a little.

There are four aspects that are worth exploring and that all build on each other.

Chapter 4 "Creating Meaningful Work and Sense of Community" looks at reconnecting your team back to the reason their work is needed and valued. There are various articles citing how transactional work has become and the corresponding dip in morale and performance. This chapter will help change both of those.

Chapter 5 "What Makes You and Your Team Members Proud?" helps you and your team think about what needs to continue, and what needs to be different, for you to be proud of the work you do. Again this builds on the previous chapter and helps raise morale and performance.

Chapter 6 "What is the Added Value Your Team Delivers?" really gets you to analyse how you are adding value to your customers and to make adjustments in areas where that is not true. This helps keep your team focussed and viable.

Chapter 7 "A Mindset of Accountability" gets you to think about how you view accountability and your role as the leader in that. Certainly leadership is shifting from the "the buck stops here, follow me" type leader to a more adult view of the work that needs to be completed and the accountabilities each person has. This chapter helps you work towards that shift which is more rewarding for everyone.

4. Creating Meaningful Work and Sense of Community

What are the benefits of doing this?

I find that many people have become disconnected from the outcome that their work gives to others. They often feel as if they are on a meaningless hamster wheel where the focus is on the task they are doing, how well they are doing it and can they do it better? Without the wider business context, perceived improvements are often short term and can actually undermine the true purpose. Eventually this leads to reduced customer satisfaction or lost revenue.

This topic is about articulating and sharing the meaningful work that you are doing with your team. It answers the questions around 'why are we doing this?' and 'what difference does it make to others?' In essence, 'why should we bother?' Connecting people to and reiterating the answers to these questions can really help people to remain motivated even when things get tough.

If people understand the impact that their work has and what happens if they don't do it then they have a broader context from which to make decisions as well as understanding how they affect others: their work colleagues and the end customer. Overall it helps create more ownership and commitment towards the work, with the focus kept on results and outcomes.

Possible pitfalls and concerns to consider

- The connection to meaningful outcomes needs to be real and this may require you to understand that linkage and the consequences for yourself, otherwise the conversation can feel quite false. Most people understand that they fit in somewhere to the organisation's overall aim although often they do not understand what that pathway looks like and the impact they really have.
- When you look at 'what does our work really do', it starts to beg the question of "if this is why we are doing it, should we be doing it this way?" Although uncomfortable in the short term, it is a very good question to answer and the topics below look to do that.
- Teams have probably had this conversation before at a superficial level so don't expect them to be that enthusiastic about having it again. Think about how you can

get them involved in the discussion and how you put in enough detail so they do get the value of the work they do.

Other relevant chapters
- Chapter 1   Understanding Their Perspective
- Chapter 17   Productive Language
- Chapter 35   Basic Meeting Outcomes, Structure and Tips

How

Covers three steps on how to do this
1. Initially gathering the information
2. Sharing the information with your team
3. Maintaining the connection

Differentiating between what activities/ tasks you do and the meaningful outcome that they deliver is a very useful exercise. Let me give an example: I was part of a programme to help an organisation improve its process of handing over completed projects. My part was to co- design and co-deliver workshops for people involved in projects whether they were providing or receiving items. I knew that five half day training events were not going to deliver much improvement if we took just an educational view. So I focussed my outcome on 'creating a conversation about better project handovers back in the work place'. I felt that if lots of people in the project were talking about doing things differently then there was a real chance that handovers would improve permanently in the longer term. My work purpose was to change the way handovers were done, not to run workshops.

Therefore, we designed the workshops differently, with three main components aimed at 'creating that conversation back at work'. Firstly, the underlying structure was a series of key topics that we wanted people to understand and start to do more of, both technically and behaviourally. Secondly, we brought together project teams and their customers which meant that they spent half a day together each week for five weeks. This allowed them to discuss a lot of issues. Thirdly, some of the participants were role models so others got to hear, from their peers, what best practice looked like. These three elements spread across five weeks with simple weekly actions made a bigger impact than we had expected.

So although my 'task' was to facilitate and train, I was firmly focussed on 'creating an environment back at the work place where best practice handovers were discussed and changes made to improve them'. Across the eighteen months numerous examples came back to us of tangible improvements that were made by those participants in many simple and effective ways. In this work I consistency checked the activities against the overall work purpose and asked myself if the activity would help to deliver this work purpose.

1. Initially gathering the information

First you need to sit down and collect the information that allows you to answer these questions:

"What is the meaningful outcome of my work /my team's work?"

o What does it allow other people to do or to have? And therefore, what can they do?

o What difference are we trying to make?

o How does my work affect the customer?

o What happens if this work does not get done?

In a realistic, step by step way connect your work to that of others: Follow it through until you get to the final customer(s). Some roles will be easier than others. Wherever possible get real facts and examples for the consequences of the work not being done or being sub-standard. This may mean that you or some of your team will need to go and ask the people affected. Getting your team to do this will create the most awareness for them.

2. Sharing the information with your team

You will need between thirty and sixty minutes and it could be part of a regular team meeting. Preferably, display the information as a diagram on several pieces of flipchart paper stuck together or on an A0 sized piece of drawing paper. This can then be put up on a meeting room wall where everyone can stand around it and easily read it. This works better than creating a PowerPoint slide which is often very difficult for people to read. Also the team can make amendments or clarifications by either writing on the sheet or by adding 'sticky notes' to it. In this way they will be involved in its creation rather than sitting and passively looking at a screen.

As they read the information, ask people:

o What they think about the work they do, now they can see it all in one place?

o What surprises them about how their work affects others and the customer?

If you are hearing comments such as 'well I never knew that' then people are making useful connections that can be used in future meetings.

Once these questions have been explored, ask them:

- How would you sum up what the purpose of your work is?

Get them to discuss this in pairs/ trios for five minutes and write down their thoughts on a flipchart.

Put all the various thoughts up on the wall so everyone can read then. Then discuss all the options until you come up with one that everyone can 'live with'. I say 'live with' rather than one that everyone 'agrees with' as that may take a lot of time and not really add much more value.

Some meaningful work purpose examples summed up by teams:

- We're here so the scientists can come in everyday and just get on with their work: We are at the very heart of the business. (Facilities Management)
- Our work will enable this publisher to open a whole new chapter in its history and springboard its growth. (IT Platform)
- We solve difficult problems so that our customers continue to benefit from us. (Business Improvement)
- We help de-stress people, reassure them and let them get on with their day. (Call Centre Operator)

3. Maintaining the connection

Once the connection to meaningful work is made then make sure that it is remembered across the year; during meetings and especially when things are tough. Whenever possible, link the work, the tasks, the meetings to the meaningful outcome.

> **Exercise**: Think back across the last two months: When did you definitely and clearly link your team's activities to the real effect it has on others, including customers?
>
> **Exercise**: How could the team's work purpose be displayed or used within the team's communications? For example, at the bottom of their emails.

Also getting feedback from your customers about your team's work is a valuable way to keep them connected to the real reasons that they are doing the tasks and activities each day. This can be as simple as asking various 'customers' these three questions:

- What do you like about what we are doing?
- What could we do less of or differently?
- What would you like us to do more of?

Wherever possible get each person to ask one or two customers these questions once a year. Then collate all the answers to each question. In a team meeting these answers can be shared. Then you and the team can decide what actions you would like to take, if any. It is also courteous to provide feedback and progress updates to the customers who were interviewed.

5. What Makes You and Your Team Members Proud?

What are the benefits of doing this?

Finding out what makes people proud about the work they do is an effective way to understand what motivates them to do their best every day. In the next topic you can use this information with the work purpose to evaluate which activities are adding real value.

It helps you understand further as well why your people do what they do and not necessarily what you would do. It also allows you to think about who is currently best suited to which aspects of the work. For example, someone who is proud only when they do a perfect job may not be very suited to jobs requiring a quick solution. On the other hand, an accountant who is proud that their figures are 100% correct every time may suit a job with attention to detail.

Overall, if people have pride in their work then they keep going when things get tough and they put in the extra effort. It may also help you understand what is currently missing for them, if they feel they don't have much pride in their work. The conversations below will give you an indication of morale within your team and some pointers as to what could be done to improve it.

Possible pitfalls and concerns to consider

- Asking someone what makes them proud about the work they do, may feel like a strange question, so they may feel a bit suspicious or embarrassed about answering it. I find it useful to have my own answer to the question and to ensure that it is genuine. Sometimes it is better to ask people individually although they miss out on hearing what others say.
- Some people may give negative answers: In these cases, I attempt to get them to think about pride again. A negative answer or an inability to answer the question may suggest that they don't feel much pride in their work at the moment. Gently push for what makes them proud and allow them to say what they think.
- When asked, people may say nothing: That's ok. I would give my answer and then see if anyone has anything to say.

Other relevant chapters
- Chapter 13   Questions That Create a Step Change in Thinking
- Chapter 15   Listening With Your Eyes, Ears and Intuition
- Chapter 35   Basic Meeting Outcomes, Structure and Tips

How

This could be a part of a team meeting or completed after a discussion on Work Purpose.

1. Ask the question

Either individually or in pairs, ask:

- Given the purpose of our work, what makes you proud about the work you are doing?

Another way you could put the question is to ask what a 'good day' looks like for them. Ignoring trite answers, you can start to build up a picture of what 'good work' would be for them.

You can also ask

- What would you be doing differently if you felt even prouder?
- What happens to make you feel less proud of your work?

2. Allow them to think about their answer

Allow people 5-10 minutes to think about these questions and to write down their thoughts.

3. Analyse the answers

Then get each person or pair to give their answers. Write up the key points onto a flipchart so you can see the common themes emerging.

4. Actions going forwards

From the above discussion, you and the team can decide what actions you would like to take. This can be as simple as asking these three questions:

"Given that we have just explored what makes us proud and less proud,

- What should we keep doing?
- What could we do less of or differently?
- What could we to do more of?

Put all the answers onto a flipchart so everyone can see them and then agree which ones you are going to take forwards.

6. What is the Added Value Your Team Delivers?

What are the benefits of doing this?

A colleague of mine once said "people get activity muddled up with progress". It's a great thought as people feel the need to be seen to be, or to be overly busy although I am not sure that they stop and think about what progress they are actually making: Does this task add significant value? My coachees tell me how busy they are and how they don't have enough time to do everything. I think that this has always been true and will always be true: After all we all have the same amount of time, 168 hours every week. So the conversation I have with my coachees is not about time, it is about 'what they think is important and what they value'. Given that there is 'lots you can do', you need to look at how you decide 'what you will do'.

Once you have discussed how your work affects others and the ultimate customer, you can then decide, given the amount of time that you have, what things you will do that do add value. In this way you will focus on what is valuable to do and make progress, which is very satisfying. It will also begin to give you solid and consistent business results.

Possible pitfalls and concerns to consider

- In deciding what is valuable to do to achieve your meaningful work, you will also need to consider what it is that senior managers may be demanding, as this is not always in alignment with your meaningful work. In any manager's role there will always be a tension to manage between different stakeholders and having solid information to back you up will be critical in these cases.

- Manager's often worry that people will use a discussion on 'what is the added value for us?' to do work that the organisation does not want them to do. In my years as a line manager and coach I have rarely found this to be the case. In fact, teams tend to be quite cautious. Key people in the team, those that are in tune with the organisation's needs and who the team listen to, are useful in these situations. Spend time with them deciding how you can involve the whole team in deciding what activities add value and which don't.

- When you start to look at how activities add value to the organisation and its customers you may find that it uncovers some uncomfortable questions around 'does it add value?' so be prepared to handle those discussions.

Other relevant chapters
- Chapter 11   Questions That Invite Others to Contribute
- Chapter 35   Basic Meeting Outcomes, Structures and Tips
- Chapter 45   Having Difficult Conversations

How

1. Sorting activities

Have four flipcharts on the wall, labelled:

A. Definitely required to deliver meaningful outcome to customer – not yet done

B. Definitely required to deliver meaningful outcome to customer – currently being done

C. Not sure how much it is required/ what difference it makes

D. Nice to have/ not really required/ wastes time & effort

Looking at your outputs from the Meaningful Work exercise in Chapter 4, write down on sticky notes, all the activities that are definitely required to deliver that benefit to the customer: One activity per sticky note.

Now, one by one, agree whether the activity goes on flipchart A or B.

Next write down all the other current activities that your team does that have not been written down: One activity per sticky note. Now, one by one, agree whether the activity goes on flipchart B, C or D.

Review the output from the topic above on what makes you and your team members proud. Then add any further sticky notes if required.

2. Creating a plan

Over time your aim would be to start doing the activities on flipchart A, continue doing the activities on flipchart B, find out whether the activities on flipchart C go onto flipchart B or D and stop doing the activities on flipchart D.

You can use steps 2-6 in Chapter 48 "Little and Often Improvements" to help you make the changes.

3. Embedding value adding activities

Remember to review the activities on flipcharts A-B each year, to see if they are still relevant. Also monitor that the change in activities is producing a change in your team's performance.

7. A Mindset of Accountability

What are the benefits of doing this?

The first step in making people accountable is for you to truly believe that they should be. This belief will subtly affect how you behave. Accountability is about getting people to do the job they are paid to do without you having to chase them, do parts of it for them or sort out the problems they have created. In essence they feel ownership for the work themselves. If your team 'step up to the mark' then things will happen quicker and people will look to overcome obstacles rather than hide behind them. You will have more time to lead the team and do more proactive work. Over time performance and morale should increase.

Also there are times when you are not the best person to make the decision or do the work. Someone in your team may be abler and would take greater ownership. Realising and embracing this leads to true accountability that demonstrates and builds trust.

Possible pitfalls and concerns to consider

- Hierarchy: As the boss it can be quite easy to think that you have to make all the decisions or that all the decisions need to go through you. Reflect on how much of a bottleneck you have become to getting the work done? Also think about whether the decision is robust if it is made by you? Do you really understand the situation enough given that you have many other things to focus on? What is the role of the person in their job if you make this decision?

- Feeling out of control: Changing your management style overnight probably isn't a good idea and usually means you'll quickly revert back and conclude that it didn't work very well. Plan out how you will learn to need less control yourself. Which situation does not really need it? Where you do need that information to ensure that the accountabilities are robust where? Over time it should feel as if there is more control as the whole team will feel accountable and problems will be resolved before you hear about them.

- The team do not care about the work getting done on time. It often feels as if you seem to be the only one that cares about how and when the work gets done. This is a sure sign that they do not feel accountable for their work (under-managed) or that they feel over managed. They are becoming 'childlike'. Remember you need to demonstrate over time that you do want them to be accountable and will not revert back to your old style of managing them.

- What do I do? Many managers are concerned that if their people are delivering the work themselves that they will no longer have a role. To me that feels as if the manager equates their role as having to do someone else's tasks rather than working on developing the team to do the work themselves. As the manager, look at your own job description: Are you working on every element as much as you would like? Most managers tell me that they don't have enough time to do their own jobs so freeing time up should be useful to most managers.

- Saying it and not actually doing it: Managers speak a lot about accountability and responsibility and yet in action they seldom do something that really makes the other person feel accountable. Think about what you actually do to make someone accountable and where you inadvertently take it away? If a mistake occurs how do you react? Does that take away accountability?

- Aggressive - Passive: Some managers feel that they will be considered weak if they give accountability to their people. Giving accountability is not letting go or abdicating responsibility. It is not about being passive. It is about being assertive and treating people like adults. It is about being clear on what you do and what they do. For example, you need that person to make the decision but it does not mean that you need to make it for them when they should. If they are unable to make the decision, then sort out their ability to make the decision rather than making it for them. Otherwise next time it will happen again, and again, as they have no need to learn how to make decisions if you always step in to do it for them.

Other relevant chapters

- Chapter 8   Making People Feel Stronger
- Chapter 33   Delegating and Holding Others Accountable
- Chapter 44   Personal Development Plans That Add Value

How

Covers four steps on how to do this

1. Assign your people
2. What next?
3. Prepare for the conversation with them

4. Review

Accountability is about getting to the place where people make the decisions that they should make. There are a number of reasons for them being the right person to make a decision:
- It leads to the most useful outcome for the work
- They have the most complete knowledge of the situation
- They complete the work on time as they have set the timescale
- They understand and have to deal with the consequences of their actions, whether they are positive or negative.

To be accountable they need to understand their accountabilities and the consequences associated with the work. They also need to be allowed to learn and to have to handle the consequences of any problems.

Overall they have to be allowed to be accountable by you. You will need to think about how to manage the tensions that this will create in you so that you can withhold from stepping in too soon and yet manage situations where the consequences of something going wrong are quite serious. Often we have learned to err on the side of caution so you need to work with your team on how they can help to minimise your anxieties and your need to step in. Useful things to do are to put in check points and getting them to take you through their thinking or their plan. It is amazing what our people can do if we just get out of their way.

Therefore, you need to have a plan that builds accountability with your people. Plan it and work on that plan as the rewards for everyone far outweigh the possible issues. At first true accountability can be quite scary although it is also quite energising.

Mistakes are the true test of your resolve to make your people accountable and will be carefully watched by everyone. People will make mistakes, as do you from time to time, and how you respond is important as it will either help the person learn and strengthen their abilities or it will take the accountability away from them. Most people will know they have made a mistake as there are consequences so they need to know these. Then see if they respond to sorting out the mistake. If they do, then let them do it and withhold the urge to take control.

If you feel you must act, then ask them questions first:
- What are they going to do?

- o How will they know it has been resolved?
- o What else do they need to do?
- o What have they learned from this?
- o What will they do differently next time?

In this way you are helping them to explore the mistake, resolve it in a robust way and learn from it for next time whilst leaving the accountability with them. If they ask you to help then think about whether this is valuable to them and the situation, now and in the long term? Are they ducking their accountabilities? Are you really the right person to help or do you just want to 'save the day'?

1. Assign your people

Think about their role: its accountabilities, competency and deliverables. Write down a list of your team's names and put each person into one of the categories below:

A. At or close to (100%) delivering their outcomes and has ownership for their role. Competent; has soundly demonstrated their decision making; knows what needs to be done and does it. Keeps me appropriately updated and does not need me to sanction things. May ask for my advice although does not need my approval.

B. Nearly there and I should probably let go more to allow them full accountability or I need to get them to realise they don't need my approval.

C. Needs developing further - it would be risky for me to let go of some areas.

D. Not certain that they will ever be able to fully deliver in this role without my continued support: struggles with the quality of the work and it would be risky for me to step aside. Has demonstrated that their decision making is not sound. I doubt this person will be able to do this role on their own.

E. Not sure which of the above they are.

2. What next?

Now for each category think about these questions:

A. Allow these people to continue in this way. What is different for you about these people that allows you to give them accountability? What can you learn about yourself that would be useful to think about in the context of your other people?

B. Are these people clear about this gap? What are they going to do to get to category A on this list? What do you need to do differently?

C. Are you clear about this gap? Are they clear about this gap? What are they going to do to get to category A on this list? What do you need to do differently?

D. Are these people clear about the situation? Do they understand the consequences if this continues? What do they want to do (and what is their plan for this)? What do you need to do in light of their decision/ plan?

E. What do you need to do to find out where they are on the list?

3. Prepare for the conversation with them

For each person who is Category B to D on the list, prepare for the conversation you would like to have with them using these chapters:

Chapter 29 Designing a Conversation to Influence

Chapter 44 Personal Development Plans That Add Value

Chapter 45 Having Difficult Conversations

4. Review

Every 3-4 months review your people again as in Step 1 and review what you have been doing to build accountability. The review exercise below could be completed by yourself or with a colleague. It will help you reflect on what you have done and build your ability to develop accountable people.

> Reviewing building accountability:
> 1. What have you done to build accountability with your team?
> 2. What has gone well?
> 3. What hasn't gone as you wanted it to?
> 4. What can you learn from this?
> 5. What have you learned about yourself?
> 6. What will you do going forwards?

Inspiring People

When people walk away from you, do they feel stronger? Do your actions demonstrate you value people? Do they feel treated like an adult? An equal? These are the questions tackled in the next three chapters.

Chapter 8 "Making People Feel Stronger" covers what I feel is the essence of being an inspiring leader. When I have asked managers if they think they are inspirational they tend to shy away. When I ask them if they feel they can make people feel stronger they tend to reply that they feel that they can. For me, that is what inspiring leaders do, they make people feel stronger and this chapter covers how to do that.

Chapter 9 "How You Train People Through Your Actions" is a thought provoking chapter on how you are inadvertently training your people in how they should respond to you and in want you want. Often your team's behaviour is a reflection of the way you manage them so this chapter helps you think about the implications of that and what you can do differently.

Chapter 10 "Handling Negativity" is about reflecting on the level of negativity in your team and how to handle it if it is a problem as an atmosphere of negativity is certain to affect everyone.

8. Making People Feel Stronger

What are the benefits of doing this?

Many managers create dependency upon themselves with their teams. Whilst this may give the leader a sense of being needed and being invaluable, it also creates a bottleneck in decision making and a 'dumbing down' of the team's thinking and capabilities. This slows down the performance of the team, makes you feel as if everything has to go through you and that your team doesn't seem to think for themselves very much.

When I have read about and discussed inspirational leaders, for me, there seems to be a common theme: Whether the leader is famous or infamous, they appear to make people feel stronger. I think that we can all have people walking away from a conversation with us feeling stronger. If you would like your team to have more capability and commitment to do their work then one element to start with, is how you are making them stronger within themselves.

Possible pitfalls and concerns to consider

- Managers are concerned that making people feel stronger means that they only have talk about positive things or put a positive spin on things but long term this weakens the team. Their sense of what they are capable of and reality becomes distorted. Often when true reality becomes apparent it is very hard to take, as in effect they have been wrapped up in cotton wool. This weakens their resilience to change and problems so managers need to be open and honest about the situation.
- Making people feel stronger is not about abdicating responsibility or just saying yes to them. It is about asking robust questions, sharing your insights or giving feedback in a business-like way with the intent to help rather than just point out deficiencies. Think about whether you would like to be treated in the way that you treat others.

Other relevant chapters
- Chapters 11-13   Questioning for Robustness
- Chapter 17   Productive Language
- Chapters 21-23   Feedback That Develops People

How

Covers

What 'feeling stronger' means

An exercise to help you develop in this

What 'feeling stronger' means

When someone walks away from a conversation, with you, ask yourself: "Do they feel stronger in some way?" Then ask yourself: "How do I know that?"

> **Exercise**: Think about someone that you have had a conversation with that you made you feel stronger. What was it that they said to you in the conversations where you walked away feeling stronger and more motivated?

Managers can create a dependency on themselves, for example by: -
- solving the problem for the person because it seems quicker
- giving your opinion without asking them for their view
- withholding certain information or vetting it out
- being vague about situations; giving poor feedback
- making decisions that they are better qualified to make because you are the boss
- not treating people as adults
- being overly cautious or holding back because you are worried about (handling) their reaction
- not having quality time for them
- not giving praise or reinforcement feedback

'Feeling stronger' does not mean that it always has to be a positive conversation about how wonderful they are. Neither does it mean that you have to be overly helpful as that makes people dependant rather than strong. By strong I mean that they can handle work in a more robust and resilient way:
- They can think better for themselves
- they are now more self-aware about how they come across

- they can think through a problem without you
- they have more confidence and more self believe
- they can solve more complicated problems
- they can handle more difficult people
- they realise the seriousness of their situation and the consequences of it
- they understand the consequences of their actions
- they understand a certain situation better or have found a different perspective on something
- they found out they could do something they didn't think they could do
- anything that grows their self-awareness, self-confidence, robustness and capability to handle their work in a mature and adult manner

Sometimes walking away 'feeling stronger' means that they now know how poor their performance is and the consequences of that. It might seem strange to think of that as making them feel stronger but for me they are stronger as they are now very clear about the situation. This means that they can choose what to do about it. Before they were unaware of the full situation so things were going to happen and outcomes reached that they had very little control over. This person is now being treated as an adult with facts to face and choices to make. You have empowered them to influence the outcome.

An exercise to help you develop in this

Think of a specific and recent conversation with one of your team.
How much stronger did they feel when they walked away?
0---------------------------------5---------------------------------------10
No   Definitely
How do you know that?

What could you have done, during that conversation, to make them feel even stronger – one point higher? Anything which grows their self-awareness, self-confidence, robustness and capability to handle their work in a mature and adult manner.

---

9. How You Train People Through Your Actions

What are the benefits of doing this?

For this topic, these old adages come to mind: 'words are cheap' and 'actions speak louder than words'.

- Could your team be more innovative? How did you respond last time they made a mistake?
- Is your team delaying telling you about things that have gone wrong or that might go wrong? How did you respond the last time something went wrong?
- Do your people feel energised and confident? How did you respond last time when someone put in extra effort/ had an idea?

If you are asking people to do something and they are not doing it, then it might be useful to reflect on what your actions are really telling them rather than the words you are saying. I first came across it when Sari Robinson showed it to me. It has been a useful exercise with many managers ever since. Once in a team meeting, our Director moaned that we weren't being very creative and that we weren't proffering any ideas. It was true, we had gone quiet. This was because four people had put forward ideas that he then belittled in front of everyone. It didn't instil a sense that ideas were there to be built on, to be explored and developed. We all got the message that he was there to criticise our ideas, and us, in front of others. That made us nervous of being belittled and the ideas simply dried up.

This chapter gets you to think about how you are training your people without realising it and how to do this more purposefully to get the outcomes you would prefer.

Possible pitfalls and concerns to consider

- Changing the way you react can take time as often we have in-built reactions especially when the situation is especially emotional for us. Reflecting on how you react and how you would like that to be different will take a number of attempts so it is ok if you revert back to old habits in particularly tough situations. Overall, stick with reflecting on your reactions and what you are starting to do differently and the changes will happen. It may take up to 12 weeks to fully embed the changes.

- Experiment with different responses to find out which reaction gets what outcome, given different situations and different people. Also get other people's views on these reactions so you understand the effect they are having.
- People may say that you are behaving differently and it won't last or 'it's not you'. That's ok. They can have a view. Maybe they like the old you as it gives them someone to blame when you react badly to something they have got wrong. Find someone who will support you in this change and listen to them. Overall stay with it, as demonstrating your persistence is a good way to silence critics.

Other relevant chapters
- Chapter 8   Making People Feel Stronger
- Chapter 24 Maintaining a Positive Outlook When Life Knocks You
- Chapter 25 Detach to Get Things in Perspective

How

Covers

How reactions affect outcomes

Exercise: Your reactions and their effect

Developing useful reactions

How reactions affect outcomes

When something happens, how you react can affect the outcome as much as what actually happened. For example:

When something goes wrong do you:	Possible Immediate consequences:	Possible Long Term Effect:
Do you blame people and get visibly annoyed?	Person does just enough to sort it out and not get blamed further.	People hold back on telling you things they think you won't want to hear which means they get uncovered later when they are costlier to resolve.
Do you say that's ok and I'll sort it out?	You sort it out although resent having to put in the extra time to do it and other work you have gets delayed.	People think that they don't have to bother as you'll sort out the problems. Or you overreact next time due to the resentment.
Do you ask questions, discuss options, explore consequences and ask how they are going to sort it out themselves?	Person takes ownership for the problem thus is more committed to sorting it out properly and not having it happen again.	People think through the situation, as mistakes happen, and what needs to be done by them going forwards. Next time they can apply this thinking for themselves.

I heard about one project team meeting where people were encouraged to speak up about what was not working so that things could be improved over time. Interestingly though, in each case, the person who raised the issue became the person who was appointed to sort it out. The consequence was that people learnt to keep quiet to avoid having to fix the problems. This was probably not what the project leader intended. Their initial intention to solve things was great and then their actions unintentionally created the opposite outcome. I wonder what unwritten rules you are unintentionally creating. Do they give you the outcomes you'd like? Do they make people feel stronger?

Your team, and others, will be watching how you respond to different things and then using that information to decide how to handle things in the future.

Something happens   **&**   how I respond to it   →   will affect the outcome (This time & future ones)

Something went wrong   **&**   I got angry with them   →   they would have sorted it properly but now will do the least they can.

They did a great job   **&**   I said thank you to them   →   they smiled and felt proud of what they did. Next time they will put in effort as well.

So when something happens, pause and think about what outcome you would like and therefore how you need to react to what has happened to get it. Reflecting on how you react to certain situations is a good way of changing how you could react in the future. This exercise will help you to do that.

Exercise: Your reactions and their effect

Look at each of these scenarios, and think about how you <u>do</u> react / what you say in these situations. (Be honest as you will learn more.)
1. You arrive late to a meeting in which there are several participants more senior than yourself, including your line manager.
2. In a project review meeting, a person wants to talk about things covered in the pre-meeting briefing document rather than focus on the meeting agenda.
3. Your work depends on a task being completed by a member of another team. This person seems to be avoiding doing what you ask.

Now find at least one other person and share with them how you reacted to these three scenarios. Find out from them, the answers to these questions:

How would they have responded to the scenario themselves?

What outcome did you want? Are you likely to get your desired outcome?

What could you change about your reaction to get that outcome?

Exercise: Some thoughts

i. You arrive late to a meeting in which there are several participants more senior than yourself, including your line manager.

   Did you want to enter the room with least disruption? Walk in, concisely apologise for being late, look round to find a chair and sit down.

   Did you want to make an entrance? Walk in and give a full blown account of what a trauma you have had getting there.

ii. In a review meeting, a person wants to talk about things covered in the pre-meeting briefing document rather than focus on the meeting agenda.

   Did you want to understand why they were behaving that way? (Perhaps they had not got the pre-briefing document). Become curious and ask them some questions to understand the purpose of wanting to talk about these items.

   Do you want to get the meeting back on track? Reiterate that the pre-briefing document was sent out and what the purpose of this meeting is. Check that everyone is happy with this and agree to talk to the person after the meeting about what they want to talk about.

   Do you allow yourself to get annoyed by this person's behaviour rather than finding out what is causing it and the meeting deteriorates due to the hostile atmosphere?

iii. Your work depends on a task being completed by a member of another team. This person seems to be avoiding doing what you ask.

   Do you want to get the work back on track? Use chapter 2's template to 'stand in the other person's shoes' to get a different perspective. Prepare for the conversation using the structure in chapter 33. Allow them to hear what you need and find out from them what is stopping the work from progressing.

   Do allow yourself to get annoyed by this person's behaviour rather than finding out what is causing it. Walk into their office and accuse them of delaying the work. They become angry and their goodwill is lost.

Developing useful reactions

Reflecting on your reactions in general:
1. What was the situation?

2. What was the outcome you wanted to have happen – immediately and in the longer term?

3. How would you need to react to have that outcome happen?

4. What needs to be different for you to react like that?

Situation: Preparing your reaction
1. What is the situation going to be?

2. What is the outcome you want to have happen?
   a. Immediately?
   b. In the longer term?

3. How would you need to react to have those outcomes happen?

4. How have you reacted previously / expect to react?
   c. What has made you react that way?
   d. What are you learning about yourself from this?

5. What needs to be different for you react as you would like to (3)?
   e. What do you need to do to make that happen?

Situation: Reviewing how you actually reacted afterwards
1. What happened (how did you react)?

2. What did you do well?

3. What didn't go as you wanted it to?
   a. What can you learn from this?

4. What have you learned about yourself?

5. What will you do next time?

10. Handling Negativity

What are the benefits of doing this?

Chris Argyris, Professor Emeritus at Harvard Business School says that as human beings, we have a tendency towards being negative. Looking at the newspapers and news broadcasts, I feel I am inclined to agree with him. Fear is a primitive feeling because it motivates us to prioritise things that keep us safe. In the work place you want people to feel pride in what they do and safe enough to make mistakes so they can learn and be innovative. Therefore, too much unfounded negativity can cause problems and undermine good work. Teasing out rational concerns from unfounded negativity maintains a healthy atmosphere and good team morale. Ignoring or denying negativity is often reflected in a drop in performance over time and may cause undue anxiety to those who allow themselves to be drawn in by it.

Possible pitfalls and concerns to consider

- As a manager and role model ignoring negativity can be seen as condoning it or simply confirming the something bad is true. Both of these can have unhelpful outcomes. Firstly, condoning negativity may mean that you lose your more positive team members as they feel they would prefer to be part of a positive team. Unknowingly confirming a rumour may cause unnecessary stress and reactions which then have to be resolved as well.

- Sometimes managers attempt to offset the negativity through joviality or humour. Often this deepens the problem as in many ways because it creates a reflection of the original negativity. It becomes a game of 'my turn, your turn' or they think it is not being taken seriously

- Managers don't wish to be seen as not allowing people to air their concerns or they feel that they may just get into a defensive argument. These are both valid concerns and this chapter looks at giving you a way of avoiding these outcomes.

- Lots of negativity can be draining to handle and it may get worse when you start to address the problem before it gets better. Finding a mentor or supportive colleague may be a useful option whilst you do this.

Other relevant chapters

- Chapter 9   How You Train People Through Your Actions
- Chapter 12   Questions to Help Overcome Unhelpful Perceptions and Thinking
- Chapter 45   Having Difficult Conversations

How

Covers four ways of handling negativity

    Refrain from doing it yourself

    Refrain from joining in with others

    Tackle it there and then

    Prevention is better than cure

A good place to start with is yourself: How often do you say negative things about work or others? On balance, how much do you think you embellish an issue or build up unfounded issues? Then think about how you would like to create a climate where concerns can be aired and discussed before they become divisive. Here are some thoughts on handling negativity within your team.

Refrain from doing it yourself

- Openly moaning or criticising: Although you may not do this very often, reflect upon how often your team hear you doing this? What are they inferring from your behaviour about what they can do? How much do they like hearing you say things like this? How much confidence or reassurance does it give them? Do they wonder if you speak about them in this way when they are not there? Basically, you need to stop doing it as you are a manager. Being realistic is one thing and being negative is another.
- Discussing issues with colleagues and being overheard: Sometimes concerns or disappointments need to be discussed. It may be that you want to talk to a colleague about something that you do not agree with. It is a good idea to find an appropriate place to do this. Somewhere you can speak openly and not be overheard or have to speak quietly. Also using the structure in Chapter 29 to prepare for and have this conversation will help you keep the conversation based around facts and reduce the risk of you embellishing the negativity of the situation.

Refrain from joining in with others

- Wanting to be part of a group: It can be hard to go against the behaviour of the group although as a manager you need balance this with being a role model for the group as well. Remaining neutral and leaving the group setting is a good way of handling this. It signals that you will not be part of the conversation and that it is not something that you wish to spend your time on.

- Forgetting where you are or reacting without thinking: It can be quite easy to be caught off guard as you walk through a coffee area or a canteen, especially if people are using humour with their negative comments. It is so easy to smile, nod or laugh with them before you can catch yourself. Reflect upon these situations and think about how you would like to handle them differently in the future.

Tackle it there and then

- Use the questions in chapter 12 to get back to facts and understand the scope of concern. If you are hearing the same negative story or one person is particularly outspoken then prepare for how you want to respond next time you hear the comment. These questions will be helpful as will the preparation outlined in chapter 45, 'Having Difficult Conversations'. Have a mindset of exploration towards what it could be about and ask questions to discover if there is a real concern. Then you can work out how you would like to address that appropriately.

- Tackle the comment in a team meeting. If you feel that the rumour needs dispelling, then it may be useful to have a proper conversation with your team about it in a team meeting. Again it is useful to prepare for this meeting: What outcome do you want from the conversation? What facts do they need to know? What questions and concerns will they have? How will you answer those? Use a colleague as a sounding board and run through your proposed team meeting conversation with them.

Prevention is better than cure

- Team meetings are a good place to encourage people to air any concerns or raise any rumours that they have heard. Handling these in a factual manner means that the team becomes better at handling what could be potential conflict situations as well as learning to ask questions about the 'rumours' themselves. If possible, get the items raised before the meeting so that you have enough time to prepare for the conversation on them. If one is raised during the meeting and you feel unprepared

to answer it then say so; agree a date when you will have the conversation with them and stick to it.
- In one to one meetings encourage people to raise issues or concerns. Again handle these in a factual way and be careful about how you react to them as people will learn how to behave in the future from your response.

Capabilities for Connecting With People

Part II of the book is about developing six key skill sets that will enhance how you put into practice the applications in Part III. As with any skill you can apply it for different reasons. For example, you can facilitate a meeting tightly to control the conversation and the outcome so you do not feel out of control. You can facilitate a meeting to manipulate it to put you in a favourable position. Or you can facilitate a meeting to encourage open discussions and gain commitment to the agreed outcomes. All of these have different intentions although they use the same skill set. Therefore, Part II builds on the mindsets discussed in Part I. Developing these skills, and those mindsets, is a powerful combination that will create adult behaviour in everyone, improve decision making and create more innovative thinking.

Firstly, we cover fundamental skills for bringing out the best in people.

- **Questioning for Robustness**
- **Listening Productively**
- **Language That is Influential**

They give you a means to have conversations that explore, understand, challenge and openly discuss work in a way that does not blame, undermine or alienate people. They also give you ways to hold people to account and make it difficult for them to cover up poor work or shift the blame to others.

Then we move onto:

- **Feedback That Develops People**
- **Maintaining Your Composure**
- **Building Enduring Relationships**

Each of these I feel are important skills to have. They are often spoken about but less often demonstrated. I have found them valuable skills to have as they enhanced my ability to manage and work with people.

Remember it is useful to have a partner who is also working on these skills to provide learning support and encouragement.

Questioning for Robustness

Telling someone what to do, in the short term, is quicker although those people struggle to do it for themselves next time the situation arises. So in the long term it is less effective and the cycle of 'tell-do' repeats itself. Also many people find that asking questions does not seem to work well so they shift to giving opinions. One of the reasons that asking questions is not effective is that they only scratch the surface. They ask a question, get an answer and move on. Initially this may seem sensible although there is little understanding as to the foundation, robustness and nature of the information gleaned thus rich and pertinent information remains undiscovered.

I feel that people go to level 1 with their questions and that you need to go to level 3 at least, if not level 4. By this I mean,

Level 1: ask an initial question and get an answer

Level 2: ask another question about the first answer

Level 3 and 4: Then ask another question from the second answer and so on until you get some insightful information.

In this way, you uncover useful information that means that your questioning delivered something of value and then you will do it more often. This level of questioning helps to strengthen people as they really have to think and piece together the answers to your questions. Therefore, their awareness is expanded. This is why people can solve their own problems from this style of questioning: They see it from a new perspective and make different connections.

Listening and questioning are like the proverbial 'chicken & egg' situation – they are intricately entwined with each other and work best when blended together. These two skills are the main stay of a manager's ability to engage people and when underpinned with the mindsets from Part I will quickly build trusting relationships and open up rich conversations.

Here we are looking at three areas of questions that will give you a wide repertoire of questions and provide reasons for the questions.

Chapter 11 "Questions That Invite Others to Contribute" covers general questions that will be really helpful to you in everyday situations. They will form 50-75% of your questions.

Chapter 12 "Questions to Help Overcome Unhelpful Perceptions and Thinking" looks at questions really designed to put detail back into people's answers. This can be really useful if they are being unintentionally or intentionally vague. They are great for yearly appraisal and development meetings.

Chapter 13 "Questions That Create a Step Change in Thinking" will look at Rich Questions that are aimed at making a step change in the person's thinking.

The biggest mistake that managers make is to use loaded or deliberately pre-chosen questions to guide the person to giving the answer the manager had already decided upon. I am sure we have all seen it happen. Any manager who does this is kidding themselves if they think the other person didn't feel coerced into an answer. Often these managers think questions are a way of getting the other person to feel as if it was 'their idea' when in fact all along that person knows they are being forced along a path. The answer to this situation is to just be honest. You have a burning idea or solution that you want them to do, so just say it. If you can, own up to the fact that it is your idea and maybe you are being a bit blinkered or a little quick in proffering it. At least the person doesn't feel manipulated by you and your honesty will be refreshing to them.

Although I am choosing questions as I hear what the other person has to say, I also have my favourite ones, such as "What will happen if you do nothing?" My favourite questions change over time as I hear new ones from other people which is one of the benefits of training coaches and working with other coaches. My mainstay questions are "Tell me more about that?" and "What do you mean by that?" Learn these if nothing else and ask them often. You'll be interested in what you learn and how valuable that is.

11. Questions That Invite Others to Contribute

What are the benefits of doing this?

This skill is the crux of a manager's ability to develop people who are engaged, committed and competent so that they think and act robustly to get the desired outcomes. If you learn to ask questions of your people, not only will you know and understand more, so will they. Knowing what they are thinking, how they are planning to do things, understanding their logic for doing something, will give you far more confidence in them and the outcome than telling and controlling ever can. Also as people grow they will take on their accountability in the fullest ways possible and feel valued. Questioning to explore and help others to become robust in their thinking is a task that managers can do more often as they reduce other less valuable tasks that they are currently doing.

If there are only two chapters that you read in this book, then read this chapter and chapter 15 on Listening. These are at the heart of a good coaching style and reform meetings as much as one to one conversations. The benefits are that you will feel more in control managerially whilst your people feel more in control of what they are doing as well.

Possible pitfalls and concerns to consider

- The analogy that is often used here is that of fishing in that you are not here to catch fish for your people but to teach them to catch fish for themselves. This can be uncomfortable for many managers as it is one step removed and therefore less easy to link your efforts to the 'fish being caught'. People in general prefer short cycle feedback: I do something and here is the result. In this case the equivalent is that 'you taught them to fish and later they caught a fish'. If you feel motivated by seeing others develop and doing things they could not do before then you will fare well with this style of managing people.
- They say nothing or say they don't know: Often when you go from telling to asking this happens as people expect you to do the thinking and answer the questions. Firstly, they have learned if they don't answer then you will so you will need to hold back from answering. Secondly, they are probably not good at thinking or they are worried their answer may make them look silly or get criticised. Therefore, you may

need to work on your relationship with this person before you get free flowing answers. Rich Questions in chapter 13 will help. When I ask a question and someone says that they don't know, my next question is usually "And if you did know, what would you say?" It is amazing how often they then give me an answer.

- It takes too long: It may take too long in the short term but usually not in the long term. This is the tension that you will always need to handle as a manager so again stand back and reflect: Am I always telling even when I could have asked a question? Could they have easily told me what I told them? Am I answering the same questions over and over again? If so, you need to carve out some time to change this dynamic.

- They expect me to tell them: Just because they expect something doesn't mean that you have to do it. It is unreasonable within the current workplace to expect to know more than all your team know and to be able to do their current jobs better than they can. Jobs are more complex and are changing daily in today's workplace. Your people are the current experts (or should be) and your expertise is in unleashing their expertise so they deliver their work. Over time your people will change their expectations of what you are there to do.

- They can blame you if you tell them: At the moment, a number of your people probably prefer you telling them what to do as that means they are not accountable if it fails. They can passively say they did what you told them. Also, this can be used as a way of doing less. Obstacles just mean that they can give up and come back to ask you what to do now. Reflect on how much of your time this is taking up.

- They will think that I don't know very much and I'll lose credibility: This is a genuine concern for many managers especially if they have built their authority upon holding a lot of the information. Again, people are entitled to think whatever they want. Although that does not mean that they won't change their expectations if given a more preferable option. Using a mentor will help you to handle your own feelings until you build a different authority model based upon getting them to explore their own thinking. Create a reputation for asking thought provoking and insightful questions that people find useful.

- I will be seen as weak and passive if I don't have an opinion: Again, there is a balance here as sometimes it will be useful for you to give your opinion. However, we have a lot of 'tell' role models and therefore we often give an opinion without thinking. Therefore, consider whether you really should give an opinion or whether you should ask questions. Maybe ask questions and then give an opinion if it is still appropriate. Generally skilled questioners are far from being weak. On the contrary, they are often hardnosed people as the questions they ask are quite demanding to answer as they get people to own up to things or push their thinking beyond its current boundaries. Personally, I love being with those people as I feel so much stronger and valued afterwards.

Other relevant chapters
- Chapter 1   Understanding Their Perspective
- Chapter 9   How You Train People Through Your Actions
- Chapter 14   Holding Eye Contact and Silences

How

Covers three steps to do this.

Being curious about what you don't know or understand is a good place to start when asking questions. A useful attitude to adopt is the curious one of "What is happening that I don't understand because from what I currently know I would not be doing what they are doing?". Rather than "Why don't they just do ... as that is what I would do?" Questions firstly open up the topic to gain a wider perspective before they bring the conversation to a conclusion. This is the dynamic you are looking for:

1. Open up the topic
2. Explore/ probe/ clarify/ expand
3. Conclude the conversation

Sometimes even this simple structure is not required so in these cases just ask 'What' and 'How' type questions.

Also, look to replace as many 'why' questions with 'what' and 'how' questions. 'Why' questions tend to create defensiveness in the other person as in many cases 'why' questions have been used to criticise and judge them across the years. Usually said with a tone of voice that you know is not well intentioned. Even at an early age 'why' questions are used in this way, for example, "why haven't you tucked your school shirt in?", "Why did you do that?", "Why haven't you done your homework?" etc., etc.

So 'Why did you do that?' may become 'What was your thinking behind doing this?' or 'What were your reasons for doing it this way?' Again, your tone is important and you need the intention behind your questions to be that of understanding and exploring rather than judging and blaming.

1. 'Opening up' the topic

This could be as simple as getting some context about the situation or just clarifying what the person is trying to do.

a. Tell me more (about this)?

b. (Is there) Anything else?

Questions a. and b. asked several times before you move on to step 2 will get you almost all of the information they (and you) need and you may never use Steps 2 & 3. Eventually the person will say that there is nothing else, that that is it. Until they do so I tend to keep asking "Anything else?" It feels strange to me as I am conscious that I have asked the same question 3, 4 or 5 times in a row. Interestingly though the person I am asking invariably has no awareness that that has happened as they are focussed on their thinking and their answers.

c. What are you trying to do?

d. What do you want from me?

Questions c. & d. are other useful questions when 'opening up' the topic so that you understand what they would like from you and what they are trying to achieve. It is surprising how often people are not very clear about that for themselves. Thus they may be trying to solve 'everything' or are focussed on things that are not directly related to the outcome they are looking to get.

e. And?

"And?" is a great question as it just prompts the person for more without any suggestions.

Remember to leave enough time for someone to answer your questions before you jump in to fill the silence. Often it seems longer for you as you are waiting for an answer whereas they are embroiled in their thinking. Chapter 14 will help if you have trouble holding silences.

Often I will prefix my questions with a short phrase just to soften them otherwise some of the questions I use can seem a bit sharp if just delivered on their own. For example, "What were your reasons for doing that?" still feels a bit judgmental so I lead in with "Hmm, I was just wondering what your reasons were for doing that?" Statements like "I was just wondering ...", "I'm curious..." and "Just help me out as I'm a bit confused about..." are great ways to lead into questions. They ensure that the question is about helping them rather than judging them and they work best when you use them genuinely.

2. Exploring/ Probing/ Clarifying/ Expanding

Now you have a wider perspective and deeper understanding, it is useful to get the person to explore their own thinking a bit more and before you add your opinion. These are good areas to explore further: -

- What are they particularly interested in or preoccupied with?
- Where I am confused as I don't know enough or I feel they have said something that conflicts with or contradicts something else they have said?
- Aspects where I am genuinely curious about it?
- An aspect that I feel they are avoiding or skirting around?

This is where I find most people do not go deep enough with their questioning so dig down with your questions. Starting with Question a. is useful and then use Questions b, c & d to dig further.

a. Tell me a bit more about (that)?
b. What do you mean by...?
c. Anything else/ Is there anything else about...?
d. And?

Really explore until they/you

- Uncover something that gives them insight to move forwards
- Uncover the true issue, reason or blocker

3. Concluding the conversation

Another interesting thing I find about a lot of management conversations is that they do not properly conclude. They kind of dry up or attention is switched. Maybe managers don't think that they need to clarify "so what are you going to do now?" Maybe they think that it's obvious. Unfortunately, it is amazing how often it doesn't seem that it was obvious. Maybe the person feels that the manager doesn't care as he didn't seem interested in 'what next'.

Also concluding really checks out what the person has understood and taken from the conversation which is also good learning for you as you discover how you have or haven't helped. It may also uncover further issues such as; 'I know what to do but I have a problem with doing it'. This can be due to lack of confidence.

In most cases you want to check what they are now going to do, by when, what could stop them doing it and how they'll handle that. The following questions may help.

a. What are you going to do given our conversation?

b. When will you do that by?

c. What could stop you doing it?

   i. How would you handle that?

This is another useful question for concluding a conversation.

d. "How will you know when you have achieved it/ completed it?"

It gets the person to really think about what outcome they are looking for. Again this may get an unexpected answer and may mean that the conversation needs revisiting but at least you know.

Practice asking questions

Practice asking questions whenever you can: Write down some on the top of your notebook page or on the meeting agenda sheet. Think about what questions it would be useful to ask in advance of a meeting and write them down. Have a favourite question each day and look for opportunities to ask it.

Also reflect on how it went using this template.

> Reviewing:
> 1. How did they go?
>
> 2. What prevented you from asking questions?
>
> 3. What will you do differently next time?

Practicing, learning from that and doing more is a good way to embed questions into your repertoire. Once people start complimenting you on how useful the conversation was, the more you will want to ask questions.

12. Questions to Help Overcome Unhelpful Perceptions and Thinking

What are the benefits of doing this?

NLP (Neuro Linguistic Programming) advocates that during our daily lives we have a lot of information that comes to us through our five senses. In order to be able to handle this amount of information we have ways of filtering it. These filters are developed through our lives from our experiences, our role models, our values and our beliefs. In essence, these filters create the way we perceive and respond to life.

Epictetus, a great philosopher and teacher, said: "Men are disturbed not by things, but by the view which they take of them".

These styles of questions help you to influence people who have views that are limiting and unhelpful, in a useful way. These views, and people, can often waste valuable time and energy in the workplace instead of focussing on satisfying work and outcomes. These questions help the conversation to focus on clarity and reality rather than smoke screens and wallowing in 'what can't be done'.

In meetings and conversations these questions help cut through some of the deflection and side-tracking tactics of others which are being used in manipulative ways and are unhelpful for progressing business outcomes. These questions also 'train' others to be more concise and factual.

In annual reviews and difficult conversations, they help you keep the conversation on track and be able to uncover the full picture of the situation. They are skilful in retrieving the pertinent filtered-out information rather than allowing people to avoid giving it.

In difficult times they help create a sensible path of action that raises morale and gives the group a goal to focus on. They also help contain possible destructive small talk that undermines many teams and projects.

The benefits of becoming skilful with these questions are that you are able to get to the real situation quickly in a factual way and in meetings you have a higher chance of disarming people who distort things to suit their outcomes. You 'train' people to be factual from the beginning and conversations become more useful and satisfying for everyone.

Possible pitfalls and concerns to consider

- These questions feel direct and can be razor sharp. Therefore, they are best used in limited amounts or by positioning them well. By positioning I mean, that the question is prefixed: For example, "I was just wondering, what would happen if we could work in this new way?"

- Initially people can respond quite negatively to these questions as they tend to put people on the spot. Therefore, it is important to have good intentions and remain curious when using them. Over time people will see that you are not trying to trick or undermine them and also that you will not condone their previous unhelpful ways.

- The questions work best when you use the actual words and phrases of the person. Keep them as close as possible to what was said without elaboration. Also refrain from answering the question yourself or by giving suggested answers at the end of the question: Keep it simple.

Other relevant chapters
- Chapter 1   Understanding Their Perspective
- Chapter 14   Holding Eye Contact and Silences
- Chapter 27   Building Rapport

How

Covers three questions sets which help overcome unhelpful perception and thinking

    Deletions – questions to put back the detail

    Generalisations – questions to create doubt in their certainty

    Distortions – questions to get them to prove it

In his work, Noam Chomsky [ref] (linguist, philosopher and cognitive scientist), discusses the three ways that we filter out information from our surroundings so that we can cope with our experience of life. These filters are Deletion, Generalisation and Distortion.

The diagram below illustrates the filtering process, starting with the millions of pieces of data come to us every second through our five senses. To cut it down to a manageable amount we generalise, delete and distort the information, thus filtering out information that is not important to us. The information that is left is internally represented (a thought) in our mind that then produces our (emotional) state of mind, which in turn affects our physiology and therefore, the way we behave.

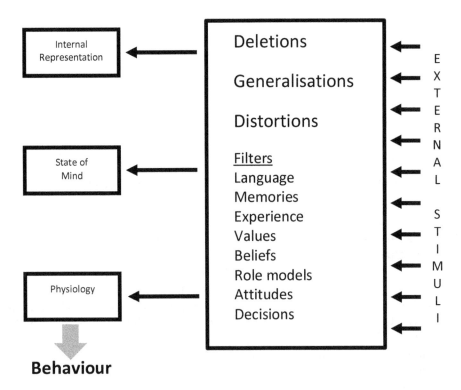

These filters are developed from our values, experiences, role models, beliefs and characteristics. It is these filters that shape our view and experience of the world. They are the constraints that we put upon ourselves to manage daily life. They can be useful to us or limit us. If they limit us then challenging them will influence how we experience the world, in a useful way.

People who genuinely engage with others focus on using these filters well and helping others to develop healthy filter patterns. They do this with positive intentions rather than being judgmental.

Let us take a deeper look at each of the three filters.

Deletions – questions to put back the detail

Deleting is a way of cutting down the information so we don't overload ourselves and the result is that lots of detail is lost. Usually the brain filters out things that it thinks are less important. This filter is useful to us otherwise meetings may take even longer than they currently do, with every piece of detail being spoken. However, when vagary is being used as a way of avoiding having to do something or is hindering progress, then it is worth challenging and retrieving the missing details.

To recover the useful information, use these questions:

What ...?

How ...?

Who ...?

When ...?

Where ...?

Questions starting with these words tend to force the person to give the required missing information, rather than allowing them to evade doing so. Also words such as 'specifically' and 'actual' focus the question further.

A worked Deletion example:

Here is a vague statement that someone may say:

"Head Office doesn't appreciate the problems we have!"

It is quite difficult to get the person to do anything with this statement as it lacks ownership. Also it would be difficult to ask useful questions as your questions would need to be vague themselves "What could you do?" and this risks having detrimental answers: "Why should I bother if they can't!"

Questions that you could ask to find out the missing detail:	
• Who specifically do you mean at head office?	• My boss
• What specifically don't they appreciate?	• How much I have to do and the effort I put in to do it.
• How do you know that they don't appreciate the problems that you have?	• They were angry I hadn't completed the report even though they knew I had to do this HR update.
• What actual problems don't they appreciate?	• It took 4 hrs to update one person's new pay details.
• What actual problems do you have?	• I had to do it before the 4pm deadline and I had left quite late before starting it.
• Who are 'we'?	• By 'we' I mean 'me'.

Now there is more detail to work with:

"My boss does not appreciate how much I have to do and the effort I put in to do it. He was angry I hadn't completed the report even though he knew I had to do this HR update. I needed to do the HR update before 4pm. It took 4 hrs to update one person's new pay details and I had left it quite late before starting it."

Only after retrieving more detail, can you begin to ask the person what they could do themselves to help improve this situation. These questions make the situation more reasonable and give them various avenues where they could do something. This in turn makes them feel more in control of the situation and less helpless. If you regularly use these questions, then this person will start to proffer more factual information from the start and over time will also start to think in this way themselves.

> **Deletion Exercise:**
> Here is a vague statement that someone may say:
> "It takes a lot of extra time, time that the team could be spending on more useful things!"
> What questions could you ask to find out the missing detail?
> -
> -
> -
>
> (See end of chapter for possible questions)
>
> **Your example:**
> What is a recent example for you, of someone being vague? Write it here.
>
> " _____
> _____ "
>
> What questions could you ask to find out the missing detail?

Two simple questions that I find in general conversation are really valuable for maintaining a useful level of detail and information gathering, are these:

- "What do you mean by that?"
- "Tell me a bit more about that?"

I am frequently relieved that I have asked one of those questions otherwise I would have started off down a solution route too early. Also, this would have wasted time working on a solution that wouldn't have worked very well. In many conversations we ask a question, get an answer and then move on: Going two levels deeper is often worth the effort as people feel listened to and the situation becomes clearer with that level of exploration. Therefore, I may initially ask "What do you mean by that?" and then once they have answered I ask "Tell me more about …?" having picked one aspect of their answer. It is amazing how these two questions can shed quite a different light on the initial comment and save a lot of time and effort.

Generalisations - questions to create doubt in their certainty

Generalisation is where you make a single or minor experience universal. This can be helpful in life; for example, when we see one chair we can easily identify other items that are also chairs rather than having to learn every variation of chair. It is unhelpful when it becomes detrimental; for example, 'Every meeting is a waste of time'; 'Nobody listens to me'.

Generalisations are also about the rules you assume that help you to navigate life: Often they act to limit or stop possible options or drive certain behaviour. Rules such as 'You must stop at a red traffic light in the UK'; 'You should clean your teeth every morning and evening' are helpful in general. Phrases such as 'we have to do that!', 'you can't do that!' or 'that shouldn't happen!' are possible indications where the generalisations have become entrenched or jaundiced. When generalisations are being used to block progress, shut down options or people tend to believe that their view is 'the right one' then in these cases it is worth challenging and creating doubt in that 'rigid' belief.

Questions to create doubt in universal experiences are simple to generate, as you can use the universal word as the question:

Never?

Always?

Everybody?

Nobody?

All?

Questions to create doubt in the 'right rules' include:

- What would happen if you did/ didn't?
- What would happen if you could / couldn't?
- What would happen if you didn't have to/ had to?

Most statements have a number of Deletions in them. I find that it is better to tackle any Generalisations first as this shifts the belief of the person about being able to do something. Afterwards it is easier to get them to recover the lost information using Deletion questions.

12. Questions to Help Overcome Unhelpful Perceptions and Thinking

A worked Generalisation example:

Here is a 'right' statement that someone may say:

"We never get what we want!"

This statement is quite difficult to get the person to do anything with as they won't want to talk about what they could do whilst they believe it will 'never' happen.

Firstly, you need to create doubt in that belief and then you can use Deletion questions to recover the missing detail.

If you attempt to use Deletion questions first whilst they believe it will 'never' happen they will see that as a pointless conversation and be evasive or sanctimonious.

Question to ask to create doubt in the belief:	Response:
• Never?	Never!
• Never? (You may need to ask a third time if you get the first response)	Yes, never! Or "Ok, well not 'never' but it is very difficult and I can't see it happening."
• Really, Never?	Ok, well not 'never' but it is very difficult and I can't see it happening.

Now there is some doubt about 'never' you can work on the "can't", which limits the possible options and drives behaviour away from action.

Now the statement is:

"Ok, well not 'never' but it is very difficult and I can't see it happening!"

Again a simple question to create even more doubt is to ask:

"What would you see if it could happen?"

In many cases this gets the person to focus their attention away from current reality and its perceived and real constraints, into a future where it is different and it is how they would like it to be. Often this changes the dynamic and they start to create possibility that something could be done to make it happen.

Once they describe what it would be like, you can ask them what small steps they could take towards that happening. Again they move from being helpless and 'done to' to having something they feel they can do and take control of.

Generalisation Exercise 1:

Here is a 'right' statement that someone may say:

"Nobody ever listens to me!"

What questions could you ask to create doubt in the two beliefs?

(See end of chapter for possible questions)

> **Generalisation Exercise 2**:
> Here is a 'right' statement that someone may say:
>
> "We have to do it that way!"
>
> What questions could you ask to create doubt in the rule (belief)?
>
> (See end of chapter for possible questions)
>
> **Your example**:
> What is a recent example for you, of someone generalising to block the progress or close down options? Write it here.
>
> What questions could you ask to create doubt in their belief?

Distortions - questions to get them to prove it

Distortion is where we change the information to fit our model of the world; to fit what suits us. In our day to day lives we are rarely conscious of this happening although investigations start to show how much we routinely do this. Distortion can happen in a number of ways: we can 'mind read' what someone is thinking or what will happen; shift responsibility from us to others; and we can create interpretations and linkages (cause and effect) that do not really exist.

Generous distortions are helpful in an engaging mindset; for example, if someone is late for a deadline. If we assume (mind reading) that they tried very hard and had unforeseen difficulty that allows us to start the conversation, with that person, with a mindset of curiosity as to what happened. This is likely to make the person feel safe and explain what really did happen. In contrast, in many meetings, I find that distortion (cause and effect - 'this means that') is used manipulatively where blame is moved around and reality can be hard to pin point. The other person rises to defend their position and the conversation is lost or becomes adversarial when asking a question would have been a powerful option.

Where distortion is being used to avoid taking responsibility or action then challenge the distortion by asking questions that get them to prove what they are saying with solid facts.

Questions to get the other person to prove what they are saying are:

o How do you know ...?

o How does ...?

- What are your reasons for thinking …?
- How does (X) mean (Y)?

Most statements have a number of 'Deletions' in them. I find that it is better to tackle any 'Distortions' first as this clarifies the real facts. Afterwards it is easier to get them to recover the lost information using Deletion questions.

A worked Distortion example:
Here is a distorted statement that someone may say:

> "I know the boss won't like this report!"

This statement is a mind-read and it can cause a lot of unnecessary anxiety and extra work. It may also stop people from putting in the real effort needed so it becomes a self-fulfilling prophecy. It is almost as if they are getting their excuses lined up, anticipating failure, so they can say 'I told you so'. This emotional energy would be better focussed on getting the report written well.

The easiest question, staying true to their statement, is;

> "How do you know the boss won't like this report?"

Once you have some more information you can use Deletion questions to discover the real problem behind this statement and what actions they could take.

A worked Distortion example:
Here is a distorted statement that someone may say:

> "He causes me to have to double check my work!"

This statement is a shifting of responsibility and it is quite difficult to get the person to do anything with it as they feel that it is out of their control and in the control of the other person. Sometimes it is used as an excuse for poor behaviour.

The easiest questions to shift the responsibility back are:

> "What does he do, that causes you to double check your work?"

And then,

> "When he does that, how could you choose to interpret it differently?"

The second question is a tougher question to ask. It may be useful to talk about how different people respond to the same behaviour in different ways: If someone shouts, then one person may go quiet, another may shout back and another may ask the person to calm down. Then ask the second question in the context of being able to choose how people affect you or about how you can learn to become more resilient to that behaviour.

A worked Distortion example:

Here is a distorted statement that someone may say:

> "You asked to use the machine before it was fully commissioned and now the main power supply has failed, that's your problem to fix."

This statement is linking two things to avoid having to fix a machine: It uses cause and effect when there is none or when it is quite tenuous. People often rely on the tenuous link to cause enough doubt in the other person so that they are reluctant to check out the assumption. It is surprising how often this works. It is usually worth checking out: They may be correct, partly correct or not correct. Asking the question factually is often worth it.

The question to ask is:

> "How does the fact that we asked to use the machine before it was fully commissioned, mean that the failed main power supply is our problem to fix?"

This question may meet with some bluster from the person and you may need to firmly ask the question again until you get a reasonable reply: Stand your ground and do not allow them to side step the question or change subjects.

Distortion Exercise 1: (Mind reading - assumption)

Here is a 'mind-reading' statement that someone may say:

> "I know they think we are just trying to get away with doing as little as possible!"

What question could you ask to get them prove the statement and find out how true it is?

(See end of chapter for possible questions)

Distortion Exercise 2: (Shifting responsibility – not my fault)

Here is a 'shifting responsibility' statement that someone may say:

> "He makes me nervous!"

What questions could you ask to get them prove the statement and take back responsibility for their reaction?

And then,

(See end of chapter for possible questions)

Distortion Exercise 3: (Cause and effect)

Here is a 'Cause and effect' statement that someone may say:

> "Because you didn't fund that project last year, you'll have to do it this year!"

What question could you ask to get them prove the statement and find out how true it is?

(See end of chapter for possible questions)

12. Questions to Help Overcome Unhelpful Perceptions and Thinking

Your example:
What is a recent example for you, of someone using distortion to avoid taking responsibility or action? Write it here.

"_____
_____"

What questions could you ask to get them to prove what they are saying with solid facts?

Larger Exercise:
Here is an excerpt from a conversation that I had with a colleague. See if you can identify which filters are being used and what questions may be useful to ask this person to help her get from 'victim' to being able to do something herself.

"My boss really annoys me. I know he doesn't think I can handle this larger second phase of the project as he has taken it on himself even though I have been working on the previous phase. I'm really good at this work and bad communication from management just makes it worse. I always handle these situations badly. I just can't work out what to say to him. Anyway I shouldn't need to say anything to him. He should come and talk to me"

	Filter / Questions
My boss really annoys me.	
I know he doesn't think I can handle this larger second phase of the project as he has taken it on himself even though I have been working on the previous phase.	
I'm really good at this work and bad communication from management just makes it worse.	
I always handle these situations badly.	
I just can't work out what to say to him.	
Anyway I shouldn't need to say anything to him. He should come and talk to me.	
	(See end of chapter for possible questions)

Previous exercises: Possible questions you could ask

These are not all the possible answers.

Deletion Exercise: Possible questions

Here is a vague statement that someone may say:

"It takes a lot of extra time, time that the team could be spending on more useful things!"

Questions that you could ask to find out the missing detail:
- What specifically takes a lot of extra time?
- What is 'it'?
- How much actual extra time?
- Who do you mean by 'the team'?
- Which specific members could be spending more time on useful things?
- What useful things?
- How do you know that they are more useful?
- Who says that they are more useful?

Generalisation Exercise 1: Possible questions

Here is a 'right' statement that someone may say:

"Nobody ever listens to me!"

What questions could you ask to create doubt in the two beliefs?
- Nobody?
- Ever?

Generalisation Exercise 2: Possible questions

Here is a 'right' statement that someone may say:

"We have to do it that way!"

What questions could you ask to create doubt in the rule (belief)?
- What would happen if we didn't?
- Says who?

Distortion Exercise 1: (Mind reading - assumption) Possible questions

Here is a 'mind-reading' statement that someone may say:

"I know they think we are just trying to get away with doing as little as possible!"

What question could you ask to get them prove the statement and find out how true it is?
- How do you know that they think you are just trying to get away with doing as little as possible?

Distortion Exercise 2: (Shifting responsibility – not my fault) Possible questions

Here is a 'shifting responsibility' statement that someone may say:

"He makes me nervous!"

What questions could you ask to get them prove the statement and take back responsibility for their reaction?
- What is it that he does to make you nervous?

And then,
- When he does ...... how could you choose to react differently?

12. Questions to Help Overcome Unhelpful Perceptions and Thinking

Distortion Exercise 3: (Cause and effect) Possible questions
Here is a 'Cause and effect 'statement that someone may say:
"Because you didn't fund that project last year, you'll have to do it this year!"
- What question could you ask to get them prove the statement and find out how true it is?
- How does the fact that the project wasn't funded last year mean that it should be done this year?

Larger Exercise: Possible questions	
My boss really annoys me.	This is a distortion where the responsibility has been shifted. The technical question is "What is it that your boss does that you choose to get annoyed about?" Although I would not actually use that, it has the embedded assumption that you are in control of how you choose to respond to his behaviour and could therefore choose to respond differently. Probably a better way to handle this is using two questions "What is it that your boss does that annoys you?" And then to get from victim mode into taking responsibility for your reaction "How could you choose to react differently to that? "or "How could you view that differently so it does not annoy you?"
I know he doesn't think I can handle this larger second phase of the project as he has taken it on himself even though I have been working on the previous phase.	This is an X means Y statement. The easy question is "How does X mean Y?" so that would be "How does the fact he has taken on the larger second phase himself mean that he doesn't think you can handle it?" Afterwards, you could also ask: "How does the fact that you worked on the previous phase mean that you should work on the larger second phase?"
I'm really good at this work and bad communication from management just makes it worse.	There are lots of deletions in this statement. What, Where, who, how questions get people to put the detail back in. So ask: "Who is management?" "Worse than what?" What specific type of communication do you mean?" "What specific work is that?" "How do you know that you are really good at this work?" "How do you know it makes it worse?"
I always handle these situations badly.	There are lots of generalizations in these statements. Ask "Always?"
I just can't work out what to say to him.	Ask "What would happen if you could work out what to say to him?"
Anyway I shouldn't need to say anything to him. He should come and talk to me.	Ask "Says who?" or "What would happen if he shouldn't have to?

13. Questions That Create a Step Change in Thinking

What are the benefits of doing this?

Standard what and how questions will help people think better although there are times when they seem to be only scratching the surface. Rich Questions are much more powerful and thought provoking questions that tend to get to the real issue or insight quicker. They are bolder than the usual what and how questions and allow people less 'wriggle-room' with the answers. Often they will create a step change in someone's thinking or awareness.

Being able to skilfully ask Rich Questions will really help your team to think deeply about their work and will allow them to get to the real problems and solutions quicker. Conversations will become less superficial and more meaningful.

Possible pitfalls and concerns to consider

- You need to purposely practice these types of questions as they take a bit of getting used to and the benefits from using them are worth the effort. Initially it is a good idea to prepare them for a specific meeting or conversation.
- They feel intrusive or 'pushy': I think that we are too courteous with our questions to others and with a curious mindset deeper questions can be asked more often. These questions are probably closer to the ones a trusted friend may ask you: They are challenging and with your best interests at heart. Perhaps, the question that you may be avoiding answering but you know you really need to face up to it.
- They feel awkward and obvious: Often when we try something new it can feel cumbersome and clumsy. Keep practicing and they will become more natural.

Other relevant chapters

- Chapter 14   Holding Eye Contact and Silences
- Chapter 18   But, And, Although and Others
- Chapter 27   Building Rapport

How

Covers three different styles of rich questioning

> The Unfamiliar Question
>
> The Unexpected Question
>
> The Unavoidable Question

Some years ago, I was running a presentation skills workshop. We had spoken about the use of rich language, as a way to engage your audience: The speeches of Martin Luther King are outstanding examples of this. One participant, Steve, was naturally very good at rich language. He enthralled us all for fifteen minutes with nothing other than his words and a copy of the book he was recommending. What struck me most as I avidly listened was the unfamiliar choice of some of his words and phrases. These leapt out of the presentation and really grabbed my attention. They fascinated me and created a richer image of what Steve was saying, rather than the dull thud of the stale and over-used phrases we have heard so many times before.

One phrase in particular stands out from the rest: It was the use of the word 'fine' instead of 'good'. A single word made such a difference to my attention, my thoughts and my engagement. If Steve had said

"… and this book makes a good introduction to the sci-fi fantasy genre…"

it would have glided over my ears without a second thought. However, he chose to say

"… and this book makes a fine introduction in to the sci-fi fantasy genre…"

It was unexpected and unfamiliar. It grabbed my attention and the cogs in my brain whirred into action in an effort to define "a fine introduction" and to differentiate it from merely "a good introduction".

Picking up on the theme of familiar verses unfamiliar, Martin Seligman in "Authentic Happiness" talks about how 'treats' become common-place and the norm if they are over used. They lose their excitement and the 'treat' is lost. It is the concept of 'unfamiliar' and 'unexpected' that I find I apply to my questions. I often find that the person responds with richer and more pertinent answers. They compel people to think, as the answers cannot be pulled from the pile of standard responses that require only a moment of thought to deliver. Rich Questions demand rich answers that are unfamiliar and sometimes, unexpected. They require searching thought. They make and break connections and do not always have answers but always provoke thought.

These questions move people forwards. If you feel that progress could be quicker if only you could ask some pertinent questions, then Rich Questions will be useful to you. Sometimes a good thought-provoking question where there is a search for an answer, even if no answer is found, is worth far more than a quick indifferent response. The person's subconscious will go on searching and searching and a rich answer bubbles up at a later point.

There are 3 main forms of Rich Questions that I use:

- Unfamiliar Questions have an unfamiliar word that grabs your thoughts and focuses in on the situation.
- Unexpected Questions jump out in front of your attention and turn you around to look at things from a different place.
- Unavoidable Questions take you beyond the decision or deadline and force you to look back at the choices you made.

The Unfamiliar Question

During a conversation we tend to know the types of questions to expect: "What did you do well?", "What could you have done better?" These questions have become common place and unconsciously we tend not to bother to think about them so much. We often assume we know the answers: The expected answers. They are also generic questions that lead to generic answers. However, an Unfamiliar Question has at least one word that captures the attention and makes the person think about their response. It heightens the question, for example, "What was the most significant action that you took?"

These questions give rise to a different answer. One that has been thought through and has dug into the depths of your memory thus making new connections and moving the person forwards. It also leaves the subconscious to deliberate over the new possibilities.

The unfamiliar element needs to home into the essence of what is required. It defines what will really make a difference to the topic being explored. These questions also tend to put the emotion back into the discussion.

So "What concerns do you have?" may become:

"What really scares you about this?"

And, "What did you do well?" may become:

"If you were in the audience, what was the most impressive moment?"

Unfamiliar Questions are specific and heightened questions to that person at that moment and therefore the answers to them are more tailored and pertinent to the conversation. This can often save time as two questions can be replaced by one question.

For example: "What will make this project successful?" and "Which of these is the most important?" could be replaced by "What 3 things are essential for this project to be truly successful?" The use of 'essential' and 'truly' focus and heighten the question.

People frequently use metaphors and analogies when they are talking. These provide you with lots of material to use for your Unfamiliar Questions and words that connect directly to the person's world and thinking. Using the person's words makes Unfamiliar Questions the most successful.

Examples of Unfamiliar Questions

(in the context of work) "What keeps you awake at night?"

"What are you most proud about?"

"What was that 'cherry on the cake' that made the most significant difference?"

"What are you dreading the most?

"Forgetting the current reality, what do you really want to do?"

Exercise:
Think about a recent conversation. Write down two questions that you asked someone:
1.

2.

Now make each question richer: Make them Unfamiliar Questions
1.

2.

Think about a meeting in the next few days where an Unfamiliar Question would be valuable to ask. What is that question going to be?

The Unexpected Question

The Unexpected Question disrupts an unhelpful train of thought. It catches the person by surprise, jumping out in front of them and taking them to a different view point; giving them a different angle. You metaphorically pick them up and put them somewhere else. It is this shifting in prospective that causes people to make connections and gain new insights. By asking an Unexpected Question people can make radical shifts in their progress. Unexpected Questions shatter the assumptions that we are reinforcing in an attempt to gain a new and useful insight; a way forward.

Therefore, if I have been working with a person and something goes awry: If there is a dip in energy, a momentary hesitation that could be the deciding moment between giving up and success. I'll ask:

"How could this be the best thing that could have happened?"

A bit of a surprise question for a number of people, but said with the simple intention to enable progress. My thought with this question is that it is only at the point when you start to think about "What can I do now?" or "How can I move forward?" that the conversation is useful and regains momentum.

Sometimes I work with someone who has a particular person that is being less than helpful in a project. The usual train of thought is to condemn the person, to look to minimise their impact, even side-line them. The Unexpected Question asks:

"How can this person be outstandingly useful to you?"

Again my intention comes for the fact that sometimes your worst detractor becomes your greatest advocate if they 'see the light'. Or that destructive people become constructive, once their energies are channelled in the same direction as the project. Often we cannot change the people we want in a project team, especially in such a matrix-managed world. We can, more easily, change our view of them and it is amazing how often they in turn reciprocate and change.

Overall, Unexpected Questions stop you wallowing in an unhelpful train of thought where you feel powerless and attempt to put you back in control. This invariably increases energy and commitment.

Examples of Unexpected Questions

"When it fails what will have caught you out?"

Context: Is their thinking too optimistic

"What is life trying to teach you?"

Context: Block/ frustration occurs

"What advice would you give to someone in this situation?"

"What actual choices do you have to make?"

Context: You can't just add more

"How does being unfamiliar with this area, make you the best manager for it?"

> **Exercise:**
> Think about a recent conversation. What Unexpected Question(s) would have been helpful to ask?
>
> •
>
> •
>
> Think about a meeting in the next few days where an Unexpected Question would be valuable to ask. What is that question going to be?
>
> •
>
> •

The Unavoidable Question

Sometimes, when working with a person, there is going to be a point in time, in the future, where an event will happen: A fork in the road and one or other of the routes will have to be taken. These questions are very useful if someone has not faced up to that decision and contemplated fully which of the alternatives they may prefer or what could be the real decider that ensures the success of their chosen path. Unavoidable Questions are invaluable for exploring these areas before the fork in the road occurs.

They usually work in sets of two or more questions, depending on the number of alternatives. Essentially they are the actual alternatives that the person is facing. The ones that are going to happen. Yet many people act as if somehow that point will never be reached. As if life will continue and the fork will remain always in the future.

Unavoidable Questions will not allow you to maintain a position of 'nothing will happen' or 'I can procrastinate for ever'. They force you to go beyond the decision, the deadline. They turn you around to look back and face the decisions/ choices that you made, for better or for worse, otherwise it is just a hypothetical conversation about endless 'what ifs' and 'perhaps'. These questions get you to experience what will really make a difference and give you a taste of how each route may feel once taken. Another useful question is: "What will happen if you do nothing?" which may be a good first question in getting them to realise that if they are passive then life will decide for them.

When I use Unavoidable Questions, I set them up with the person as they are not as succinct as the previous questions. These questions require a scene setting intro that works best if it triggers the person's feelings as if each alternative had been made.

A simple example of where Unavoidable Questions work well is in working towards getting another job. In this example the person really wants to get this job and I want them to think hard about their preparation so that they are successful. At some point there will be a fork in the road: The day they find out whether they have got the job. If possible I would ask the person when they expected to find out the result of the interview and where they might be when they receive the news. Then I set the scene, pose the first question and get a response. Then I set the second scene, pose the second question and get that response. For example:

The First Alternative: "Ok, it is Thursday morning and you have just put down the phone at your desk. You sit back in your chair. Oh no! You've just found out that you didn't get the job. How do you feel? (Their response) Now, what do you really, really wish you'd done that you didn't do?

The Second Alternative: "Ok, it is Thursday morning and you have just put down the phone at your desk. You sit back in your chair. Great! You've just found out that you have got the job. How do you feel? (Their response) Now, what are you really, really glad that you did do that you nearly didn't do?

How the scene setting element and the questions are delivered can be significant as I want the person to feel the difference in each alternative. In the example above, the first alternative I deliver in a flat and down-beat tone. The second alternative, I say with excitement and encouragement. This adds to their thinking as it connects a feeling to the questions. Often they come uncover a vital piece of preparation that needs to be done.

Another example is where the person does not know which alternative they might want to take: Not sure if I do want this job or not. A modified form of the Unavoidable Questions above is helpful in helping them understand which option they want to choose. It is important this time that each alternative is said with equal tone and clarity so that both options are fairly weighted. For example:

The First Alternative: "Ok, it is Thursday morning and you have just put down the phone at your desk. You sit back in your chair. You've just found out that you didn't get the job. How do you feel?

The Second Alternative: "Ok, it is Thursday morning and you have just put down the phone at your desk. You sit back in your chair. You've just found out that you have got the job. How do you feel?

Finally, I simply ask, "What do you know now?"

From this they often gain valuable insights into how they feel about each alternative option.

My intention with Unavoidable Questions is to unearth vital actions that will heavily weight the outcome in favour of what the person wants or get them to find information so they can decide before it's too late. So many times I hear people say "I knew I should have done …" or "gosh, I'm really glad I did … I nearly didn't do that." To enable the most robust action plan it is worth uncovering these actions before the fork in the road and not leave it totally to chance.

> **Exercise:**
> Think about a situation where someone needs to think about the options they have and the decisions they need to make. What would be the two, or more, useful Unavoidable Questions to ask them?
> 1.
> 2.
> How will you 'set the scene' for each question so that they really feel as if they are in that situation as you ask the question?
> 1.
> 2.

Overall I find Rich Questions are a useful addition to go with the standard and fundamental questions. If you follow the person's train of thought and use their own brand of words and phrases, Rich Questions will come naturally. Like anything that is rich, if used excessively they may prove too much for the person's appetite.

Being inspiring as a manager means providing a stimulating environment where thoughts are uncovered, created, debated, viewed, explored and progressed. I believe that just as rich language from a presenter creates an inspired audience, Rich Questions from a manager create an inspired team.

Finally, ask yourself these questions:
- "What will happen if I do nothing?"
- "If I knew you couldn't fail what would I do differently?"
- "What choices do I have to make?"

Listening Productively

Listening goes hand in hand with asking questions. Ask an insightful question and then listen to the answer. By listening well to what the answer is you can ask another insightful question. By listening to what people say, it is much easier to ask questions and to understand what they are really saying. Listening means that they feel you are listening to them rather than you saying that you are listening to them. Listening forms a connection with the person and it is amazing how you may hear things you have not really heard before.

Chapter 14 "Holding Eye Contact and Silences" discusses how to hold eye contact and silences well. I have found that these often go together. People who find it difficult to hold silences also find maintaining reasonable eye contact harder. Now you can really focus on the person,

Chapter 15 "Listening With Your Eyes, Ears and Intuition" is about the art of listening itself and what that entails through listening with your ears, eyes and intuition.

Chapter 16 "Listening That Invites Others to Contribute" looks at 'how you listen' affects the person you are listening to and what they may or may not be willing to share with you because of that.

14. Holding Eye Contact and Silences

What are the benefits of doing this?

Have you been in a situation where someone has asked you a really good question. It's really made you think and you are just about to answer it when either they answer it for you or they move on: Frustrating isn't it? As a manager, it is worth realising that you need to give people time to think about and then answer the question you have asked them. Also pausing trains people to realise that you are expecting an answer as I am sure that some people just wait as they know their manager will answer the question for them. This perpetuates the 'learned helplessness' and dependency on the manager. The manager remains frustrated and critical of their team for not 'thinking for themselves' but in reality they are given little time to actually do that. Remember some people take time to think before they respond, so give them time.

The real benefit, apart from giving them time to think, is that the person feels listened to and respected as you wait for them. It also creates a safe environment where it is ok to have time to think. Thinking time is something that I feel we are currently really missing in the workplace. It is do, do, do all the time! So where is the 'thinking' time? The time to reflect on how things are and consider what could be done differently? Also if you consider someone to be 'very quiet' then they will definitely need space to think about their answer and then to say it. By doing this, I often find that 'quiet' people can be amazingly chatty. Overall you are allowing people the space to do their own thinking and develop their own solutions.

From your side, people with poor eye contact are invariably considered to be nervous or to be hiding something. Conversely, people who are comfortable with silence and eye contact are often considered to have gravitas. If you have had feedback that you do not seem to be very confident then consider how good your eye contact is.

Possible pitfalls and concerns to consider

- Although you wait quietly for someone to answer, you are impatient for them to answer. Usually the other person will feel your impatience and this will cause an amount of stress in them which will affect the conversation. Learn to let go, enjoy the pause and wait patiently for them to answer.
- Whilst waiting you start to read notes or write something in your notes: Withhold the urge to do something else while you wait for them to answer as they will take

that as a signal of disinterest. At the very least it will distract their attention away from their thoughts.

- The other person will feel uncomfortable: I have only found this to be true if I have been uncomfortable myself. When I am comfortable about it that seems to transmit to the other person. If the person is uncomfortable then hold the silence just a bit longer as it will help that person feel more comfortable with holding silences. I will then ask another question rather than answer for them as I really want them to answer it for themselves and build their confidence in these situations.

Other relevant chapters
- Chapter 3   People and Their Differences
- Chapter 26   Being Your Own Best Friend
- Chapter 27   Building Rapport

How

Covers three different ways of improving eye contact and holding silences

As a manager it would be useful to be able to hold the silence just a little bit longer than you feel it is comfortable to do so. Whilst avoiding the tendency to jump in too soon to 'save' the other person or to put an end to our own discomfort. The same goes for eye contact: Be happy to hold it just a bit longer than usual and be comfortable in totally focussing on the person as they talk. Focussing on them means looking at their face but not always directly into their eyes: Focussing around the 'eyes-nose-top lip' area will work.

Practicing helps with both silences and eye contact. Initially find someone safe to work with and then as you feel more comfortable find someone a bit riskier to practice with. As you feel more and more comfortable then broaden out to holding silences and eye contact on more challenging people or in more challenging situations.

Remember this is about stretching our boundaries so forgive yourself if you have a bad day and it feels less comfortable. Once you feel more robust then do it more.

Practice one

Sit across from your colleague and look at them for one minute without breaking eye contact. Get them to time it. If you break eye contact with them, get them to start the one-minute timing again. Once you can comfortably do one-minute move on to Practice two.

Practice two

Put two chairs facing each other, close together. You sit in one and your colleague in the other. You should be directly looking at each other. Your knees should be only a few centimetres apart. Now look at the person, in silence, for 15minutes: yes 15 minutes. It is an amazing experience as people's faces change dramatically as you look at them. When I did his I found that after 3 or 4 minutes I needed to have a quick giggle, but once that was over I held the silence for the remaining time.

Practice three

Write down an insightful question and a few variations of this question. Sit next to the person and ask the question. Wait until they answer - as long as it takes, just wait. If they say 'I don't know' then try a slightly different way of asking the question and wait for their answer. Practice this once a day for a week and then see if you need to practice for another week. You will know this as you should start to notice how much better and comfortable you are at holding the silences in other conversations.

Tips

- Sit next to people or at 45 degrees rather than opposite them. This feels more as if you are working together on something rather than in opposition to each other as your seating may subconsciously suggest.
- Counting to 15 is a little bit crude but it gives you something to occupy your mind and forces you to wait. Hopefully by then they will have said something and you'll have learned for yourself that it is worth the wait. Increase the counting to 20 if you need to.
- During the silence take time to reflect on the conversation and how it is going? How do you feel about it? How do you think they feel about it? How do you know that?
- Enjoy the silence as welcomed 'downtime' and the emotional space it gives you.
- During the silence notice what is going on around you at that moment although without moving your eyes too much.

If I feel that whilst I am waiting for their response, they feel anxious because I am silently focussing on them, then I will look away for a bit. I look in the same direction as them, in my lap or just in front of me. I am careful that it does not look as if I have become impatient or disinterested. I use the time to think about what this means for the conversation we are having.

15. Listening With Your Eyes, Ears and Intuition

What are the benefits of doing this?

When people feel listened to they feel understood and valued. Once they have been allowed to say what they wanted to say then usually they will listen to you and other people's views. Sometimes they will then let go of their wishes as they feel they have been properly heard. Many are not unreasonable at all once they feel they have been allowed to have their say.

Also when you really hear what they are saying it is often different to what you thought you heard or were going to hear. Listening well can save a lot of time and misunderstanding not doing the wrong thing and by understanding what the real issues are. Listening well also instils trust in the team and builds relationships.

Finally, you learn a lot about the person when you listen. You learn about what drives them, their values and beliefs, and how they view the world. This is really helpful to you when you wish to motivate them or when problems arise. Similarly, they will listen to you differently and understand what you are saying better.

Possible pitfalls and concerns to consider

- It will take too much time: There is a balance to be struck but once people understand that you will spend time listening to them they will become more succinct. Reflect on when you could have listened well and how often you are doing it. As we tend towards speaking ourselves because it seems quicker, you should challenge yourself on why you felt you did not have enough time to listen well.

- People will talk for far too long: Initially this may happen although they will learn that people will not tolerate that, especially in meetings. They will then temper the amount that they say and the quality of what they say. If they do not, then you can use questions to pull out the significant points and close the conversation.

- What if they have nothing to say: For me this says a lot about the quality of the relationship rather than about them having nothing to say. It is true though that some people are more succinct and say less but rarely do they have nothing to say. If people are less willing to open up to you then think about what you need to do to improve your relationship with them so that they feel safe to talk more.

- They want to hear my thoughts first: Yes, they may want this and it doesn't mean that you have to do that. If they want your thoughts first, then pause and consider why they want them first: Do they want to tailor their response from what you say; are they dependant on you and is it wise to continue condoning that? If you do decide to give your thoughts first, then reflect afterwards on how that helped or hindered the outcome and their long term development.
- I might not like what I hear: This is true. Sometimes what we learn can be painful personally or mean that we now have a problem we didn't have. Well at least you know and now you can do something about it if you wish to before it gets any worse.

Other relevant chapters
- Chapter 1   Understanding Their Perspective
- Chapter 3   People and Their Differences
- Chapter 27   Building Rapport

How

Covers four topics that will enhance the quality of your listening

Clear your mind and focus fully on them

Maintain your attention on them

What am I hearing, noticing and feeling?

What is my intuition telling me?

Clear your mind and focus fully on them

When you are about to listen to someone clear your mind of other conversations and the work that you are doing. Mentally pause that work and 'put it down' to clear your mind. I do this by really noticing something about the features of the person talking to me, for example the contours of their face. Then I focus my attention on them: I bring them into focus not only visually but also in my mind. They become the central point of my vision and awareness. I blur out everything else and then I don't get distracted by it. People notice if your attention is not on them even if you are looking at them. Sometimes I feel as if people are looking through me or that their focal point is behind me or just to my side. Also people can see that vacant look on your face when you think they won't realise that although you are looking at them you are really thinking about something else. It is simply better to be honest and either say you are not listening or clear your mind and focus fully on them.

If they interrupt you working on the computer or something else, then stop what you are doing. Unless it is vital don't be tempted to say, 'give me a moment, I just need to finish this'. It almost certainly can wait and they will notice that you have stopped for them rather than them having to wait like 'school children' whilst 'teacher' is finishing off something more important than they are. By stopping you give them the message that they are important and valued. It is a simple thing to do and one that can get good results. Otherwise agree a time when you can meet and listen properly.

Maintain your attention on them

It is very easy to allow yourself to be distracted by a person walking by or at the sound of a phone ringing. This is usually very frustrating for the speaker and gives them the message, intended or not, that they are not as important as what distracted you or that you aren't very interested in what they are saying. Practice ignoring these: Focus on an object or spot on the in front of you and fix your gaze on it. As things happen around you maintain your gaze and your attention on that object or spot as if nothing else exists. Set a timer and see how long you can maintain your attention for. You'll know when you get distracted. Once you can do it, it becomes very easy to ignore other things and just listen to the person. When I am fully listening to someone and my phone rings in my bag, not a muscle in my body moves to acknowledge it. It is as if I have heard nothing at all.

What am I hearing, noticing and feeling?

I recognise that when I am truly listening to someone that I use more than my ears. Here are some thoughts, questions and examples for you to consider when you are listening to someone. I find they also help with my attention.

Hearing

Tone and volume changes, emphasis on certain words or phrases may tell you what's important to them or where there is doubt or hesitation. These are places to explore with questions perhaps or connections to be made with events that have happened, or not. Lots of apologies, for example, or the way things are phrased (optimistically or pessimistically for example) give you an insight into how they are viewing the situation or the effect it is having upon them. What useful questions might this prompt you to ask?

Noticing

Smiles, frowns, glances away, eyes down, eyes up, hands moving or still, shoulders slumped or upright, fidgeting or rigidity, eye contact. What message am I interpreting from these? What questions would it be useful to ask to help checkout my interpretation? How might this be affecting the person and the situation?

Sometimes what people say and how they are being at the time seem to be in conflict. Often how they are being is the authentic version. I remember during an exercise in one training session I attended, I was saying that I would speak to Steve whilst gently shaking my head from side to side. I was totally unaware that I was shaking my head. My partner spotted the verbal 'yes' and 'behavioural 'no'. Once challenged I admitted that I was nervous about speaking to him about it. That led to a conversation about my conflict and what how I was really feeling. I was then, and still am, amazed that I had not been aware that I was doing that.

Feeling

How am I feeling as I listen? Nervous, fearful, comfortable, energised, excited - am I feeling as they do? Would it be useful to say how I am feeling? Is it helpful or unhelpful to feel as they do? Or do I need to think about how to change the feeling, for both of us?

Or am I feeling concerned, frustrated or calmed by this conversation, although they are feeling quite differently? Would it be useful to say how I am feeling? Is it helpful or unhelpful to feel as I do? Or do I need to think about how to change my feeling before it interferes with the conversation?

What is my intuition telling me?

When I am listening I also put the conversation into a bigger context as well as drawing upon my knowledge and past experience. It is a bit like forensic investigation where a letter can look quite different when put under a special lamp that highlights the different inks used and enhances other pressure marks. Therefore, I might think about some of the following: -

- o What aren't they saying what you may have expected them, or someone else, to say during this conversation?
- o Are they congruent - are they contradicting themselves or an earlier conversation?
- o What is not being said - what is left unspoken or avoided? Could this be the true issue?

- What insights do these give you? What questions may you ask because of these insights? Also it can be useful to think about how happy they are to talk freely.
- How guarded or open are they being? What can you do to help them feel safer to be open?

16. Listening That Invites Others to Contribute

What are the benefits of doing this?

Have you ever noticed that you tell some people more things than others, that it feels safer and more worthwhile to do so? Have you noticed how much doing that helps move things along and engenders more trust? This is because how someone chooses to engage when listening to you affects what you are prepared to say to them.

Often people listen to you because they have to or for their own benefit or to quickly solve your issue. It is rare that someone gives you quality listening time and attention whilst you are talking. Many coaching training programmes focus on this aspect as coaches need to quickly create a safe environment where coachees feel comfortable to be open about their situation and what needs to be different. A line manager that creates that same safe environment is rewarded by hearing far more about the thinking of their people, hearing about problems sooner and being able to usefully help the person develop their own solutions. Overall everyone wins: The manager knows more about what is really happening and how people feel. The team appreciates being genuinely listened to and finds that they can often solve their own issues once they have been helped to thoroughly think about the situation.

Possible pitfalls and concerns to consider

- It takes time: Although the initial conversation will probably take longer, the solution is often more robust and well implemented. It is a shame that even today we have time to resolve things multiple times because we didn't have enough time to have the initial conversation properly. I suppose people feel vindicated as they are 'doing something'.
- I tend to interrupt and I can't change: It is true that change takes practice and there is also a lot of evidence that people can change and change quite radically. There seems to be a general thought that it takes six weeks to break a habit and six weeks to embed the new one. It is embedded at the point it becomes automatic and effortless.
- The conversation of two monologues: Be careful of falling into the trap of asking just enough questions until you think you understand the problem and then telling

them want they should do. I call this the conversation of two monologues where they tell you the problem and you tell them the solution. Often the solution is from your perspective and about what you would do from the limited information you have, as you are focussed on problem solving rather than fully understanding the situation. In many cases the other person does not even get to say what their solution was. It leaves them feeling frustrated, low on commitment and struggling to carry out someone else's idea. Often it leads to unresolved problems due to inadequate or incorrect solutions being implemented.

- People will know that I don't behave like that during a conversation: Initially they may be nervous and wonder if this is a long term change although overall they will prefer you engaging with them. Persevere and maintain your focus on changing. In a few months they'll have moved on to.

Other relevant chapters
- Chapter 1   Understanding Their Perspective
- Chapter 3   People and Their Differences
- Chapter 15   Listening With Your Eyes, Ears and Intuition

How

Covers

Exploring rather than solving

Practicing exploring

Exploring rather than solving

From my experience, feedback, training and the reading that I have done over the years it feels as if the first question people have in their mind when someone is starting a conversation with them is, "are they actively engaging with me in this conversation?" Once you know that someone is then I think that the second question is whether it is for your benefit or their own. Therefore, what you are aiming to do is to engage with someone by putting other thoughts aside and focussing on helping them to think about and explore their issue. Exploring is a key word as by helping them to thoroughly explore their thinking they often come up with a way to solve it or a valuable insight that significantly changes their perspective on it.

The feeling of satisfaction and commitment this creates is rewarding for both of you and in many ways it starts with your mindset, a mindset of curiosity. A mindset that thinks:

"Having listened so far to what you have said, I would be doing X but you are not, therefore what is it that I am missing? If I truly understood the situation from your viewpoint, then I would understand why you are not doing X and what could be different. This would put me in a better position to help you develop a solution that works for you and solves the real problem."

You also need a mind-set that respects the other person for who they are and what they bring to the conversation, as a peer and a fellow human being. In a peer relationship it is easier for each person to feel safe and comfortable to be honest about their thoughts without fear of blame or retaliation. As you demonstrate respect and genuine interest for others, people feel safe enough to be honest. People speak up so the real issues become known and solved. Therefore, your version of reality is closer to reality. In effect it is a collaborative conversation where your role is to provoke robust thinking in the other person until they have uncovered all the information they need to solve the problem once and once only. This requires a holistic understanding of the situation, what led up to it, other people's influence and any other factors involved.

If you are exploring a situation/ issue/ problem, then afterwards you would be able to tell someone else:

- What has happened in the past?
- How has this developed?
- How the person feels?
- What are they worried about?
- How they see the situation?
- What have they done already?
- What is stopping them doing more?
- Other people involved
- Relationships between these people
- How everyone feels?
- How everyone sees it and what would they like to happen?
- Other people who are not involved who should be
- What would the person like to have happen?

To engage more collaboratively you need to practice exploring the situation as then you fully understand why the situation exists and why it is where it is. It is a bit like piecing all the jigsaw pieces together to get the full picture of the puzzle before acting upon it unwisely.

Here are some useful questions to help you explore: -

- What has happened?
- What have you done so far?
- How do you feel about this?
- What would you like to have happen?
- Who else is involved?
- What is their perspective?
- How do they feel about it?
- What would they like to happen?
- How do other people feel about that?
- What are you assuming that is (stopping) you from ......?
- What are the consequences of doing nothing?
- What choices do you have to make?
- What needs to be different for ...?
- What happens if ...?
- And can you ...?
- What do you mean by (that)?
- Tell me more (about ...)?
- Is there anything else (about ...)?
- And then what happened/happens?

Practicing exploring

1. Find someone who you feel comfortable to talk with.
2. Get them to talk about a work issue, problem or challenge they currently have.
3. Allow them to talk freely for at least 3-4mins
4. Now think about what you are curious about. Ask some of the questions and allow them the space to answer.
    - What has happened?

- What have you done so far?
- How do you feel about this?
- What would you like to have happen?
- Who else is involved?
- What is their perspective?
- How do they feel about it?
- What would they like to happen?
- How do other people feel about that?
- What are you assuming that is (stopping) you from ......?
- What are the consequences of doing nothing?
- What choices do you have to make?
- What needs to be different for ...?
- What happens if ...?
- And can you ...?
- What do you mean by (that)?
- Tell me more (about ...)?
- Is there anything else (about ...)?
- And then what happened/happens?

5. Remain engaged and ask the questions until either they have solved it for themselves or you really understand the situation holistically.
6. Reflect on the conversation:

> Reviewing:
> 1. How well did you explore, as opposed to focus on solving the problem?
> 2. What challenged you?
> 3. What helped?
> 4. What will you do differently next time to explore more?

7. Repeat this exercise with other people until you feel able to explore what is happening to get a full understanding of the situation. This will help them to solve more of their own problems or for you to work with them from a well-informed place.

Language That is Influential

Sometimes with the best intentions in the world, what managers say significantly undermines that intention. Here is a simple example from a meeting I was at yesterday. The manager wanted to create participation in the meeting as generally people say very little. After they had been presented to for 40mins, the manager asked "Does anyone have any questions...no?" Although slightly better than "I don't suppose anyone has any questions?" which I have heard said, it does not really invite or enhance participation. Better questions might be: "What questions do you have?" or "Who has the first question?" followed by enough space, silence, to allow people to think of a question and then feel brave enough to ask it.

As a coach when I raise the manager's awareness to what they are saying they can be shocked by how different it is from what they meant. Sometimes they are self-aware enough to admit to their underlying concerns that they thought they had hidden well but came through loud and clear to everyone else. In the example above, many managers would rather not invite questions as they may not want to hear them or are worried about how to answer them. I think it then becomes an unconscious habit where we are subtly giving out 'don't engage fully' signals.

So the topics in these chapters are all about how your language can enable rather than hinder.

Chapter 17 "Productive Language" is about using language that is easy to understand and conveys what you meant it to. This means people are clearer about what you want or where they stand.

Chapter 18 "But, And, Although and Others" is a simple chapter looking at some key words that we use a lot and can significantly alter how the listener feels from what we said.

Chapter 19 "Reframing Perceptions" covers how we can usefully use language to reposition a situation or event, when someone's thinking is limiting them.

Chapter 20 "Using Analogies and Stories" looks at the use of these as they are powerful ways to convey messages and engage others which is useful in meetings as well as presentations.

17. Productive Language

What are the benefits of doing this?

By Productive Language I mean language that

- motivates
- is clean and clear - to the point
- has no mixed messages
- sounds as if you mean it

When I am coaching managers who need to handle a performance issue, the first thing I check out is what they have actually said to the poor performer about the situation. I do this because invariably the poor performing part of the message has been lost, toned down, counter balanced or confusingly stated so that it is unlikely that the poor performer really understands their situation. This often causes the situation to get worse and become more difficult to handle. It is frequently the fear of this happening that causes the manager to use such language in the first place. On the other hand, if they had been straight forward and clear about the poor performance message then it would have gone a lot better. The person would have understood the severity of the situation which would have enabled them to make some adult choices about what options they have and what they were going to do. In short it creates ownership.

So if you find that people don't seem to get what you are saying or you are not getting the results and reactions that you intended then this chapter will help you become clearer with your language. People will prefer that. Although to be clear, we are not talking about being 'blunt' or 'terse', just unambiguous.

This chapter will also help with gravitas as that is partly picked up by others through the words we use and how we construct our sentences. Take these two sentences for example and think about how you perceive the two speakers.

a. I was just wondering if, well perhaps, we maybe ought to have a look at the figures again as I'm not sure if we took last year's changes into account, but maybe we did.

b. I think we should relook at the figures as I am not certain that we took last year's changes into account.

Overall this chapter looks to ensure that your language supports your intentions which in turn will be easier for your team to act upon and convert into results.

Possible pitfalls and concerns to consider

- People's language is influenced more than we think by our unconscious and therefore non-productive language can be due to an underlying concern or fear about how the person may respond or your own abilities to handle the situation. An experienced colleague, mentor, coach or your line manager can help you work through those concerns so that you feel more confident about handling the issues.
- In being clear and clean, still keep in mind the topics from Part I that will help the language come across authentically rather than being blunt or feeling judgmental.
- Feeling the need to put in all the details and examples for every eventuality often clutters and confuses the conversation. Think about what your core message is and focus on that: What is the least I need to say? What is one solid example that clearly demonstrates my point? Only if required should you give further examples.
- Discussing multiple issues: It is better to handle the issues one by one than attempt to cover them all as this will confuse and overload the person.

Other relevant chapters
- Chapter 1   Understanding Their Perspective
- Chapter 9   How You Train People Through Your Actions
- Chapters 24-26 Maintaining Your Composure

How

Covers seven steps for a productive conversation

1. What do you want to happen?
2. Creating your concise message
3. Supporting evidence and facts
4. Checking its robust
5. Making it authentic
6. Reviewing all your thoughts
7. Afterwards

1. What do you want to happen?

Firstly, understand what you want to happen after the person has heard what you have to say?

- What is your intention by saying this? Is it honourable?
- What is the outcome that you want from this conversation?

2. Creating your concise message

Write down concisely the message you need the other person to hear and understand.

- Does this sum up the key element(s) of the message? Does it achieve the outcome you wanted above?
- Are there really two or three messages here? If so, do they all need to be said?
- Can one or more be said later?
- If you could only say one which one would it be?

3. Supporting evidence and facts

Write down what supporting evidence, facts, figures and events you have. Be objective and remove any opinions or judgments.

For example, "You have arrived 30minutes late to the last five meetings" is much clearer and objective than "You were late yet again for the meeting".

The second statement implies a judgment and that is what the person will respond to and what tends to cause problems. They are unable to do that with the first statement.

Also "Congratulations, you are our top student. Since we started this course 10 years ago this is the first time someone has achieved 8 A grades. You should be proud" is more satisfying for the student than "Wow you are wonderful as you're our best student ever". Although energising they might be left wondering if you really meant it or feeling it was a rather 'sugar coated'.

- So what is your supporting evidence?

4. Checking its robust

Is this enough information to convey the message well? Is it conflicting or does it make the message clear? Are you certain about the information? Can you check it or do you need more?

- Is there one example or fact that conveys the message well, that really 'lands' the message?
- Does it really need anything else?
- What is the least you can say to convey the message well?

5. Making it authentic

Can you have this conversation authentically? Are you feeling that you are robust in your intention and the evidence you have to back it up?

- Are you convinced it will achieve the outcome you intend? If not what needs to be different?
- Can you make those changes? If not who could work with you on this until you feel able to have this conversation authentically and robustly?

6. Reviewing all your thoughts

Reviewing all your thoughts from Steps 1 to 5, write down what you are going to say to the person in bullet point format.

- After you say this and have the ensuing conversation, will you achieve the outcome and action you stated in Step 1?
- If not, what needs to be different? If you are unsure, who could help you?

7. Afterwards

Use this template to review how productive your language was.

Reviewing:

1. What happened?

2. What did you do well?

3. What didn't go as you wanted it to?

4. What can you learn from this?

5. What have you learned about yourself?

6. What will you do next time?

18. But, And, Although and Others

What are the benefits of doing this?

Sometimes it is the simple little words that make a big difference on what you intended to convey and what the other person felt you conveyed. Being conscious of these four words is an easy way to enhance your relationship with others.

Possible pitfalls and concerns to consider

- Is it that simple/ does it really make a difference? Yes, and yes. We have enough complex things in our life so let's be grateful for something simple that can make a difference.

Other relevant chapters

- Chapter 3   People and Their Differences
- Chapter 8   Making People Feel Stronger
- Chapter 9   How You Train People Through Your Actions

How

Covers

But / And / Although

Could / Can

Why?

But / And / Although

For many people, anything before the 'but' has very little meaning in the message heard. It is the words after the 'but' that are felt most. This can be useful if someone has said that they would find a task difficult as you can agree with them and neatly emphasis something more positive using 'but'. For example, "Yes it may be a difficult task but I feel that once you have understood it you will find it easier to do."

In general, we seem to use 'but' a lot and mostly when it is unhelpful. Take the statement "I am a team player but I can work on my own." What we tend to infer from this is that they prefer working on their own. Now take this version: "I am a team player and I can work on my own." It feels a lot more balanced, feeling as if they'd be happy to do both. Yet most people say the former sentence without thinking about it.

This leads us on to;

"Overall you have done a good job but I feel there were some aspects you could have done better."

For most people the 'well done' part gets lost and they are left feeling they did a bad job. Using 'and' gives a better balance

"Overall you have done a good job and I feel there were some aspects you could have done better."

'Although' enhances the 'well done' part even further

"Overall you have done a good job although I feel there were some aspects you could have done better."

Written on a page like this it may seem a little like playing with semantics but to the listener it makes a difference. Of course you could say "There were some aspects that you could have done better but overall you have done a great job."

Could / Can

Sometimes if a person is doubtful or anxious about doing something, the use of the word 'can' brings to mind all the problems associated with doing it. It reinforces the anxiety and thus the brain becomes narrow in its focus and thinking as the fight/flight response is triggered. Whereas the use of the word 'could' first creates a conversation of possibilities before a final choice is made. Often when possibilities are being explored the mind becomes more open and creative to solutions, therefore a new idea is created that 'can' be done. So if someone has a problem, 'what could you do?' is a good question before 'What can you do?' to open up people's thinking, make them more optimistic and less daunted by the practicalities that face them. The same is true for 'might' and 'will': "What might your options be?" followed afterwards by "So out of those suggestions, what will you do?"

Why?

For a lot of people, a 'why' question makes us feel defensive when it is used to question us personally. The question of "why does the moon go round the earth?" or the "5 Whys" asked for problem solving work perfectly well. However, if you ask "why did you make that decision?" then people can feel quite defensive even if the person asking the question is well meaning. Usually this happens because during our lives we have had a lot of experiences where 'why' has been used to challenge or undermine us and we start to fear the question. For a lot of people, it starts at school with 'why haven't you done your homework?' If this is said in a menacing way when we are young, then that can be quite intimidating for a child and tends to create quite an emotional connection between 'Why?' and feeling fear or anxiety.

This is the reason a lot of people react badly to being asked 'why they did or didn't do something?' It is not the question itself, it is the 'emotional baggage' that has been collected when younger that we are unconsciously responding to. Therefore, however well asked, a 'why' question tends to make people feel unsafe and it is useful to replace it with a 'what' or 'how' question instead.

For example,

"Why did you make that decision?"

"What were the reasons behind the decision?"

"What factors led to that decision?"

19. Reframing Perceptions

What are the benefits of doing this?

Reframing is way of enabling people to create doubt in their unhelpful perspective of something, a limiting belief or assumption they have. This can help with confidence, getting work completed and building new relationships. Sometimes people get blinkered and just need someone else to help them open up their thinking. When it works well it can have an instant effective just like switching on a light and being able to see things that could not be seen before.

When someone makes a statement such as, "I'm not very good at that." Rather than trying to convince them that they are good at it, which is tempting to do, use a reframe instead. The reframe is different as it gets the person to have to view things differently whereas convincing feels as if you are telling the person that their view is wrong. Reframing allows them to come to that conclusion for themselves or at least it puts some doubt into it.

Reframing one thing can also have an influence on how that person views other related things. It seems to start to broaden out their overall perspective and their ability to be able to do that.

Possible pitfalls and concerns to consider

- I am never going to be able to think of these when I need them: At first this may be true and to help it is worth practicing them. If you think of a situation when reframing would have been useful then think about what reframes you could have used. Persevere and you will find that you are able to do this.

Other relevant chapters

- Chapter 1   Understanding Their Perspective
- Chapter 2   What is Driving Their Behaviour?
- Chapter 20   Using Analogies and Stories

How

Covers

Context Reframe

Content Reframe

Exercises on Reframing

Technically there are two ways that you can reframe something although I tend not to get too bothered about exactly which one I am using. Instead I am focussed on the reframing aspect itself.

Context Reframe

This is where you take the same situation or occurrence and put it into a different context. For example, a cloudy day at 23 degrees Celsius might be a miserable day in Brazil but is a lovely day in England.

When people say things like, "I am not very good in review meetings as I just tend to sit back and allow others to talk". This could be reframed as "That will be useful in our team meetings as you can observe how we are interacting as everyone else will be focused on talking." This reframe puts doubt into their negative thought. You could ask a question to get them to reframe it themselves, for example, "How could that be useful in some meetings?" or "How could that be a useful skill elsewhere?"

Context reframes are naturally used in organisations when talking about the skills of a person. Someone who is very task focussed may be great doing a specialist role on his own but may struggle as a team leader. A scientist or engineer is a classic example of this. Realising that their skills can be useful in certain roles and not others means that good people do not get fired just because they are in roles that don't suit them.

So this is about how could this same thing be more valuable or less problematical in a different context or situation.

Content Reframe

This is where you choose to interpret something differently so that it is more helpful to you or the person. Effectively you look to change the meaning of something. This is especially useful if someone has chosen to focus on something in a negative way and where someone else might have viewed it differently. This happens as people have different backgrounds and experiences so they have built up different views of things and how life works for them. In chapter 12 we looked at how people filter information and one of these filters was Distortion, where they fit the facts to their view of life. When people distort things they often do so by pretending to know what the other person is thinking or by making assumptions although they do not really know if those are true or not.

So if someone has something happen to them and they are viewing it in an unhelpful way that is causing problems with their work then a Content Reframe may be useful. It may be that they make a comment like, "He's not keen on my proposal as he took 2 weeks to reply to my email" could be reframed as "Maybe he took 2 weeks to read it thoroughly because he really wants to support it by understanding all the detail". Or maybe someone says "I can't possibly remind him as he may think I am being pushy" could be reframed to "It might be good to remind him as he may be embarrassed if he forgets".

You can also ask a question so that they do the reframing, a question like, "Why might he be pleased that you have reminded him?" This question works as you have introduced the perspective that he might be 'pleased' which the person was not thinking about until you asked the question.

A content reframe is useful for situations where people undermine themselves by saying things like, "I don't have a degree so I am not very good at this." The reframe question could be: "How does not having a degree mean that you are very good at this?" and make sure that they give at least one answer to this question as it helps to create doubt in their belief about not having a degree.

In many ways a Content Reframe is about shedding a different light on something to create some doubt in the person's limiting belief about it.

Exercises on Reframing

Example 1:
John is very standoffish as he only ever sends emails when it would be much better to phone me up and talk

Reframe: "Maybe John is nervous about how to have the conversation with you."

Reframe question: "What other reasons could John have for not phoning you?"

Example 2:
I am really good at managing my people and the Appraisal system just causes me problems

Reframe:

Reframe question:

Your own example 1: Reframe: Reframe question:
Your own example 2: Reframe: Reframe question:
Example 2: One possible answer I am really good at managing my people and the Appraisal system just causes me problems Reframe: Some managers wouldn't ever sit down with their people if we didn't have a yearly appraisal and maybe it is more about them than you. Reframe question: How could the Appraisal System be helpful to you? If you rarely saw your manager, how would you feel about the Appraisal system?

20. Using Analogies and Stories

What are the benefits of doing this?

You can convey a lot of meaning within a story or analogy in a way that engages the listener at a far deeper level. In many ways it allows the listener to connect with the meaning for themselves and take their own understanding from it. As humans we like to make meaning from things and we use different parts of the brain for listening to stories than we do for logical conversations. The process of interpreting the story and applying it to themselves seems to allow the person to reach their own conclusion and 'ah-ha' moment. This creates more ownership and commitment for any actions that need to be taken.

Although on one level it seems that a clear and clean message means that everyone gets the same message, in fact they rarely do. Firstly, everyone's understanding will be coloured by their previous experiences which will be quite different. Secondly it may appear logical to them but it is unlikely to connect emotionally with them. Therefore, the level of commitment will be reduced. Facts are great and facts told as a story are even greater.

Analogies work very well if people can relate to them and if a business issue can be personally connected to. For example, one company I worked at had recently changed the way its post was received. This had slowed down the arrival of parcels and some people were trying to bypass the system. This meant that there was the possibility of receiving parcels that may contain abusive substances or products. The main problem was that a lot of parcels were badly addressed. At a Town Hall the project manager made a request for everyone to help ensure that their parcels were addressed correctly by the sender and to be tolerant of the current implementation issues. He used a great analogy to do this. He said, 'imagine that a person rings on your door bell at home. When you open the door he says here is a parcel for you. It is a largish, brown wrapped parcel with just your name on it.' And then he asked 'would you take it?' I think at that moment most of us thought 'no, we wouldn't'. We got the point without having to be told it directly or lectured to about our duty as managers. After the meeting there were far fewer people moaning about the implementation issues and better addressed parcels started arriving.

So stories and analogies can get people on board rather than alienating or criticising them. They have lots of indirect suggestion in them and so you can give tougher messages.

They are a great tool to have at hand and can also give people the courage to try new things as people think "If it is possible for them then it is possible for me".

Possible pitfalls and concerns to consider

- I can't tell stories: Start with simple analogies and review how they work. Also listen to the ones other people use and then use those ones yourself. Over time you will build up your confidence and repertoire.
- It's not appropriate in a business: I would agree with you for some stories. You need to listen to the stories and analogies you hear in your business from the really good presenters and engaging managers as they will use them. Then you can decide for yourself which ones are appropriate and that you feel comfortable using.
- It takes too long: Initially it may do but it's a lot longer spending time trying to pull people along with you rather than having them willingly help you. It takes time to have to police or monitor people rather than getting them to understand, and do something differently of their own accord, through the use of a well-constructed analogy.

Other relevant chapters

- Chapter 1   Understanding Their Perspective
- Chapter 3   People and Their Differences
- Chapter 27   Building Rapport

How

Here are some ways you can build up your confidence and repertoire. Practice story telling in a safe environment and then you will find that you naturally start to use them every day.

- o What stories, metaphors, anecdotes or examples do you hear others say? Write them down and learn them for yourself.
- o Think about the message you want to convey and write this down. Write down a few possible metaphors or analogies. Ask some colleagues for their ideas and what they think of your ideas. Leave it for a while and come back to it. Carry it with you in your note book so if an idea comes to you, you can write it down.
- o Metaphors are good as they make us think differently and convey a lot in a few words. Search on the internet for different ones and make them your own.

- Think about experiences you have had and how some of these helped you learn something. Use these as stories. Sometimes I tell my own examples as if someone else had had it. I find people listen to them better if they are not always what you have done as that can sound as if you just like talking about yourself.
- What experiences do you hear about that others have had that really gets a point across well? Use those stories.
- Ask other people what analogies or stories they would use to get a point across.
- If appropriate, making it relevant and personal can be helpful.
- Some ambiguity is good as they fill in the blanks and create their own meaning.

Feedback That Develops People

Here I am going to differentiate ongoing feedback from needing to have a serious conversation about more fundamental issues or concerns around the person's behaviour or performance. If you need to do this, also read Chapter 45, 'Having Difficult Conversations'. In these chapters, think about feedback in the context of on-going reinforcement and 'nudges' to get people back on track. I feel that in the past years we have built feedback up into quite a scary thing and therefore people tend to back away from it. This leaves a void of neither knowing what's working nor what isn't.

Chapter 21 "Giving Praise" is about giving authentic praise.

Chapter 22 "Reinforcing What You Want More of" is about giving reinforcement feedback so people do more of what they do well.

Chapter 23 "Developing Through Feedback" is about giving people developmental feedback to 'nudge' them back on track or enhance their abilities.

For me, feedback has the intention of being helpful, of strengthening, and stabilising. It enables people to grow and feel confident. So before you give any type of feedback, check your intention: If it is none of the above then it is likely to be criticism, constructive or otherwise, judgmental or intending to undermine the person or weaken them. This does not mean that it always has to be nice feedback but it does have to be useful and specific which means that it works best when you have first-hand experience of what you are about to talk about.

Some helpful tips/ practical considerations when giving feedback

- Give specific information related to the feedback. Quote the actual words; state the actual actions.
- Focus on describing what happened; what objectively happened rather than putting a judgment or interpretation on it. Example: "You were 25minutes late" rather than "you were so late".
- Keep the feedback concise and focused on the area you or they want and expect to cover.
- Be very clear in giving feedback (use simple jargon-free language).
- Ensure the person receiving feedback is appropriately involved in the conversation.

- When someone comes back for more feedback, to see if they have improved after they have worked hard at improving, they will expect praise for the difference they have made and encouragement to keep going.
- The person must be able to do something with the feedback.
- Give feedback that is in line with the person's expectations and effort.
- Give the most important points first; leave smaller points to the end or leave them out.

21. Giving Praise

What are the benefits of doing this?

People like to feel and know that they are valued for what they do and are more likely to carry on doing the good things that they are praised for. Even the dourest person, deep down responds to genuine praise, even if they rebuff it when it is said. Over the years as a career coach lack of praise is one of the things I often hear about. People feel taken for granted and praise is not expensive to give. It is a simple way to remind people that you value what they do and that you notice what they do. It is an informal type of reinforcement feedback; a verbal 'well done' and it helps with motivation and morale.

Possible pitfalls and concerns to consider

- Often we might think of the praise in our head and yet are reticent to say it to the person. Mostly because we fear the reaction of being told that it is cheesy or not genuine. These are both valid consideration for the person receiving the praise as it totally devalues the praise and the person. Make sure yours is genuine, this is very important and give it to them. Conversely, their reaction may tell you more about them than about what you have said.

Other relevant chapters

- Chapter 9   How You Train People Through Your Actions
- Chapter 17   Productive Language
- Chapter 18   But, And, Although and Others

How

At the point you are sincerely thinking "wow, that's great" or "I wish they would do this more often" or something along these lines, then that is the point to say it. If the person is not with you at the time, then make a mental note to tell them when you next see them, or call them, text them or email them. It only requires a short message and in that way it is easier to be sincere. Keep it to what you thought and what made you think that.

Also stand firm despite their reaction. I firmly belief that praise strengthens people even if they are embarrassed about it or pretend otherwise. Of course if they are quite rude or very abrupt then I may think about whether I want to give them praise in future. And for yourself, if someone gives you praise, a simple 'thank you' works wonderfully; no more, no less is needed.

Exercise

Think about some praise you could have given in the past few days? What was it?
How could you give it to the person?
Reflecting after you have given the praise: How did it go? What did you learn? (What went well? Less well?) What would you do differently next time?

22. Reinforcing What You Want More Of

What are the benefits of doing this?

Reinforcement feedback is about getting people to do more of what they do well. It helps strengthen the person's results as well as their self-confidence. Therefore, they become more consistent performers and from their growing confidence they will feel able to handle more.

Knowing that there are things that you do that work well and are valued by others is a wonderful confidence boost as well as being very satisfying. From a manager's point of view, it ensures that the behaviour gets repeated and allows people to hone that ability as well. After all we really want people to do more of what they are good at and what adds value – don't we?

Reinforcement feedback is sadly missing in many workplaces and the focus tends to be on pointing out mistakes that need to be improved upon. Also when reinforcement feedback is given it is frequently vague in its nature, so it is easy to accidentally stop doing things that actually worked very well and gave a lot of benefit.

Possible pitfalls and concerns to consider

- The common mistake often made in giving reinforcement feedback is that it is too general and therefore harder to repeat. If you want someone to repeat what they did then you need to be quite specific when you talk about it. It is very easy to say "that was good" but when you are giving feedback you need to say specifically what it was that they did that made you think "that was good". Otherwise they will have little idea as to what they actually did well making it very difficult to repeat it next time. Also it may not appear very genuine.

- We don't give people anywhere near enough reinforcement feedback. How often do you think "she did well today in that meeting" or "he did well ...." and then forget about it? At the point you think it make a note of it and then you have the detail to hand so that you can give the feedback. It acts as an aide-memoir as well as a reminder to say it.

- People often worry about appearing insincere and are put off by that. If you are quite specific, it is unlikely to come across as insincere since you have put effort into the comment.

Other relevant chapters
- Chapter 5   What Makes You and Your Team Members Proud?
- Chapter 17   Productive Language
- Chapter 18   But, And, Although and Others

How

It is quite easy to think about how well someone has done something but unless you actually tell them they are unlikely to know you think that. In many cases because of the lack of reinforcement feedback they do not feel appreciated and may stop doing the very thing that works well. So the best time to give reinforcement feedback is at the time it happens, when they do something well, or as soon after as possible.

This is a useful format to use:

1. **State the specific situation so that the person can understand exactly what you are referring to.**
2. **Give specific and clear details about what it was that they did that you liked.**
3. **Give the real and beneficial effect it had on you. How did you feel?**

Notice that to do this, you must have seen or experienced what the person did yourself. This is more powerful and more credible.

Exercise

Think of a recent situation where you would like to give someone some reinforcement feedback.
What was the specific situation where they did something that you would like them to do more of?
What would you like the person to do more of? Again, be specific and clear about what it is.
State the real and beneficial effect it had on you: be specific. It is especially valuable if you can say how it made you feel or what value you got from it.
Now plan when you are going to give this feedback to the person? What needs to happen for this feedback to be received usefully by the person?

Reflecting after you have given the feedback:
How did it go? (What went well? Less well?)

What did you learn?

What would you do differently next time?

23. Developing Through Feedback

What are the benefits of doing this?

For a number of years, I worked with a trainer called Chad and I really enjoyed working with him. One of the reasons for this was that he was very good at giving developmental feedback. I really looked forward to it as it helped me deliver the training workshop with more ease and effectiveness. So what was Chad's magical ingredient? Well it was the fact that his developmental feedback was always given as a hint or tip on how to make it work. It came from the intention of helping rather than detailing out what I had done wrong and why. Usually I already knew something hadn't quite worked so what I really wanted to know was, what to do differently and why that would work.

As a simple example, during the workshop we ran an exercise called the 'Ugli Fruit'. It was designed to demonstrate how easy it is to get drawn into 'quick solution finding' when exploring a problem and its consequences would give a true win-win outcome. When I did the exercise people were realising their mistake in the first part of the exercise which lessened the impact of the learning. Just before I ran it on the second workshop, Chad said to me, "Keep the pace moving in the first part and keep it a bit shorter then you'll find they don't work it out so early and their learning will be richer in the debrief." It was great, I knew it hadn't worked very well but I hadn't worked out what to do differently. From then on I kept the conversation moving faster, the exercise worked much better and the learning was richer for the participants.

Possible pitfalls and concerns to consider

- As with Reinforcement feedback, developmental feedback needs to be specific so it works best if you have experienced it for yourself. Otherwise it can be perceived as criticism rather than useful feedback.
- It needs to be something that the person can do something about so think about how far you are asking someone to stretch or change 'who' they are. Also think about what support they may need in doing this. Overall consider: Is the benefit of changing this worth the effort it may take? Are you really that bothered? Also change is best done in smaller more manageable steps that the person believes they can make so take this into consideration.
- Developmental Feedback needs to be tempered as it is very easy to give a person lots of 'what they can do to improve help'. This will feel to the other person like

nothing is good about what they did even if you do it with positive intent. As guidance, give one piece of Developmental Feedback to every three pieces of Reinforcement Feedback. Either, find more of what they are doing that works, or hold back on your desire to improve lots of things at once and think about which one piece really adds value.

- Most commonly people refrain from giving developmental feedback because they are worried about the reaction that they will get and how they handle that. Although it may be a moment of discomfort for you both, think about how much discomfort will arise from not addressing it. I find that if my intentions are good and I follow the guidelines then the overriding feeling is one of appreciation. Also if you are focussed on giving someone a suggestion about how to do it differently, it is often met with an open mind.

Other relevant chapters

- Chapter 1   Understanding Their Perspective
- Chapter 2   What is Driving Their Behaviour?
- Chapter 17   Productive Language

How

Chad modelled how to give developmental feedback wonderfully.

The format is:

1. Wherever possible give the developmental feedback just as it is required. Or recall the specific situation.

2. Be specific and clear about what needs to be done differently or what works rather than what went wrong.

3. Give the benefits that doing this will have.

There are a few other things to note about developmental feedback.

- Firstly, Chad's attitude was one of positive intent: to help me and the participants.
- Secondly, he was very specific about the situation and what to do differently. He refrained from telling me what I did wrong. He kept it simple which had a better chance of working. That meant that I could consolidate the feedback and move on rather than having to handle making a lot of changes all at once.
- Also it is easy to give lots of developmental feedback which, even when given as a hint or tip, can become overwhelming and starts to feel like everything needs to be

improved. So think about what is the most valuable aspect: What is really needed here rather than what are all the things I could give feedback on. In the long run, it is better to do one thing at a time. So think of developmental feedback as an ongoing exercise of helping someone improve and develop with your intention being to help the person truly grow rather just get the problems off your chest.

Sometimes, things really don't work well and that type of conversation is probably better handled by reading Chapter 45, 'Having Difficult Conversations'. Although the intention is still positive and the format similar, it is a wider ranging conversation and I feel it deserves a more consideration.

Exercise

Think of a recent situation where you would like to give someone some developmental feedback.
What was the specific situation: What was the context where it happened rather than what went wrong?
What would you like the person to do next time? Be specific and clear about what it would be useful to do instead.
State the main benefit of doing this. Think about what the person would consider a benefit as it may be different to what you may consider beneficial.
Now plan when you are going to give this feedback to the person. What needs to happen for this feedback to be received usefully by the person?
Reflecting after you have given the feedback: How did it go? (What went well? Less well?) What did you learn? What would you do differently next time?

Maintaining Your Composure

As a line manager you are a role model for your people and they will follow your example and the tone you set. This means that you need to have a good mindset whenever you are with someone. It comes with the promotion: It's just no one tells you it is part of the job specification. Marcus Buckingham, in "First Break all the rules", says that people join companies and leave line managers. In my work helping people to find new jobs, I have found little to contradict that.

I feel that there are three aspects to maintaining yourself.

Chapter 24 "Maintaining a Positive Outlook When Life Knocks You" is on how we handle the days when we're feeling a bit off or a bit 'can't be bothered'. Most people have days like this so this chapter looks at how you can pull yourself out of feeling that way and get yourself going again.

Chapter 25 "Detach to Get Things in Perspective" is about how you detach yourself when things are getting on top of you and it feels a bit overwhelming. Or when you have got too wedded to something and it seems to be the most significant thing that you cannot get past or let go of.

Chapter 26 "Being Your Own Best Friend" is about ensuring your brain is on your side rather than being destructive in what it is thinking about. It is about not undermining yourself and being your own best friend.

The good thing about practicing the aspects in these chapters is that they consolidate and so become more natural.

24. Maintaining a Positive Outlook When Life Knocks You

What are the benefits of doing this?

Being able to maintain yourself to be more optimistic means that you handle what life throws at you better. Also you look and feel more approachable to others so they won't be nervous about talking to you about things that they really need to discuss.

Overall it is good for your health too as you will have less anxiety and frustration. Your thinking will improve as you will feel less threatened by circumstances and your brain will be more open to creative thinking and outside opportunities. When you feel threatened or anxious your brain reduces the blood flow to the neocortex, rational brain region, so your thinking ability really does shut down.

Possible pitfalls and concerns to consider

- Do people really do these things? Yes, they do. A lot of these techniques come from sport's coaching or from the field of psychology. No one else needs to know that you are using them and many of them are just whether you choose to focus your thinking in a negative or positive way. Some of them you will be already doing without knowing it although you may be using them in an unhelpful way. I say to people, 'it's your brain, take control of it and make it work for you'.
- They take time I have not got: Initially this may be true although with a more positive mindset you are likely to cause fewer problems which saves time. Also with practice they will become easier.

Other relevant chapters

- Chapter 3   People and Their Differences
- Chapter 5   What Makes You and Your Team Members Proud?
- Chapter 46   Taking Individuals Through Change

How

Covers

Simple things to help

Rational Analysis: Sorting fact from fiction

Positive Listings

Visualising feeling good

Anchoring

Simple things to help

Visual Aid

Have a picture or an item by your desk that makes you feel good or smile whenever you look at it.

Useful thoughts

Remember some really good feedback you have received: If it is an email print it out.

Remember when someone you respect gave you a compliment.

Remember something nice someone said to you.

Music

Listen to songs that make you really feel good, happy or uplifted.

Do something different

Do something that makes you feel good: Take a walk, read a book or chat to a friend.

Do something that you can achieve; a small win.

Do something that you are in control of such as, tidy your office. Anything simple.

Rational Analysis: Sorting fact from fiction

This is a simple technique that gets you to write down all the facts you have, or think you have, about a situation so you can understand which is which.

1. On a piece of paper draw a line down the centre of it to create two columns. Head one column "Known Fact" and head the other column "Assumptions to check out".
2. Simply write down all that you are thinking or worried about in the appropriate column.
3. For the Known Facts write down how you know them to prove it is a known fact or that it is not.

4. In the second column, cross out items that you now realise are fiction and are probably not true.
5. For the remaining items, in the second column, write down how you are going to find out if they are a fact or an assumption you have made.

Looking at the columns, now how do you feel about the situation?

Once you have found out if the remaining items are fact or assumption, how do feel about the situation?

Positive listings

Fear is a good survival emotion. It has kept us alive and thriving for many thousands of years. Therefore, we have a tendency to be cautious or fearful before we tend to look at positive things. In balance looking at what could go wrong and what needs to happen to make it successful is a valuable combination. However, focussing predominately on what could go wrong and what you fear does not create a positive atmosphere in the long term. If you have a tendency to focus only on that then forcing yourself to write down some of the positive things and times where things go well is useful.

The exercise is simple and is best completed daily for 12 weeks. The benefits should speak for themselves and you will notice them in yourself as well as in feedback from others.

There are a number of different variations, you can pick one of these or create one that works for you. They all follow the same method.

1. Choose the time of day that you will do this. Put it in your diary or choose a time when it is easy to remember, say on the train home.
2. Have a notebook or a tablet, etc. to write in.
3. Choose whether you will write down 3 things, 5 things or the list of things you have that day until you have no more.
4. Choose what you will list:
    o What you did well today
    o What strengths or skills you had today
    o Things you feel proud of today
    o Good things you noticed today – from you/ from others/ around you
    o Things of beauty or that made you smile
    o Things you did and want to do more of
5. Now write them down.

6. Once a week, review all the lists you have written that week and ask yourself, what do you notice as you read them?

At the end of 12 weeks reflect on what you have learned by using the questions in the box

> Reviewing:
> 1. What difference have you noticed?
>
> 2. What worked?
>
> 3. What didn't go as you wanted it to?
>   a. What can you learn from this?
>
> 4. What have you learned about yourself?
>
> 5. What do you need to do going forwards?

Visualising feeling good

Visualisation can be used for creating a confident and positive feeling to maintain your confidence. It is simple to do and can be done anywhere so it is easy to fit into a busy day.

Whenever you need to, remember vividly a memory of a time when:

- something really good happened;
- you felt really good about yourself;
- you felt really proud about something

Recall that memory, that specific time, in your mind's eye, as if you were looking through your own eyes:

- See what you saw,
- Hear what you heard
- Feel what you felt.

Really let that feeling come back and it will immediately enhance your mood.

Anchoring

This is about our natural power of association and happens to us all the time without us being aware of it. Think about something that you have done recently that you really enjoyed, that made you laugh a lot. Recall what it was and what you saw or heard: See it and hear it as if you were there again. Did you smile as you recalled the memory?

If it was a good enough feeling, then most people will smile and feel good again. The converse is true as well: For example, take someone who does not like cold calling, as they go to pick up the phone they feel anxious, remembering the last bad conversation they had and the difficult one before that. This one turns out no better so another bad call on the phone. Then they find even when they need to make a phone call to a friend just to catch up and say 'hi' that they start to feel anxious as they pick up the phone. Often they know they feel anxious but cannot understand why. They have anchored the anxious feeling to the phone so subconsciously it reminds them of that feeling whenever they pick it up.

So we anchor positive or negative feelings and it can happen over time with multiple experiences, such as the phone. Or it can happen with one larger emotional experience such as something that makes you laugh a lot.

If we are purposeful with anchoring it can be a way for us to create useful states of mind when we need them. Although I hate the smell of cigarette smoke, when I smell a single cigar I feel great, I cannot help it. This is because when I was a child my father only smoked a cigar on two days of the year: Christmas Day and Boxing Day. For a child they are a wonderful two days and so subconsciously it has created a powerful anchor that I was unaware of at the time.

Anchoring also allows us to dispel less useful states of mind when they hinder our performance. I have used it a lot when helping people feel less nervous when giving a presentation. Let us have a look at anchoring and how to create helpful ones of our own.

Anchoring depends on five main things:
- You need a memory of a good strong positive emotion to use.
- The anchor needs to be something unique: Something you can remember when you need it but not something that you remember all the time as it will lose its effectiveness or you may use it inappropriately. For example, touching your elbow, a specific knuckle, a picture or song.
- You need an anchor you can replicate time and time again.
- To build up an anchor you need to repeat Step 3 at least 5 times so that it is strong and repeatable.
- You need to follow the method in Step 3 so that you start and remove the stimulus at the correct point to create a clean anchor.

1. To create an anchor, you need to think of a specific memory when you felt the same emotion strongly

Specific memories that are useful could be when you were feeling: -

Supremely confident	That you couldn't stop laughing	Full of energy
Really powerful	Deeply loved	You 'Could have it all'

To see how strong the emotion is, recall the memory. Really immerse yourself in remembering the memory: See everything you saw and hear all the sounds you heard. Relive it. Now how did it feel? Was it a strong positive feeling? If it was then that is a good memory. If it was a bit faint or you could not maintain your focus on remembering it then choose a different memory.

Notice that the feeling does not come back straight away. It takes a bit of time for the feeling to build up. Also as your mind starts to wander to the next thought the feeling starts to fade away and the next thought will come into your head with its own feeling attached. It looks a bit like the simplistic diagram below.

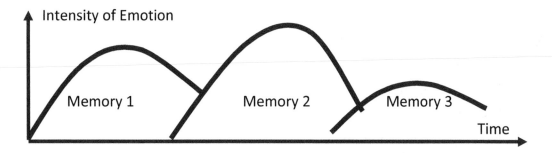

2. Choose what your trigger is going to be

It needs to be something you can use in many situations without other people knowing. You can start with something tangible, such as my song, and then recall it in your head. So when I recall the music I feel good and when I hear it on the radio, I feel really good. If it is a picture, then can you carry it around with you? Maybe you can remember the picture and have the original on your desk or in your wallet.

A very common trigger is the pressing of the left-hand little fingernail onto the top of the left-hand thumb. This is easy to do and is not a commonly done during the day. Other people have objects that they carry in their pockets and can use at any time. One coachee I met carried a short letter from his young daughter with him. Reading it made him feel great pride and he just needed to touch it in his pocket if he needed a boost of confidence.

3. Now to put it all together

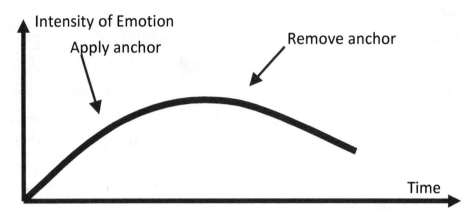

a. Recall your memory. Really immerse yourself in remembering the memory: See everything you saw and hear all the sounds you heard. Re-live it.

b. As the feeling gets stronger then apply your anchor. For example, pick up the object; look at the picture; say the words; press your little finger onto your thumb. Remember to do it exactly the same way each time.

c. Just at the point you feel the emotion start to drop then remove the anchor: put down the object; turn over the picture, etc.

d. Now clear your mind. The simplest way to do this is to say your telephone number backwards out loud.

e. Now repeat i. to iv. four more times.

f. Finally wait for at least an hour and then trigger your anchor; that is, look at the picture; say the words; pick up the object; press your little finger onto your thumb. How do you feel? If you have created a strong anchor, then you will get the same positive feeling as the memory.

4. Using and topping up your anchor

If you need a boost or to help you feel more confident then trigger your anchor and notice the change in you. Many people use them without realising they have an anchor. They just know that a certain memory helps them feel better about themselves and they are clever enough to use it purposefully.

If you use your anchor too often then it can fade. There are two ways to keep it topped up. Firstly, you can repeat a. to e. again. The other way is when you are feeling really good about something then trigger your anchor so you are creating the anchor in real time rather than going through a-e. Just remember to remove it before the feeling fades away.

The reason for doing that is so that the anchor is not contaminated by the feeling of the next thought.

Anchors can also be locations in a room which is worth considering if you are having a series of difficult meetings with someone. I once had an operative who I was having some very challenging conversations with. At our fifth meeting, which was actually good news as he was progressing by then, I noticed he'd gone quite pale as we entered the meeting room. I asked him if he was ok and he said that it was the room and could we use a different one which we did. I realised that we had used the same room for the previous four very difficult conversations and that had created a negative anchor for him in whereby he started to relive those conversations again.

Collapsing unwanted anchors

Sometimes anchors get created without you realising it and they can have strong negative feelings associated with them. In these cases, it would be useful to reduce the anchor and make the feeling neutral. There are a number of ways to do this.

- If it is a place or a time then arrange to do something really great in that place or at that time, where you feel extremely good about it. If the positive feeling is larger than the negative one, then the anchor will reduce. You may need to repeat it a number of times for it to become neutral.

- If it is an object such as the telephone, then firstly create a really strong positive anchor as in Step 3. Next as you pick up the telephone trigger the strong positive anchor to dispel the negative feeling. The positive anchor must be larger than the negative anchor for this to be successful. You must fire the positive anchor before the negative feeling starts. So if as you see the telephone you feel bad then trigger the positive anchor just before you look at the telephone. Repeat reducing the anchor 5 or 6 times until the 'telephone' creates a neutral feeling.

25. Detaching to Get Things in Perspective

What are the benefits of doing this?

From time to time, it is useful to stand back and look at things from a detached perspective otherwise life can become overwhelming. If we become too busy and fill our life with things to do, then life becomes very reactive and we become less creative and open minded. Therefore, we need some time to stand back; to think and be curious. This will open up our mind again such that we are receptive to other thoughts; other experiences and learning.

Sometimes we become badly affected by something and find it difficult to stop those thoughts intruding into our daily thinking. This can have a knock-on effect to how we behave and our decision-making. Detaching ourselves also stops us becoming 'wedded' to a specific way or an idea when we should really let it go or allow others to become involved and shape the way forward. Overall, the benefits are that we and our team remain engaged in value-adding meaningful work in a collaborative manner.

Possible pitfalls and concerns to consider

- Taking time to pause and think, feels like a waste of time. Time that could be used to do tasks but thinking is work and very valuable work. It is time to stand back and survey, to pull yourself back to the reason why you are doing this and what difference it is supposed to make. It is time to reflect on what you have learned and could do differently? Time to bring things back on course or think about the impact you are having on others. It may be easier initially for you to write yourself a few questions and then think about those.

- When I read these detachment techniques they feel a bit strange and uncomfortable to do. I am worried about what people may think. The six techniques are quite varied and I suggest that you start with the one(s) that you find most drawn to. Have a go with at least two of them to find out which works for you or in which situation you may use each one. Once you are comfortable with these techniques then you may feel more comfortable to try the others. They will work differently for each of us and we will have our own preferences. The real secret is to use one when we are feeling overwhelmed or stuck.

Other relevant chapters
- Chapter 2   What is Driving Their Behaviour?
- Chapter 19   Reframing Perceptions
- Chapter 31   Adding Value as a Leader

How

Covers seven different methods for helping you get things back in perspective

    Importance and pride

    What can I control and influence?

    10 minutes, 10 days, 10 years

    Seeing yourself as another person

    Three Questions to ask

    Viewing it in perspective

    Reducing your irritability

Importance and pride

As you think about the situation, write down the one thing that's really important about it or the work. What would make you truly proud of it or the outcome you'd like?

What can I control and influence?

Draw three concentric circles on an A4 piece of paper. Label the centre circle "I can control", label the next ring out "I can influence" and label the outer ring "I cannot affect". Thinking about the situation or work, put the different elements under one of the three headings. This exercise is good to help you let go of things you cannot affect. Think about how much you can influence some things and about what you really can control, as often we get stressed by trying to control things that we cannot affect nor have very little influence over.

10 minutes, 10 days, 10 years

Thinking about the situation or work. Write down, how you will feel about it in 10 minutes time? Write down how you will feel about it in 10 days' time? And write down how you will feel about it in 10 years' time?

Seeing yourself as another person

Stand and look at yourself in the situation, as if you were another person. This is most effective if you stand or sit so you can look at where you were sitting as the other person would. This physically detaches you from the situation, which helps to emotionally detach yourself.

Ask yourself,

- What advice or thoughts might you have for this other person?
- How do you feel when you look at them?
- How do you think they feel?
- What questions do you have for this other person?

Three questions to ask

Thinking about the situation or work, ask yourself these questions:

- What would a trusted friend say or ask?
- What would I say if this was some else?
- What would my partner or manager say to me?

Viewing it in perspective

Sit back in your chair and defocus your vision. Now in your head, metaphorically float backwards out into space. Keeping float until you can see the whole world in front of your mind's eye, about the size of a large ball. Now in the context of the whole world and life, think about the situation or your work.

Reducing your irritability

If you are prone to getting easily irritated by people and their actions, then I would suggest having a look at the book "Overcoming Anger" by Windy Dryden. He will help you discover which little rule you have created about what people 'should' do, in your opinion. He also has a way of getting you to construct a more useful and resilient statement instead.

26. Being Your Own Best Friend

What are the benefits of doing this?

Tim Gallwey in the "The Inner Game of Tennis" talks about the inner game because it is about the conversation that you are having with yourself inside your head. His suggests that it is often this voice that hinders or helps us most on what we want to do or how we go about something. He very much agrees with "whether you think you can or you think you can't, you'll be right". I feel that this also applies just as much to imagining what will happen and then seeing it go wrong in your mind's eye.

I often laugh with people and say that it is their brain and it might be useful to get it to help them rather than hinder them. I laugh, as I know only too well how my brain can seem to have a will of its own and not be my own best friend at times. Learning and using the two techniques below has helped me expand my boundaries. Although there are times when I am hindering myself, with doubt or anxiety, these are a lot less often and less destructive than they used to be. Usually I can gain back control and consciously using these techniques, pull myself into self-talk or images that are helpful. The two techniques are about using visualisation to help you picture success and about using that 'little voice in your head' to help you feel good about yourself and what you are doing.

Possible pitfalls and concerns to consider

- They take practice: The brain dislikes change as it is very energy thirsty so it has well-formed habits that take minimal energy to do. Neuroscience is also showing us how amazingly the brain can change with practice. Often I feel that my participants are looking for that 'magic pill' so they can change without any effort on their behalf, like becoming a concert pianist over night because you have fallen in love with the idea of it. Without practice nearly everyone would struggle to play a piano well. So change takes practice. However, the more you practice the quicker you change. Three months seems to be the time scale most spoken about. Six weeks to lose a habit and six weeks to embed the new one so it is the new norm where you will be using these techniques without thinking about it.

Other relevant chapters
- Chapter 5   What Makes You and Your Team Members Proud?
- Chapter 19   Reframing Perceptions
- Chapter 46   Taking Individuals Through Change

How

Covers

> Visualisation: Seeing it all go wrong or all go well
>
> Self-talk that hinders or helps

Visualisation: Seeing it all go wrong or all go well

There has been a lot of research conducted on the use of visualisation in sports practice. It has been found that the same brain pathways are used when it is visualised as for when it is actually done. This seems to be backed up by the recent Neuroscience research. Thus repeated visualisation practice can begin to create the neural pathways so it will be easier when you come to actually do it. Of course this can work in two ways. If you imagine yourself getting something wrong, then you are pre-programming yourself for failure. If you imagine yourself doing it well then you are pre-programming yourself for success.

I suppose this is how a 'self-fulfilling' mindset comes about. If you are concerned, then it can be easy to imagine it going wrong and you run that scenario through your head over and over. This not only begins to programme your actions; it also makes you anxious which in turn starts to limit your thinking ability. This is the time to 'grab yourself' and realise that you need to focus your brain differently by focussing your brain on imagining what it would be like to do it well or to do it successfully.

1. Find yourself somewhere quiet where you are happy to shut your eyes.
2. In your mind, visualise yourself doing whatever it is, in the way that you would really like it to be. Visualise the situation as if it were actually happening:
   - What are you seeing?
   - What are you hearing and saying?
   - What are others saying?
   - What are you (and others) feeling?

Really immerse yourself into the image and the feelings.

3. Repeat this every day for 5-10mins for at least 14 days.

Self-talk that hinders or helps

The other way that people make themselves feel nervous or bad is through self-talk: The little voice in your head. It is amazing how much of a critic this voice can be. Often we would not say such things to a friend and it would be useful to apply that to ourselves. After all there are enough other people to be critical of us let alone ourselves. Usually this self-talk has been created early on in our life by our role models and when we were able to tone it down or ignore it. Sometimes it is our own 'less than generous thinking' based on our own self-esteem and self-set standards. Therefore, it can creep into our heads at the most unhelpful moments.

Here are two simple techniques to reduce self-talk that hinders us.

Technique 1: Dealing with the 'little voice in your head'

- Move it so that it's coming from your big toe or little finger.
- Make the voice really quiet or muffled.
- Make it so that it sounds like a silly cartoon character voice?

What affect do these have on how you feel?

Use whichever one neutralises or reduces the feeling you have. Maybe you have another way of changing the voice so that it neutralises the feeling, if so use that.

Once you have quietened the unhelpful self-talk, you can now create a new voice: One that is your 'best friend'.

- Create another voice, someone you respect or a friend. What would they say that is helpful and boosts your confidence?
- Imagine them saying that helpful phase, loudly and clearly. Adjust how they say it until it makes you feel good every time you imagine them saying it.
- For the next 14 days practice saying it to yourself. Make sure that you remember to practice by having a diary note or doing it at the same time each day.

Technique 2: Start to think helpful thoughts towards yourself

- Say to yourself what you would say to a friend to be helpful to them and to give them confidence.
- Think of a situation and practice what useful things you are going to say to yourself to keep yourself calm.

Building Enduring Relationships

We are tribal and community animals at heart and thus relationships are important to us as human beings. The reason this topic is at the end of Part II is that all previous chapters are in some way about creating effective relationships. In essence I feel that when we are talking about trust we are talking about the strength of a relationship; it's a measure of relationship. People will respond to you on the strength of your relationship with them. How far they are prepared to go tells you how strong the relationship you have with them is. As a manager, apart from managing your team, you are working within your peer group whom you need to influence. The strength of your relationship will fundamentally affect your ability to influence others although it will vary from person to person.

Emotional Intelligence, rather than intellect, appears to be the greater indicator of management success long-term and building relationships is a vital element of that. Relationships get the work done quicker and help to remove obstacles that could otherwise hinder your progress so it is worth investing time and effort in your ability to build successful relationships.

There are four different chapters to help you develop your relationships.

Chapter 27 "Building Rapport" covers how to build rapport with people in the most simplistic and succinct way.

Chapter 28 "Looking at the Situation From Different Perspectives" is a method of looking at the relationship from different points of view which is helpful if the relationship becomes problematical.

Chapter 29 "Designing a Conversation to Influence" is a pragmatic way to prepare for an influencing conversation and is good business case preparation.

Chapter 30 "Giving Someone the Benefit of the Doubt" outlines five steps to help you give people the benefit of the doubt which can sometimes mean the difference between mending a relationship or having it breakdown.

27. Building Rapport

What are the benefits of doing this?

'Rapport' is one of those words that is frequently used and yet little is discussed about how you do it. Basically Rapport is about whether I feel connected or disconnected from you: It is about communication at a deeper level. What it does not mean is that if you have rapport with someone that they will do what you want or vice versa. It means that you will have an open and honest conversation with each other where it feels safer to do that. You may end up disagreeing but you will feel mutually respectful of each other's views if you have rapport.

Without rapport communication can be severely impacted and resistance is often a sign that there is a lack of rapport. Six simple rapport techniques, from NLP, will give you the ability to relate to others in a way that creates a climate of trust and understanding. Once you have rapport much else will be forgiven, conversations will be useful and your ability to influence will improve. Rapport is also covered very well in many NLP books such as 'Influencing with Integrity' by Zeborde.

Possible pitfalls and concerns to consider

- It feels awkward doing some of these elements: It may do at first and especially when they are practiced out of context. However, it is worth remembering that these are the things that people in rapport do. That you do when you are with someone you like and trust. I found it easiest to start with the ones I felt most comfortable with. Initially I used them in a safe place and then ventured out as I got braver. I was amazed at the difference it made.
- The other person will notice me doing them: I have not found that to be the case as the other person just feels comfortable with someone who is like them. In meetings watch how many of these elements you see other people doing, without knowing it, and the other person does not notice that either.

Other relevant chapters
- Chapter 1   Understanding Their Perspective
- Chapter 3   People and Their Differences
- Chapter 15   Listening With Your Eyes, Ears and Intuition

How

Covers six main keys to building rapport and related topics

    Match their language

    Match and mirror their movements

    Match their voice

    Match their breathing

    Match their chunk size: big picture or detail

    Match their experience

    Practise

    Signs of rapport

    Uses

The field of NLP (Neuro Linguistic Programming) researches and models various human aspects and then brings them down to their very essence. Rapport is based on the principle of 'what is the difference that makes the difference'. This can give us some very simple and useful models; Rapport building is one of those.

It starts with a simple premise of 'like me - like you' or 'dislike me - dislike you': People initially like people like themselves and give them more benefit of the doubt. People initially dislike people dislike themselves and are more cautious of them. Conversely if you like someone you tend to want to be more like them and if you dislike someone you tend to distance yourself by becoming less like them. For example, notice how people wear different clothing to fit in with different groups. Notice also how people who are good at engaging with people subtly change what they talk about and how they talk about it to different people. So the six main keys to building rapport are what we currently do every day with the people we relate to. Each one is explained below with exercises to help you develop that skill.

Match their language

This is about the words they choose to use and the way they construct their sentences. In its simplest form, people often have their own favourite phrases and ways to say things, consciously or not, and these are the ones to use.

In an email, someone may use 'Dear Deni .... kind regards, Peter ', therefore I tend to use the same, 'Dear Peter....... kind regards, Deni, rather than 'Hi Peter.......regards Deni' which is my natural tendency.

When speaking, someone may say 'you know' a lot. Although I do not use this phrase myself, I would purposefully use it more often with them. Subconsciously they will notice it being used and they will think "that person is like me as they use that phrase too". This gets them into the 'like me - like you' mindset and hence they will start to be more generous towards you, and what you are saying. When you are first building a relationship being given the benefit of the doubt can be very helpful.

In its simplest form 'matching their language' is about using their way of saying things rather than your way of saying things. It is the same as the business words used by a company. Do you have Staff, Employees or Associates where you work? In reality they are all the same, paid people to do their work. Each company has their preference and you are probably seen as an outsider if you choose to use the wrong one. There are many more for a new employee or consultant to remember before they will be fully accepted.

In NLP and from Howard Gardener's Multiple Intelligences, comes the idea that people have three main ways of storing information and thinking. These are as pictures (visual), sounds (auditory) and feelings (kinaesthetic). We also store information as tastes and smells which is less useful in this context. Auditory has two distinct variations. Some people are auditory in that they store sounds and words. Whereas, some people are Auditory Digital and only the words are important to them, not tone or sounds.

So if they remember a meeting:

o Visual people see the room, the people in it and recall the slides.
o Auditory people hear the noises inside and outside the room, including the conversations had.
o Auditory Digital people remember the words used.
o Kinaesthetic people re-live the atmosphere and how they and others were feeling. Feeling includes emotions and sense-wise, for example that they were cold or the chair was too hard.

Their main preference(s) is also highlighted in their language. To build rapport it is useful to understand which main preference the other person has and then to use that type of language yourself. As you are very likely to have a preference yourself, those are the people that you are easiest you build rapport with.

Many good NLP books or websites have lots of information on these so I will only give you a summarised view below. I feel that it is enough for you to be able to use it for rapport building.

You can infer a person's main preference in a number of ways although be open minded as people tend to be a blend of them. Use it as a good starting point and look at these aspects:

- where their eyes look
- their hand movements
- their breathing position and rate
- the tone of their voice
- the speed of their talking & what they say
- some times their seating position

The table below gives you an over of each one for visual, auditory and kinaesthetic people for guidance.

Visual	Auditory	Kinaesthetic / Feelings
Eyes look up (to get information) a lot	Eyes look left and right (to get information) a lot	Eyes look down to their right (to get information) a lot
Hands move a lot up in front of face – as if painting a picture		Usually very little hand movement or considered
Fast breathing, high up in chest / throat	Rhythmical breathing, mid chest	Slow breathing, low in chest.
Higher pitched	Melodic	Lower pitched
Fast talker		Slow talker
Sits upright, often leaning forward, slightly alert		Sits relaxed and slightly reclined
Uses these words: See Look Picture Appear Clarity Imagine Focus See you later Looks like Clear cut	Uses these words: Sounds Talk Discuss Speak about Listen Unheard of Loud & Clear Sounds like Babbles on Speak to you soon	Uses these words: Feel Solid Grasp of Handle Warm / hot / cold Touch Hold Wound up Keep calm Get a grasp of

If you are in doubt use all the main types in your conversation which is also useful in group situations. Being able to flex your preference is constructive and these exercises will help you to do that.

Exercise 1

Work with a practice partner or a group of 3-4 people. You are going to tell a story between you, using each one of the preferences. Start your story with "Once upon a time …" Start with Visual and use as much visual language as you can. After you have each had 4 or 5 goes start a new story using only the Auditory preference. Then finally using only the Kinaesthetic preference. Each person usually adds to the story for about 30 seconds and then the next person takes over.

Exercise 2

Work with a practice partner or a group of 3-4 people. You are going to tell a story between you and this time you are going to rotate through each of the preferences. So the first person starts with Visual, and the next person uses Auditory. The third uses Kinaesthetic and then the next person goes back to Visual. If there are three people, then you need to work out a way where each person changes preference on their next go.

Exercise 3

Notice when you are in a meeting if someone has a strong language preference: Which one is it? Which words are they using to tell you that? Also does anyone in the meeting have their own favourite phrases or words?

Exercise 4

In an informal conversation, identify the person's preference or favourite words and change your words so that they are full of that preference or those favourite words. Afterwards reflect on what you learned and what you will do differently next time.

Now you are ready to weave other people's style into your language as you need to, to enhance the rapport between you.

Match and mirror their movements

With this you copy the movements they do: The way they sit, how they move their head, their hand movements and how they move or gesture. Matching means if they raise their right hand, you raise your right hand. Mirroring means that if they raise their right hand, you raise you left hand, as a mirror image. For our purposes they both work equally well.

When I say 'copy the movements they do' I don't necessarily mean as they do it. It would look strange if whilst they were talking and you were listening that when they moved their hands around you also moved yours around in silence at the same time. For example:

- You end up sitting the same way they are as soon as possible. So if they sit down first you can adjust as you sit down. If they shift position, then fairly quickly you can have a reason to adjust your position. It is easier if you are talking or make a comment as people often shift as they talk.
- If they move their hands in a certain way as they talk, then when you talk you use the same hand movements rather than your own ones.

So sit as they sit and adjust as they do. Adopt their gestures rather than use your own. If this feels awkward, and at first most people find it does, then just watch two good friends talking or having lunch together. You will see this happening before your eyes. And yes, you do it all the time as well when you are with someone you get on with. Have you ever noticed that you are sitting in exactly the same way as a friend or your partner? If you do, then sit differently and notice how uncomfortable that is. Or when they shift position don't change your position. Again notice how uncomfortable that is to do. That is the power of rapport and the strength of matching & mirroring.

Conversely, if someone you distrust sits down next to you in the same way you are sitting, notice how quickly you change position. You probably think you shift because it has become uncomfortable to sit like that. And yes it has but it is because you want to break the rapport rather than because the seat has become uncomfortable. Sometimes, this is not helpful and you need to override your natural tendency to want to break rapport. You need to override your natural reaction until you have gained more control and got to a more comfortable place otherwise you could have a problem with the person from the beginning: A problem that just widens the gap rather than closes it. This is especially true when you meet someone for the first time. They may remind you of someone you dislike and therefore subconsciously you'll want to break rapport which starts the relationship off on the wrong footing when neither of you really knows the other. This is a good time to override your natural reaction and force yourself to focus on the six rapport techniques. These exercises will help you to do that.

Exercise 1

Work with a practice partner. Sit about 90° apart. Sit exactly as your partner is sitting. It will feel strange at first. Get your partner to talk about something they are interested in or a challenge they have. As they talk, match & mirror the way they shift their position:

You'll gradually do this more gracefully. Use their gestures when appropriately. E.g. if they move their hands whilst talking then do this when you are talking.

Exercise 2

Start to notice how other people are matching & mirroring each other without even knowing it. Notice during meetings: Who is sitting like someone else? When one moves, does the other person shift their position as well? Is it always the same person who follows the other person? If so then the leading person is probably the more influential and if they are on your side, it is likely that the other person will be as well. Notice this in restaurants, cafes and bars. Notice as well how alike people are in their dress style, etc.

Exercise 3

Choose an informal situation where you can practice matching & mirroring during normal conversations. Choose one person and match & mirror them during your conversation with them. How brave can you be? Maybe they may remark how much they "feel like they have known you for a long time" or "how easy it is to talk with you".

Now you are ready to use matching & mirroring whenever you feel that you could do with a better connection with someone. Try it out and then reflect on how it went and what you would do differently next time.

Match their voice

By this I mean the speed of talking, the volume, the pitch and tone: As a minimum match the pace and volume of their speech. If they are very Visual, then they will probably talk quickly. If they are Kinaesthetic then they will probably talk slower. Matching the opposite style can be quite tricky although I find it easier when I am with the person. If possible, match tone and pitch. Do not copy an accent as that does not appear to work very well and will get noticed. Practicing different volumes, paces and styles can be fun to do and gives your voice more flexibility so here are some exercises to complete.

Exercise 1

Write on separate pieces of paper these words: high pitch, low pitch, loud, quiet, fast, slow, clear & precise, gruff. Give them to a partner. Talk to your partner about a hobby you have or a recent holiday. As you talk, get your partner to hold up one of the pieces of paper and then you must talk in that style. Get them to hold it up long enough for you to be able to do it well so that your partner can clearly hear the difference.

Exercise 2

Read stories to your children or grandchild remembering to create very different voices for each main character. Reading a play out loud is useful as well.

Exercise 3

In a safe conversation match the person's voice in as many ways as you can. What did you learn? What would you do differently next time?

From now on, practice matching at least the speed and volume of the other person's voice.

Match their breathing

People who are very good at building rapport will sync their breathing in with the other person. If you are in a meeting where you are not participating very much, then this can be a powerful way to build rapport. As a minimum you should approximately match the breathing of the person: fast, medium or slow. If you are matching the speed of their speech from point 3. then this is easier to do. Otherwise it is useful to watch their shoulders or their tie/ necklace as they tend to move as people breathe and to sync in with this. If someone is very excitable then they may breathe extremely quickly which might not be a good idea to match.

Exercise 1

With a partner, sit at a 90° angle to them. Get them to talk to you about something they are interested in. As they talk match your breathing to their breathing using their collar or necklace. Practice for at least 15minutes.

Exercise 2

In a meeting where you feel safe, pick a person and match their breathing. What did you learn? What would you do differently next time?

Match their chunk size

If they talk big picture, you talk big picture. If they talk detail, you talk detail. It is useful to understand if they just want to know if it's 'going well' or if they want a 'line by line' progress review. If you want to change the level at which they naturally talk then start with their chunk size and gradually shift to the level you want to discuss, shifting as fast as they will shift with you.

Exercise 1

With a partner practice talking about the same topic in detail (small chunk size) and at a much higher level (large chunk size). Have each conversation for at least 15mins. Ask your partner to rate the level of chunk size from one being small chunk to 10 being large chunk. Can you talk about a subject at one, five and ten?

Exercise 2

Now prepare for a conversation with someone who has small chunk size and someone who has large chunk size. Complete each of the conversations and review how they went. What did you learn? What would you do differently next time?

Match their experience

This is about talking about things the other person does and making your examples relevant to them rather than you. I had a boss who was very good at this. He spoke to me about my sons and would sometimes get me to think about a situation in the context of them. With the operators he spoke about football and with another manager he spoke about the motorbikes he'd seen recently. He naturally shifted to what the other person was interested in and made the conversation relevant to them.

Exercise 1

Pick an idea or suggestion. Think of three very different people (CEO, Manager, operative or administrator/ retiree, mother, teenager/ football fan, climber, artist). Prepare for how you would talk to them about the idea using their experience and what is relevant to them. Once you are ready then have the three conversations with a practice partner. Can they understand what the three people's experiences or preferences are?

Exercise 2

Prepare for a conversation with someone using their experience. Have the conversation and review how it went. What did you learn? What would you do differently next time?

Practice

Practice each one of the six Keys to Rapport separately so that you understand them and they become more natural. Then it is useful to pick real situations to practice them where it does not matter if you are not paying full attention to the conversation and you can pay attention to practicing. For example, when you are with friends or in a meeting where you do not have to contribute very much.

I found that I do three of the six really well. I do one other to some extent and I am variable with the other two. Even with this I get significant results and I feel the difference too: It makes life a lot more workable. There are some people that I do not want to be in rapport with although I am careful to not be too 'dislike' them as that has the potential to become a problem. In these cases, I find a more neutral mode works well rather than being very 'opposite' to them.

If someone becomes visibly uncomfortable when you use these techniques, then I suggest that you refrain from using them and focus back on the conversation. A small number of people subconsciously reject the attempt to connect to them. They know they suddenly feel uncomfortable although consciously they are not sure why. I have had it happen twice: one person was naturally very cautious and wary of people; the other was very logical with low interpersonal skills. With both these people I focussed back onto the quality and expertise of what I was saying and connected through my in-depth knowledge.

Signs of rapport

How do you know when you have rapport? This is a good question. In essence it is when you suddenly feel 'in tune' with the person or that you have suddenly 'clicked'. Often, I found, the person says something that indicates rapport.

They may say something. E.g. "I feel like I have known you a long time."

When you have deep rapport you will find that when you 'lead' they 'follow': This means literally, that if you move then they will move in the same way. If you shift how you are sitting, then they will shift as well to be sat like you.

Once you have rapport, you can relax as you are now both in tune with each other. If something happens in the conversation where you feel the rapport is lost, then you can concentrate on these elements again. Even on the telephone these techniques work although 'matching & mirroring posture' is not relevant.

Uses

If you are in a conversation with someone and you don't feel in rapport, then it is unlikely they will feel in rapport either. When I notice that feeling and it is getting in the way of the conversation then I think about which one or two aspects it would be useful for me to concentrate on. I have learned on many occasions that shifting my focus a little from the content of the conversation onto building rapport has been very beneficial. I usually choose to match and mirror them more. I also check my voice speed and volume as well as my speed of breathing: Is it too fast which is especially important if they are kinaesthetic? Then I focus more on their language and their experience. I keep my concentration on these main areas of rapport until I feel comfortable again and then I can put my full attention back to the content of the conversation.

If someone is being quite resistant or you find them a challenge, then I focus almost purely on rapport with minimal attention on content. Before I had learned and practice these elements I would have said that that was ridiculous. Now I have had my own personal successes and seen the difference it makes for everyone I find I am able to do it gracefully. In the end it is about building a relationship, a connection, before you start to work together.

28. Looking at the Situation From Different Perspectives

What are the benefits of doing this?

Sometimes when we are emotionally attached to a situation it can be hard to stand back and take a more objective and pragmatic view of it and the possible ways forward. For example, sometimes the outcome accidentally changes from getting a piece of work completed to not letting the other person get their way or be seen to 'win'. Neither of these views is helpful in enhancing a relationship or in getting the work completed. This reflective technique will help you get out of this entrenched situation back to an objective position.

Overall, it helps you can gain a broad and holistic perspective that will help you think beyond the other person's limitations. Ultimately this perspective adds value to future conversations and how you handle situations effectively. Not only will it increase your influencing ability, it will help improve your business gravitas.

This is also an exercise that you can train another person in, or your entire team, if they are struggling with a relationship and need a way forwards.

Possible pitfalls and concerns to consider

- Remaining seated in one place: This method works best if you physically move although that may seem strange at first however the more you use this technique the more comfortable it feels.
- I could not do this with my team as it is weird: If you think this then you will be awkward when you do it. Therefore, you'll be right and it won't work. I have done this technique with one person, with groups of up to 40 people and with Leadership Teams. Each group found it a valuable exercise to do and a number of managers subsequently completed the same exercise with their teams. If you make it a meaningful discussion, then you and they will get a lot from it.

Other relevant chapters
- Chapter 1   Understanding Their Perspective
- Chapter 2   What is Driving Their Behaviour?

- Chapter 3   People and Their Differences

How

There are four perspectives in this technique.

1st Perspective: The situation as seen by you.

2nd Perspective: The situation as seen by the other person.

3rd Perspective: The situation as seen by an observer who is not involved and who is detached from the situation.

4th Perspective: The situation as seen by a distant observer who has a wider view (as if looking down on the situation from a great height or global view).

The technique is good for resolving an issue you have or had with a person. It works best if you go back to the room where the situation happened as this will help you to think through each perspective and literally put you back into the situation.

1st Perspective

Firstly, sit or stand where you were. Sit or stand exactly as you remember and imagine the other person with you.

- What are your thoughts on the situation?
- What do you see?
- What do you hear?
- How do you feel about the situation?

2nd Perspective

Next, move to where the other person was. Sit or stand exactly how they were and look at 'yourself' (where you were just sitting or standing). Now become the other person for a few minutes: Talk as if you were them. Answer these questions using 'I' as you are being the other person.

- What are your thoughts on the situation?
- What do you see?
- What do you hear?
- How do you feel about the situation?

3rd Perspective

Now stand two or three paces from where you and the other person were. Stand so that you are an equal distance from where both of you were. You are imagining looking at yourself and the other person. As you stand there as a detached observer:

- What are your thoughts on the situation? What do you notice?
- What do you see?
- What do you hear?
- How do you feel about the situation?

(Talk about both people in the third person)

4th Perspective

Now stand as far away as possible from both where you and the other person where. You may need to stand just outside the door or outside of the room with the door closed. Now you are imagining looking at yourself and the other person. As you stand there as a distant observer:

- What are your thoughts on the situation? What do you notice?
- What do you see?
- What do you hear?
- How do you feel about the situation?

(Talk about both people in the third person)

Reflection

Now reflect on each of the four positions and write down:

- What insights you have had?
- What do you know now?
- What you are now going to do?

29. Designing a Conversation to Influence

What are the benefits of doing this?

The 'Ladder of Inference' by Chris Argyris can be used as a simple and effective way of preparing for and having a conversation with someone where you wish to influence their thinking. Using the process helps structure conversations in a way that makes it easy for the other person to fully hear what you have to say rather than quickly ending up with a polarised conversation where both of you are just stating what you think or want. It also helps you construct a solid business case with thorough preparation of the facts underpinning your assumptions and your conclusions.

Furthermore, you can create useful and exploratory questions to ask the other person that will help you understand their thinking and rational. Together these facets encourage a healthy conversation where it is easy for either or both of you to shift positions. In this way you have the best chance of coming out with a win-win solution that is focussed on a business outcome.

Possible pitfalls and concerns to consider

- Not thoroughly checking out the facts that underpin your assumptions and conclusion: Often when we are questioned about our assumptions we struggle to put forward a sound and constructive case for them. This can lead to us feeling defensive which does not make for a useful conversation or outcome. However, we usually have more data than we use or have not thoroughly checked out that our assumptions are soundly backed up. So thorough preparation can really help if you understand why it is necessary.
- Staying on your ladder too much and not understanding their ladder: In using this method it is important for you to logically build your case and then quickly get the other person to talk. In doing this make sure you spend time exploring their assumptions and data rather than justifying your own position. Keeping the conversation in real facts as much as possible helps both of you come to a sensible and business orientated outcome.
- Asking closed questions or questions that shut down the exploration: In these conversations I often hear people starting questions with "Do you think…" or "I think

that ..." or "Don't you think... ". These are not open questions; they are leading or closed questions or opinions disguised as questions. Practice asking questions starting with How, What, When, Where or Who. Often our closed or leading questions are our solution to the problem or concern we have in our heads. Therefore, ask an open question related directly to that concern or problem. Maybe voice the actual concern you have as it is much more constructive if you can do that.

Other relevant chapters
- Chapter 2   What is Driving Their Behaviour?
- Chapter 11   Questions That Invite Others to Contribute
- Chapter 12   Questions to Help Overcome Unhelpful Perceptions and Thinking

How

Covers

Creating your own ladder as preparation for a meeting

Using your ladder in the meeting

The Ladder of Inference model is covered very well on pages 242 to 259 in 'The Fifth Discipline Fieldbook' and basically covers the process of how firstly people select certain facts from all the real ones that are actually true. This filtering is due to their preferences, values and how they view the world. Next, we make assumptions based on those facts and finally we quickly reach a conclusion. As the conclusion is ours it is important to us, therefore we use that to add to the filter that selected the facts in the first place. Thus it tends to be a self-reinforcing process and one that we are pretty unaware of as it happens so fast and without us thinking about it. In daily conversations we usually start by stating the conclusion we have made and defending this rather than explaining the facts behind it.

So the first thing to question is, is your data all the actual data and to think that it is probably not. Then you are at least open to finding more of the actual data which puts you in a mindset of possibility and curiosity. From this mindset you will be more willing to listen to others which they will feel and therefore they will be more willing to explore themselves.

When we make assumptions we have started to interpret the data and therefore are starting to put a bit of ourselves into it. This means that we start to become emotionally attached. Data is data but how we interpret it allows others to begin to form an impression of us and therefore we feel more nervous about being judged by others.

Next we draw our conclusions. As we have worked this through in our mind and have really interpreted it, we have become much more emotionally attached to it. Some people feel that they have staked their reputation to some conclusions. Therefore, if you want to explore that conclusion those people are likely to take the questions very personally, as a personal attack on their ability to judge things. This is why people can react somewhat irrationally to a perfectly good question that challenges their conclusion.

Conclusions with a lot of emotional attachment often become beliefs. Our beliefs are very important to us and we tend to defend them heavily as well as looking to reinforce them.

This is an example of the process in action.

Selected data: As a graduate, I notice how much I get corrected in meetings and how senior people's ideas get built upon.

Assumptions: I am too young to know enough to contribute.

Conclusion: Stay quiet until I have enough experience.

Belief: You only know enough if you've been here for 20 years.

People get wedded to their conclusions which become obvious to them and therefore see no need to explain how they came to them. Thus when challenged they just engage in 'conclusion ping pong' ('I am right', 'no you're not', 'yes I am' etc.) and jump to defend their own conclusion rather than ask questions to get to other people's facts. However, if you can remain in amongst the data, it becomes easier to change what you think as you are less emotionally attached to it and so are they to theirs. This is the way to become more influential and keep everyone collaborating with each other.

Creating your own ladder as preparation for your meeting

The first way to use this technique is to help you construct your own ladder in preparation for the meeting.

1. Write down what you have

Take an A4 sheet of paper and write down your outcome or conclusion for the meeting. Then the assumptions that have made you draw that conclusion. Finally write down all the facts you have to back up your argument.

2. Looking at your facts

- How can you prove that it is true?
- Do you know it is valid or do you need to check it out? It is also important to check out whether a fact is really factual and not just a numerical assumption. For example, if someone says that the average yearly rainfall in Suffolk, England is 110mm, is that just pulled from the Internet and if so how reliable is it as a figure?
- Do your facts back up your assumptions? If not, do you have more data that you have not written down?
- Or perhaps you need to find out some more data so that your assumptions are soundly backed up by data?

3. Look at your assumptions

- Do they back up your conclusion? If not what else is required?
- Or perhaps now you have found different data or cleaned up your data, you have come to a different conclusion?

4. Ask a colleague to check out your thinking

- Start with giving the facts, then lead onto your assumptions and finally state your conclusion. In this way you build your case in a logical and flowing way so that the other person has the best chance of understanding your rational from facts to conclusion: You take them on the same journey you took.
- Ask your colleague whether the facts back up the assumptions and whether the assumptions back up the conclusion?
- Take on board their feedback and adjust your information accordingly.

Using the process in your meeting

Now you are fully prepared with a robust business case you are ready to have the conversation.

1. Start the conversation by giving your facts

For example:

"These are the facts I have ...."

2. Give your assumptions

For example:

"From that I made these assumptions........."

3. Give your conclusion

For example:

"Therefore this is the conclusion I came to ...."

Get through the first three steps quickly as ideally you want to get onto their ladder and then work your way down their ladder to their selected facts. Once you both have more of the actual facts, by sharing each other's, it will be easier to come to a joint and more informed conclusion.

4. Get them to talk

Once you have gone through your data, assumptions and conclusion get them to talk, so you can get to their facts, by asking them an open question, for example:

"What do you think?"

"Have I missed anything?"

5. Go down their ladder

Usually they will start by giving you an opinion, such as "I think that ...." Be careful to avoid being tempted to start defending what you have said; instead ask questions about what they have just said. Ask questions that dig below the statement and work down to their data. Questions such as these are useful?

"What is your thinking behind that?"

"What made you come to that conclusion?"

"What made you make that assumption?"

"What is your rational for that?"

"How do you know that?"

"Where did the data come from?"

Usually you will need to ask a lot of probing/ exploring questions as often one assumption is backed up by another assumption and only then will you get to the actual data. Or perhaps you'll uncover that there is not any real data to back up the assumption.

You will also need to make sure that you are being curious otherwise these questions can make the other person feel as if they are being interrogated.

30. Giving Someone the Benefit of the Doubt

What are the benefits of doing this?

Recall two people, one you trust and one you don't. What you would think about each person if both made the same mistake? It is highly likely that you would be more forgiving and generous to the former and less forgiving and more cynical of the latter. These thoughts tend to shape our reaction to the person and the incident. Invariably when we are feeling more generous to the person we are more understanding and keep a more open mind. This in turn improves our relationship with them.

If we are less generous then we may jump to a wrong conclusion too fast which can cause a lot of damage that is hard to recover from and a reputation that may not be wanted. Being open minded and sensible will allow you to handle a situation in an appropriate way without the person feeling judged.

If you feel that you get easily irritated or frustrated by people's mistakes, then also have a look at Windy Dryden's book on "Overcoming Anger". Step 1 is adapted from this book.

Possible pitfalls and concerns to consider

- In the exercises in this chapter you need to think of genuine possible reasons for the person's behaviour. If you can only think of trivial or superficial reasons, then it may be useful to complete the exercise with a colleague to see what reasons they may suggest.

Other relevant chapters

- Chapter 1   Understanding Their Perspective
- Chapter 2   What is Driving Their Behaviour?
- Chapter 9   How You Train People Through Your Actions

How

Covers five stages you can use to help you give someone the benefit of the doubt
   Remove the word 'should' from your sentences

Think about when I might behave like this

How might I feel if I was them or someone I trust in this situation?

How do I feel about the incident now?

What am I going to do now?

It is very easy to invent for yourself a number of rules that people "should" and "shouldn't" do and often it is these that stop you from giving people the benefit of the doubt. If you are feeling frustrated or annoyed by someone's actions, then see if you can identify the sentence you are telling yourself with the word 'should' in it.

For example: "I am the customer and you should sort out my problem quickly."

1. Remove the word 'should' from your sentence.

You may wish your problem could be sorted quickly although it is not always possible and pressurised people make more mistakes. Therefore, it may be useful to rephrase the sentence without using the word 'should'.

For example: -

"As the customer I would appreciate it if you would sort out my problem quickly although I understand that you may have just had a long and difficult previous call or that not everyone working in a call centre is driven to help customers to the highest standards."

2. Think about when might I behave like this?

I also think about times when I am not functioning at my best and therefore have not put in the effort I may usually have done. I find this helps me to realise that I may have made someone feel the same way and that people are not perfect no matter how much we'd like them to be.

3. How might I feel if I was them or someone I trust in this situation?

Also I wonder how I might feel if I was that person doing that job all day and handling all the different customers. If I thought about someone I trust behaving in that way, then I would come up with some plausible reason as to why they behaved like that.

4. How do I feel about the incident now?

Usually by completing these three steps I feel more balanced and generous towards the person and it only takes a moment of time to work through the three steps. If you are not feeling more generous then complete each step again making sure that your answers are really genuine, as they would be for a person you trust. Or ask a colleague what they would answer for each step and compare your thoughts to theirs.

5. What am I going to do now?

Now I am more balanced in my thinking I find that I naturally behave more appropriately for the situation.

Exercise

Here is an exercise to complete with a colleague to help you practice.

"He shouldn't have asked that question as it made me look as if I didn't know what was going on."

Step 1: Remove the word 'should' from the sentence.

Step 2: When might you behave like this?

Step 3: How might I feel if I was them in this situation or it was someone I trust?

Step 4: How do you feel about the incident now?

Step 5: What are you going to do now?

(Compare your answers to those of a colleague)

30. Giving Someone the Benefit of the Doubt

Use this template for resolving your own actual incidents

> **Your situation:** Write your "should/shouldn't" sentence here:
>
> Step 1: Remove the word 'should' from your sentence.
>
> Step 2: When might you behave like this
>
> Step 3: How might I feel if I was them in this situation or someone I trust?
>
> Step 4: How do you feel now?
>
> Step 5: What are you going to do now?

Applications to Engage People

In Part III, I want to give you step by step applications that I fundamentally believe help to bring out the best in people and that will in turn improve morale and productivity. These applications use the mindsets from Part I and the skills from Part II and I have referenced the most relevant ones for each chapter.

Every day in business, I hear senior managers and HR telling line managers to empower, to engage, to trust and to involve their people although I rarely hear them say or demonstrate how to do it. When managers ask how, the answer is often 'aren't you paid to work that out' or 'you'll think of something'. Frustrated at getting a glib response to a genuine question, managers go away and try their best with the role models they have around them whilst the focus from senior managers is all about performance and rarely about people management. On the other hand, managers may get to attend a one-day management workshop that covers topics in 30 or 60 minute sessions. This is good for introducing subjects although less useful at making managers competent in them. My intention with this part of the book is to give you the 'how to do it' so that you can become competent in each aspect yourself, if you choose to.

In the book "Making It Stick" by Brown, et al. the basic theme is that to learn something enough to make it innate you need to apply it to your real situation, struggle to apply it, then reflect, learn and reapply it. Therefore, it is ok to try out these applications knowing that you will not really understand what I am suggesting until you use it in your situation. Once you have used it, you will understand what you did not know and also how to adapt it to work for you and your team. Each time it will be easier and more beneficial, so stick with it and make it stick.

The following chapters vary in length as I have given you what I have or what I think the topic requires. Most of the pages are templates on how to do things with step-by-step guidance. When I put it all together, it fell into six natural groupings, that I put into the following order:

- **My Part as a Manager**
- **Participative Meetings to Create Ownership and Motivation**
- **Building Teams**
- **Developing Individuals**
- **Getting Your Team to Improve its Own Work**

- **Connecting With Others to Enable Your Team's Work to Happen**

Remember to have a partner who is also working on these skills as well for learning, support and encouragement.

My Part as a Manager

As a manager, you set the tone and environment for your team more than any other factor. In essence, your team is a snapshot of your leadership style. In 'First break all the rules' Marcus Buckingham cites that 80% of an employee's motivation is due to their line manager so you are an important asset to the company regardless how it might appear. With that backcloth, it is worth thinking about how you give yourself some mental space so that you have enough emotional intelligence to think before you act and to think about the consequences of that action. No one is going to tell you that you need to 'keep your head above the noise' and think about the value you are adding as all the external indicators will suggest that you need to dive in with your people and help them finish their work. At the end of the year though, you will get little thanks for doing that and lots of comments about lack of leadership style. Moreover, although it seemed like a good idea at the time you will have had less time to invest in the longer-term activities that managers need to do to ensure that their teams are gradually developing and thus improving their results. As a manager everything seems to suggest you need to 'get on with the urgent' but you have to have the conviction to give priority to what is important for the longer term and stop doing urgent and less important things.

Chapter 31 "Adding Value as a Leader" outlines some of the key areas in this book that will help you think about and develop the value you add as a leader, someone who leads rather than a leader who helps out. It also gives you a set of questions that you can use from time-to-time or regularly to reflect on the value you are adding. Very successful managers often have as many as five mentors that they have used across their career.

Chapter 32 "Time for Your People?" looks at the reality of how much time you actually spend with your people and how many times you cancel or reschedule meetings with them as this can have a damaging effect on how valued they feel.

Chapter 33 "Delegating and Holding Others Accountable" is about how to delegate and hold people accountable. It goes through methods on successfully delegating, creating accountability and holding people to account. It also thinks about whether the manager should be making all the decisions and the consequences of this or others doing so.

Chapter 34 "Communicating to Your Team" is a short chapter on communication and is meant to give you an easy way to think about your communication and what is really being communicated. It is a gentle wake-up call to get you to sharpen up what you are doing as over time we all allow things to drop off.

31. Adding Value as a Leader

What are the benefits of doing this?

Your team is often a reflection of your management style therefore thinking about how you interact with them and the type of role model you are, is important. Managers often worry about what it is they are doing if they are not doing the tasks, what they call 'the real work'. Well your team is doing their work and usually there are enough of them to complete that work. Your helping them to do it is usually counter-productive which unfortunately makes you feel that you have to help even more. If you are doing the task, then who is monitoring the overall situation? Who is developing the crucial relationships that aid the work getting completed smoothly? Who is motivating the people and facilitating their development? If these aspects are covered well, then the team is able to complete its work better. Therefore, I think that there is plenty for a manager to do rather than becoming another team member. Your task is to get the business task done through people not with you helping. Unfortunately, many environments unwittingly condone a manager helping with the work; therefore, your work reduces to doing the reactive elements of your role when in fact the proactive longer-term development ones would be more productive.

By shifting the focus of your role and adding value to the team and its development, you create a high performing team that is engaged and committed to completing its work. This allows you the time to develop the team, nurture valuable business relationships to help the team and to bring in higher-level information. If you do not create enough emotional space and time to do this, then it can be very stressful and a never-ending loop of you doing more.

Possible pitfalls and concerns to consider

- 'What do I do?' is the question that stops most managers from letting go of the task and focussing on their people. Hopefully, the words above give you enough suggestions on what you would be doing instead and how valuable this is to the team and the work.
- Giving up too soon: Changing the habits that you and your team have built up together and throughout your working lives, is not an overnight change. If there is a set back then allow yourself to be human and then get back on track, rather than

thinking that one mistake means you should give up. Successful dieters have the same mindset: One cream cake does not mean you should give up dieting; it was just a weak moment and we all have them. So back on with the diet now you have realised.

- Reacting badly at the first mistake: Think about how you will react when something does not go as planned or there is a mistake, as your reaction will be watched by everyone as an indication as to whether you have changed or not. One way is to think about how you will feel about your reaction just afterwards, a week later and six months later.

- Not having a long-term mindset and plan: A long-term aim or plan helps put the day-to-day 'ups and downs' into a different context. They also help temper your reaction to certain events by forcing you to think about the consequences of your actions at a later date.

Other relevant chapters
- Chapter 4   Creating Meaningful Work and Sense of Community
- Chapter 7   A Mindset of Accountability
- Chapter 46   Taking Individuals Through Change

How

Covers

What I am doing as a manager / leader

Reflecting on my style

Benefits of a mentor

What I am doing as a manager / leader

It is useful to think about what you are doing, if you are not doing your team's work with or for them. Currently you may be solving problems that they need to learn how to solve themselves or correcting mistakes they need to correct. Instead, you could do the following:

- Helping people's thinking to be robust and enabling them to think more for themselves by questioning, listening, giving feedback & ensuring accountability

- Bringing knowledge that they don't have access to - broader business context, understanding other managers hopes and concerns for the coming year and under-

standing how well they are meeting the needs of their customers
- Synthesising themes from the business
- Helping them to be business savvy and connecting them to useful people
- Developing a high performing and engaged team, using various chapters from this book
- Developing your people individually and managing poor performers: Making people feel stronger, delegating, giving accountability and having value-adding PDPs
- Setting direction, aligning people, inspiring and motivating them (Kotter, 1993)
- Building relationships with your peers and key stakeholders to aid your team's work

There are exercises related to the above that you can do to develop your ability in those areas in the following chapters:

Chapter 5   What Makes You and Your Team Proud?
Chapter 6   What is the Added Value Your Team Delivers?
Chapter 8   Making People Feel Stronger
Chapter 9   How You Train People Through Your Actions
Chapter 10 Handling Negativity
Chapter 11 Questions That Invite Others to Contribute
Chapter 15 Listening With Your Eyes, Ears and Intuition
Chapter 16 Listening That Invites Others to Contribute
Chapter 32 Time for Your People?

Reflecting on my style

From time to time, it is good to reflect on how you are managing your people. The simple framework below will help you to do that. There are also many other Reflective Frameworks, most notably those of Donald Gibbs, Argyris & Schon and David Kolb. The method below is adapted from my use of all of these. You might want to do the same: Try each one at least four times to see how useful it is. Then either use the one that works for you or create your own.

Thinking about your role as a line manager:

1. What's happening?

    What is working well?

    What is working less well?

On balance, which side is this tipped?

   What is your intuition telling you to be observant of?

2. What are you thinking/ feeling?

   What is affecting what you are doing?

   What is outside of this context that's affecting it?

   What do you need to let go of?

3. What is happening that you like?

   How can you do more of that?

   How can this be achieved?

   How could not having this be beneficial?

   What would you like to have happen?

   How can you do that?

   How else can this be achieved?

   How could not having this be beneficial?

4. What have you learned about yourself?

   Your values and beliefs?

   How does this help or hinder you?

   How does this learning apply to your role /work?

5. What will you do differently going forwards?

You can also use these frameworks to reflect upon meetings or conversations and other situations.

Benefits of a mentor

Mentors are extremely useful and extremely underused. Some of the benefits are that they give you time to reflect; they provoke different thinking and get you to look at things from different perspectives which really helps make your thinking robust. Usually they have a broader context than you do as they are more senior and that helps you become more astute with your decisions and ideas. They may also help you with their contacts and through their extensive experience and knowledge. Therefore, it is worth having at least one internal and one external mentor, who provide you with different perspectives and contexts for your work and role.

Ideally, internal mentors are not in your management chain and are in a different part of the organisation, which helps keep them impartial. Both mentors would usually be at least two levels higher than you are. Therefore, a Head of Department or a Senior Section Head would mentor a team leader or section manager. A Finance Manager in a large company would mentor a financial manager in a small company. In this way, they will help you put your work into a larger context. In addition, they usually have a good network of colleagues and from time to time, they may suggest it is valuable to talk with one of them.

Here are a few other tips for choosing a mentor:
- Someone you feel comfortable and open with so you do not feel restricted on what you want to say or ask.
- Someone who is useful and does not just agree with you on everything as that does not stretch your thinking
- Someone who's thoughts you value so you are taking something from the conversations
- Someone who has the time and does not continuously rearrange the meetings. Although do not decide that they are too busy as you might never ask anyone. Let them decide if they want to spend some of their valuable time mentoring you, as it might be one of the highlights of their busy day and a welcomed break from their problems.

Few people, that are mentors, have been trained as mentors so it is not a prerequisite however it does require someone who wants to help you rather than just talk about themselves. Mentors use many good coaching skills in asking thought provoking questions and listening well. In addition, they will share with you how they might, or have, approached similar situations, which can be a valuable source of information and challenge.

Usually people meet with their mentors 2 or 3 times per year for an hour. They are most productive for both of you if you prepare for the meetings. Here are a few thoughts on preparation:
- Know what you want to talk about. Given that, write down the question(s) you would like to discuss with your mentor or that you want some thoughts on different options, you want them to comment on what they notice when you talk about the subject or you want them to challenge your thinking? Otherwise, you can easily spend an hour talking about the subject but not get what you wanted from the conversation.

For example:
- I would like to talk about an on-going difficult situation I have with one of my team. I would like to think about how I am not helping the situation and what an experienced line manager might do differently.
- I feel like my team could care more about their work. I would like to discuss what you may have done with your teams to get them to care more or what other managers do.
- I had a meeting with my boss, that went badly. I would like you to listen and then help me understand how it happened.

- Next, think about what preparation you need to do before the meeting so that you get what you need from it.
  - Gather information - facts, figures, graphs, documents
  - Write down what you thought happened so you can easily talk about it in the meeting
- If possible, meet in an office rather than a cafe so you feel you can be open and honest without any distractions. Make it convenient for your mentor to minimise the impact on their time.
- Always take a notebook with you to write things down, as this is not an interview. After the meeting and once your mentor has left, write down any other information you remember.
- Let your mentor know about any outcomes from your meeting as mentor's often wonder if the meeting was useful for their mentees. It also helps them feel valued and respected.

If you are not sure who you could ask to mentor you then ask your HR Department or your line manager. Old bosses and colleagues might be useful to ask about for external mentors. Often Associations have a pool of volunteers as mentors and you can apply to be allocated one of them.

32. Time for Your People

What are the benefits of doing this?

What is important to you: People or meetings? What would your people say?

If people feel that they matter to you then they will put in effort and commitment. Morale will go up and correspondingly a few months later so will your team's business results. Every day, by what we choose to do or not to do, we tell our people how much they matter to us, and the organisation.

When times are busy and tough, that is the time to ensure that you have team meetings and 1:1 time. This will help keep morale on track and allow people to air concerns rather than create rumours and unfounded gossip. It keeps everyone updated and you can gauge how everyone is feeling which helps the team stay focussed on the results required. The analogy I use is that of maintaining a car. When we are driving many miles in our car, the car is important to us so we tend to maintain it regularly. Otherwise, we know we could be heading for a problem we could do without whilst driving. With people, we tend to do the opposite and wonder why we have problems.

I also wonder about how much less managers would have to do if they put effort into developing their people and making them feel stronger as well as finding out how they really add value.

Possible pitfalls and concerns to consider

- It is very easy to get caught up in the whirlwind of day-to-day activities. As a manager, it is wise to stand back occasionally and review what this course of action is actually delivering and what the down sides to it are. Role model line managers have time between meetings in their diary and are seldom treble booked.

- Experience has taught many managers that team meetings and 1:1 meetings do not go very well; they are difficult and awkward so managers would rather avoid them if possible. This may be true of past meetings but it does not need to be true of future meetings. Part III of this book will help you structure more participative and worthwhile meetings whilst Part II will help you handle a diversity of situations with more skill. Build your ability to make these meetings add the value that they should rather than avoiding them as this just leads to different and inevitable problems.

- Quality time does not mean lots of time. Some managers spend a lot of time with their people and it may not add much value. Prepare for your team meetings and 1:1 sessions then it will.

Other relevant chapters
- Chapter 3   People and Their Differences
- Chapter 5   What Makes You and Your Team Proud?
- Chapter 9   How You Train People Through Your Actions

How

1. How often in the last 3 months have you:

Cancelled a team meeting?	_____ out of _____ meetings
Moved/ Cancelled a 1:1 meeting with your people?	_____ out of _____ meetings
Been called out of a 1:1 meeting to deal with something 'urgent'?	_____ out of _____ meetings
Been late to a 1:1 meeting or had to shorten its duration?	_____ out of _____ meetings
Answered your phone during a 1:1 meeting?	_____ out of _____ meetings
Given sensible time to prepare for the 1:1 meeting and done that?	_____ out of _____ meetings

2. Looking at the answers to those five questions, how do you feel about the current situation?

3. How would you feel if this was how a paid external consultant was behaving?
   a. What implications does this have for you?

4. What message does it send to your people about how important you think they are?

A few thoughts:

Situation	Good Practice
Cancelled a team meeting	It does not have to be cancelled as someone else can run it if you are not there. A minimum of 10 out of 12 meetings attended by you is good.
Moved / Cancelled a 1:1 meeting?	Move/ cancel no more than one meeting in six months for that person. Move/ cancel no more than one meeting a month overall in your diary.
Been called out of a 1:1 meeting to deal with something 'urgent'?	No more than one meeting a month.
Been late to a 1:1 meeting or had to shorten its duration?	No more than one meeting a month.
Answered your phone during a 1:1 meeting?	None: turn it off or ignore it. Some extreme circumstances may mean that you need to have your phone on, for example, being the emergency duty manager.
Given sensible time to prepare for the 1:1 meeting and done that?	Every meeting although one meeting a month may not get prepared for due to valid circumstances.

5. What would you like your figures to be?

	In 2 months time?	In the long term?
Cancelled a team meeting?	_____ out of _____ meetings	_____ out of _____ meetings
Moved/ Cancelled a 1:1 meeting with your people?	_____ out of _____ meetings	_____ out of _____ meetings
Been called out of a 1:1 meeting to deal with something 'urgent'?	_____ out of _____ meetings	_____ out of _____ meetings
Been late to a 1:1 meeting or had to shorten its duration?	_____ out of _____ meetings	_____ out of _____ meetings
Answered your phone during a 1:1 meeting?	_____ out of _____ meetings	_____ out of _____ meetings
Given sensible time to prepare for the 1:1 meeting and done that?	_____ out of _____ meetings	_____ out of _____ meetings
(your own one)	_____ out of _____ meetings	_____ out of _____ meetings

6. **What are the first steps that you can and will take towards achieving your 2 month targets?**
    - What needs to happen to ensure you do those actions?
    - What could stop you dong those actions and what can you do about that?
    - Who can help you keep to your commitment on these actions and targets?

33. Delegating and Holding Others Accountable

What are the benefits of doing this?

Do you find that you care more about getting the work done than your team does? Usually the answer is 'yes' and mostly this is because you understand and feel the consequences more than your team. That is the stark reality, otherwise, your team would care as much as you do and therefore this is also the answer to the situation. Many managers feel that they need to allow their team to have any praise and that they should protect them from any criticism or negativity. These are at the heart of delegation and accountability. If we step back and look at the situation it, feels like a parent and child situation when in fact as managers it is essential to realise our team is made up of adults.

Managers who treat their people as adults gain many benefits including increased speed of decision-making and improved productivity as well as their people feeling valued and trusted. As most working people have been in an environment where it is very 'parent-child' it may take a bit of effort to get them back to working in an adult way. Some of your team may not like this as it also comes with increased accountability. They may prefer being told what to do and not having to own the consequences of not delivering. Maybe you might like to think about whether these are the type of people you want on your team and how you might handle that situation.

Overall delegating work and making people accountable will raise the quality and value of everyone's work including your own. Having people 'stand alongside you' and stepping up to do the work is worth the initial effort in demonstrating to everyone that you mean it. In this chapter, I am looking at the three components for achieving these benefits: delegating, making decisions and holding people accountable. Two useful books to read that help with delegating and making people accountable are "The Speed of Trust" by Stephen R Covey and "First Break all the Rules" by Marcus Buckingham.

Possible pitfalls and concerns to consider

- Not setting it up thoroughly enough: It is vital to spend time initially ensuring that the person really understands what the required outcome is and how they are going to do it. Importantly, this sets the person up to succeed rather than the person getting it wrong and having to correct their work, or worse, you taking it back. In the latter case, you have probably already taken a step backwards.

- Leaving it too long before checking: Think about the consequences of the person not delivering the work as required and evaluate the points where checking on progress would be a good idea. Pick a timescale where the person still has enough time to correct things if there are problems. Take into consideration the competency of the person and how much it is your need to know rather than the risk of it going wrong.
- Taking the work back if there is a problem: This mainly demonstrates to everyone that you didn't really trust the person and didn't really want them to do the work. You should only take it back as a last resort as it really undermines delegating and making people accountable.
- Favouritism: The focus for delegation and accountability should be on the job description and competence rather than who "deserves it".
- Assuming that someone will not want to do it or is too busy/ overloaded to do it: Making these assumptions is treating someone like a child. Let them tell you if they can or cannot take on the work. You will be amazed how many times they relish the work and are successful in doing it. Conversely, it is good for them to learn how to say 'no' rather than allowing themselves to become overloaded.

Other relevant chapters
- Chapter 9   How You Train People Through Your Actions
- Chapter 12   Questions to Help Overcome Unhelpful Perceptions and Thinking
- Chapter 17   Productive Language

How
Covers

Delegating to people

Decision making where it should be

Holding people accountable

Delegating to people
Assess the likelihood and consequences of the work being right first time or incorrect when it is too late. The first time of delegating or being delegated to needs to be a positive experience, otherwise you or they will be cautious about it next time. As delegation is a

long-term strategy, think about how you will handle initial mistakes so that they learn from them and want to avoid further mistakes.

Here are some thoughts on successful delegation
- Take the person through the work; slowly and with enough detail so they get it. Remember that you already understand the work but they do not so you may think it is excessive to do this when in fact it is a necessity. In the long-term, it will save time, as invariably it will take a lot more time sorting things out if this part is not done well.
  - Think of breaking it into stages and doing it stage by stage
- Be incredibly clear about the outcomes - give previous examples, a sketch or a mock up
- Check they are clear about the outcomes by getting them to take you through what they think you have asked them to do, explaining it fully.
  - Maybe do the first one together
  - Maybe do the first one in steps with checks by you before starting the next step
- Decide if and when you will meet for a review
  - Ensure it is early enough to advert or rectify any problems
- Do not assume 'I understand' means they actually do. It may mean that they understand something different to you without realising it. I have heard many conversations where I realised that the two people talking were actually having parallel conversations about different things. The conversation was general enough for them not to realise it until I asked them specifically what each one meant. Because we have a tendency to want to concur, we seldom check out minor discrepancies, which are tell-tale signs of understanding drifting apart.
- Make their thinking robust by asking questions:
  - What questions do you have?
  - Which part will you find the easiest - why?
  - Which part will you find the hardest - why?
  - What could cause you to fail to do this?
  - What will ensure that you are successful?
  - How will you avoid delivering something different to what is required?
  - How will you know along the way that you are on-track and delivering the right outcome?

- What help or support do you need from others or me?
- If you were delegating to someone, what interaction would you like to have with them and why?
- What concerns do you have?
- If you delivered an outcome you were proud of, what would have made that difference?

• When they come to you with updates, questions or to ask for help, think about how you react to the situation.
- Do you make them feel confident or undermine their confidence?
- Does it reflect their efforts? Is there enough praise and encouragement? Is there enough attention to errors or issues?
- Will they go away happy to come back again or want to avoid updating you in the future?

• Ensure they sort out any problems as this is how they learn and it helps them want to avoid having to do that next again.

• Praise their efforts and celebrate the success of the work when they have completed it or can do what is required. This reinforces how much you value them and their efforts in making this successful so that next time they will have a positive experience to build on.

Decision making where it should be

Ultimately, the person who has the responsibility for the decision should make the decision. In reality, this is not often the case, sometimes because of a lack of confidence in the person or the line manager's need to be in control or stamp their authority on things. Therefore, here are a few suggestions to help you get to a place where the responsible person actually makes the decision.

Who is the right person to do it?

(Rather than 'who will I allow to make the decision'). Deciding that you should make the decision because you are the manager is rarely the right answer to this question.

So think about these aspects instead:

• Part of their role: If it is part of their job, make them decide. If you are worried that their decision-making is not sound, then you need to work on improving it.

How can making this decision be part of improving their judgement so that next time they are more competent? Perhaps you can work together on it this time. Longer-term you need people to be able to make the decisions they are paid to make, so think about people's development needs or whether you need to manage this person out of this role.

- Ownership or commitment: The more they do, the more commitment and ownership they have. The more you do, the more this is eroded. It is as simple as that. Think about the benefits you will gain by allowing them to make more of their own decisions and how much they will learn by doing that.

- Development: Sometimes it is useful to stretch people as part of their development. Allowing them to make decisions they would not normally get to make is a useful way of building up their competency and motivation for now and the future.

- Who has the true information: Someone in a higher position of authority often does not really have the true information about the situation. Even if you are briefed you can never be told everything and often they do not know they have the information as it is more of an instinct or 'gut feeling' due to all the subtleties picked up when they are with others.

Other aspects to consider

- Handling risk: Think about the likelihood of the decision being a poor one due to the ability of the person making it. Now think about the consequences of a poor decision being made and how likely these are to happen. Finally, remember that we have a tendency to be overly risk adverse, which means people feel less trusted and have less commitment for the work. Once you have these factors you can assess how much this person can make the decision alone and how much someone needs to work alongside them or make the decision instead.

You do it ----------------------do it together----------------------they do it
Little commitment Full commitment
or ownership and ownership

- Building confidence in their decision-making: If people are not used to making their own decisions or if mistakes have been badly handled then you will have to build the person's decision-making confidence. Think about the different ways you can do this and factor these in. For example: small steps that are successful; regular reinforcement feedback; praise from others; reviewing what has worked and what could be done differently.

- They will wait for you to make the decision so do not be tempted to do that – as it demonstrates you really preferred to make it yourself. Ensure they do it by facilitating them making the decision.

- When it goes wrong or a mistake is made: This is the point where everyone watches how you react because it tells your team whether you really meant what you said or not. Therefore, think very carefully before you react about the long and short-term consequences. How you could handle the situation successfully for you both? Chapters 8 and 9 can help you with this.

Holding people accountable

Accountability happens and can happen at many levels so we are going to look at what you can do differently. It is not just accountability with a capital A but rather accountability with a small a. Think about small differences you can make that will start to add up over time. Also, look at what other managers do to get lasting and willing results.

So how do we create a culture of accountability rather than just enforcing it? Enforcing it is about punishing people who get it wrong or telling people what reward they will get for doing it. True accountability is the willingness of team members to own their work and remind one another when they are not living up to the performance standards of the group: Peer pressure is better than authoritarian punishment. For example, it is about attending meetings you have agreed to attend; sorting out your own problems; delivering work as required; pushing the right decisions upwards and making your decisions yourself.

Conversely, accountability is not just about saying to people they are accountable it is about upholding it, maintaining consequences and reinforcing what you would like more of. Accountability utilises a number of the techniques we have previously covered, but before we look at that let us think about why it is useful to have people who hold themselves and others accountable.

Think about:
- What currently happens at work due to lack of accountability and lack of people taking accountability?

- What difference would you see within your work if there was true accountability?
- What destroys your desire to be accountable?
- What makes you want to be accountable?

To hold people accountable you first need to make people accountable. Below are three aspects that help create accountability within your team. Each has a few thoughts or questions to stimulate your thinking about what you could do differently.

Who is accountable for what?
- What decisions should you actually make?
- What decisions are you making for others?
- What decisions should you pass back or upwards?

Who is telling who?
- Get them to set their own deadlines as it increases commitment and motivation. You might set some parameters as well as asking questions to ensure their plan is robust enough to deliver.
- "Yes I understand" is not checking their understanding, as you are not sure what they mean by that. Ask questions to explore this with them.
- Get them to tell you what they understand or what the outcome that they are delivering is. Ask them to tell you what they think you have said or have agreed. Get them to play it back to you and then you can see where the mismatches are before they start.

Your reaction affects the outcome
- How do you respond when things go wrong / unexpected / well?
- You train your people through your actions and reactions so have you thought about how you are training them. Would you step up to being accountable if your manager acted in the way that you respond to your team?
- Blame switches the focus away from the unaccountable person onto the 'blamer' thus losing the opportunity to create accountability.
- How could you be creating apathy and saboteurs?
- How could you be creating strong people who will step up and handle obstacles?

Exercise on creating accountability:

For a situation where you would like to create more accountability:

1. What are your thoughts from reading the three topics above?
2. What outcome do you want?
3. What actions do you need to take to do that?

Now that you have created accountable people you need to hold them to that accountability so that they care about it as much as you do. Thinking about the three topics below, and what this means for you, can help you hold your team more accountable so that they continue to feel accountable.

Talk verses action

- We often say people are responsible and then our actions take that away from them or do not enforce it. What do your actions 'say' to your team?
- Sometimes we do not tell people what accountable looks like and what they need to do so that they can take accountability: what they need to do differently and what you will do differently.
- Use these questions when there is a problem as they help maintain their accountability and stop you taking it back.
    o What are you going to do about that?
    o What do you need to do to resolve that?
    o Who do you need help from?

Questions that challenge unhelpful perceptions

- Hold the person to account, rather than allowing then to act as a victim by asking 'how, what, who, where or when' questions to explore the situation and uncover the facts.
- Keep the conversation focussed on the topic being discussed and allow the person to generate specific actions rather than you doing that.

Consequences

- Do people truly understand the consequences of the situation? Do they understand the 'knock-on' effects of them not completing their work? Have you checked that they understand the consequences? What is it they need to know so that they care about the work as much as you do?

- Can you, and do you, uphold those consequences? How? When have you demonstrated that? When should you have demonstrated that?
- What message are you giving? Is it firm & consistent or wavering? What would your team or others say? Are you being overly protective or too helpful?

Exercise:

For a situation where you would like to hold someone accountable or make them more accountable:

1. What are your thoughts from reading the three topics above?
2. What outcome do you want?
3. What actions do you need to take to do that?

34. Communicating to Your Team

What are the benefits of doing this?

Communication is so important and so superficially done: It speaks volumes whether you communicate or not. For me, this is the one area that managers underestimate the importance of and what is required, yet it is a topic that is constantly talked about. As a manager this is very much part of your role and it will take your time although this will be repaid with future time-savings. Having well informed people means they make sounder business decisions that are taken quicker because people have less need to continuously refer upwards.

Well-informed people act as adults, feel trusted and have increased commitment. This usually means that problems are overcome rather than used as reasons to stop work or slow down.

Possible pitfalls and concerns to consider

- "I don't have any new information" or "I can't tell them anything yet": Then tell this to your team rather than saying nothing at all. If you leave it, people will fill the void with their own thoughts and suspicions. It is better to have a short meeting or send a short email, saying that there is no new information. If possible, saying when you expect to get further information is good. It might be something like: "At the moment we are still working on the proposal. We had hoped to be able to tell you about the new structure by now but we are not able to as it was more complicated than expected. We anticipate that we will have it completed by the end of this month and we'll update you then."

- People have too much information these days: Yes, that can be true although I find so much of it is not required. Sometimes I get volumes of detail that I do not need because it was easier for the sender to send it all rather than cut it down. Or, people 'CC' me because they can rather than because they need to. The barrier of effort and cost that made people think about sharing information has significantly dropped or become hidden, so people send information 'because they can' rather than 'because they need to'. This means that concise useful information gets lost in amongst everything else. My advice is to think about whether you need to send it, to stop people sending you stuff you do not need and get your team to do the same.

34. Communicating to Your Team

Other relevant chapters
- Chapter 8   Making People Feel Stronger
- Chapter 17   Productive Language
- Chapter 51   Internal Networking to Improve Your Team's Work

How

Here are a few thoughts on communicating as a manager.

- Overall, talk to people and share. Share more than you think you can: Check it out if you need to and then share as much as you can.
- You are probably not communicating enough: Use meetings, emails, conversations in the corridor or when having a coffee. Little and often works well. Think of communication as a continuous process rather than a monthly meeting or blog as line manger communication is above and beyond what Corporate Communication teams are doing.
    - Use various mediums as not everyone has access to a computer.
- Communicate to your people, your manager, your peers and your stakeholders. Managers are often caught out by someone being obstructive because they are not well informed. Your role is to ensure that your people can get their work done within a helpful environment.
    - Simple, concise weekly update emails or blogs are easy to do. Make them easy to do. Get your team involved and then you have less to do.
    - If you are sharing information from a document, then indicate which page or chapter to read rather than just sending it and saying it is a 'worthwhile read'. People are more likely to read the highlighted section than the whole document.
- Emails are often hurried and misunderstood: A few simple things to think about that make a big difference. Importantly, stop and think before you press send.
    - Would you say it to the person face to face? If not, then do not send it. Faceless communication can entice us into writing things that we later regret.
    - Would you be happy for anyone to read it? If not, then do not send it. Once you send an email, it is out of your control so think about whether you would be happy for various people to read it.
    - Language: Does it sound officious? Does it use 'business-speak' or jargon or is it clear and simply worded?

- - Keep it short. Two short emails are better than a long email. If it is long, summarise at the top so people only need to read the full email if they want to.
  - Does it connect with the reader?
  - If you are feeling emotional then leave sending the email until you feel calmer. Re-read it and you may find that you rewrite all or part of it or delete it entirely.
- If you cannot talk to your team about the content of what is being discussed, then there are a few things you could tell them.
  - that it is being discussed and when a conclusion is likely to be reached if you know that
  - about the process that is being undertaken
  - about any milestones and their progress, etc.

Participative Meetings to Create Ownership and Motivation

Meetings are the lifeblood of the organisation, helping with the flow of information to and from everyone who works there. A healthy organisation has lots of flowing conversations both formal and informal, which means that decisions are made quickly and robustly. However, I think that many meetings are poorly designed, overly controlled and seem to take a lot of time to prepare for. Usually participants leave feeling frustrated, undervalued and that the meeting was a waste of time. Conversely, I think that well designed, simple meetings take less effort, engage participants and deliver results.

There are a few reality checks though such as not over packing an agenda so people can discuss issues properly; such as not having overly detailed slides and ensuring your key points are easily conveyed; or such as putting time between meetings so you are there at the start and do not have to leave before it finishes. The business norm seems to be to run back-to-back meetings with agendas that do not allow time to discuss and resolve issues with buy-in from people. Breaking that mould and creating a new norm would be a worthwhile thing to do as well as making your life easier and more productive.

Chapter 35 "Basic Meeting Outcomes, Structures and Tips" sets out to cover some of the basics of a participative meeting, to help you create an achievable agenda and get the outcomes you require.

Chapter 36 "Monthly Team Meetings" covers team meetings as I feel they are the most important meeting within an organisation and, sadly, are regularly cancelled or poorly run. This chapter helps you design and run valuable and participative meetings.

Chapters 37 "Basic Kick-Off Meetings" and **38 "Basic Review Meetings"** take you through structures for these two other common types of meetings so that everyone is fully involved in them.

David Sibbet also has some interesting material on visual meetings and graphic facilitation that are great for ideas and ways to design and run participative meetings. His website is useful and he has written a number of books on the topics.

35. Basic Meeting Outcomes, Structure and Tips

What are the benefits of doing this?

Deep inside we know that when we prepare a meeting properly it goes much better, people feel engaged and a useful outcome is achieved. A few minutes thinking about the purpose of the meeting, what realistic outcomes you want from it and who should attend are worth doing. Yet we invite people and create an agenda without wondering what we want to get from the meeting, whether the agenda delivers this or even if the agenda fits into the timescales given. Usually agendas are over-packed and it becomes about racing through the agenda items rather than a meaningful discussion to resolve the issue.

Firstly, we should be brave and cancel or stop attending meetings that we know add little value and use up a lot of our time. We need to stop pretending that we need to go to them in the hope "we'll get something from them" or that "we'll miss out". The question to ask is against our other priorities, is it really worth the time?

Putting time into structuring the meeting to achieve its objectives is the next part of saving time and gaining commitment. By preparing meetings with a defined purpose and participative structure to achieve its outcomes you find you need fewer meetings. In addition, people behave differently in them once they are convinced you will stick with the new style. It may take a few newly formatted meetings for people to trust that these meetings are different, so persevere. By doing so, you will find that your meetings get good feedback, are worthwhile and deliver the outcomes they need to.

Possible pitfalls and concerns to consider

- People are not expecting meetings to be like this so they may attempt to revert to the old style. Be firm and give this style of meeting enough time to demonstrate that it delivers longer-term benefits.
- Agenda items usually take longer than most people think, or at least want to admit to. If you rush things, then you tend to get less buy in. If you include lots of people's input, then it takes longer. You need to balance the need for buy in against the amount of time you can afford. To help decide, think about how much time you may save in implementation because you spent a bit more time in earlier stages.

- 'Death by slides': Slides are useful if they aid the speaker to get their point across, otherwise leave them out. If you are using slides for your notes, then keep them as your notes and either simplify the slides for the meeting or do not show them. It is still common for people to read their slides line by line or to put up a slide with small writing on it that no one can read. This really undermines the speaker's credibility and I often find it is because the speaker is too lazy to adjust their slides for use in a meeting: Simplify wordy slides and delete wording that is too small to read. Pictures, graphics and diagrams can convey many words and appeal to most people. If you have to have a detailed diagram, then think about using a handout for everyone instead of a slide or build the slide bit by bit.

Other relevant chapters
- Chapter 1   Understanding Their Perspective
- Chapters 11-13 Questioning for Robustness
- Chapters 17-20 Language That is Influential

How

Covers six steps on meeting preparation,
1. Write down the purpose of the meeting
2. Who needs to be invited to deliver those outcomes?
3. The agenda items
4. Allocating time to the steps and overall agenda items
5. Closing the meeting
6. Invites and your notes

Meeting preparation template

Other thoughts

1. **Write down the purpose of the meeting**

This is usually easiest to do by writing down the outcomes you want from it. Think about the end of the meeting,
- what actions were agreed and what decisions were made?
- what do you want people to do differently when they leave?
- how do you want them to feel when they leave?
- what do you want them to be saying afterwards?

If you are looking at outcomes such as 'everyone is clear on project A's scope' then think about how you will know that they are clear. Asking people 'are you clear about project A's scope?' rarely reveals the truth. Sometimes people think they are clear when they are not, some people say yes so as not to embarrass themselves or you and some people say yes as they are clear about what they think which is different to what you think. Therefore, it is better to check out people's understanding by asking them to do something that will demonstrate if they are clear or not.

Usually if people have to apply their thinking, it helps them and you understand where they are. So asking them a question about Project A's scope would help demonstrate how clear they are about it. You could ask. 'How do you think project A will affect your team?' Do not be surprised if they say it will not affect their team when you think it will. Be grateful that you have found out at this point that they are not clear about project A's scope.

If an outcome is about sharing information or presenting information, then really think about what you want them to do differently once you have done that. What is the benefit in them listening?

Now you have a list of outcomes for the meeting. Ensure at the end that the meeting you structure does indeed achieve those outcomes.

2. Who needs to be invited to deliver those outcomes?

Think carefully about whom to invite. Who cares enough about those outcomes to engage in a meaningful conversation about them? I have seen many meetings derailed by people attending who give their opinions without any consequences, as they are not affected by their actions. In these situations, it is easy to have an opinion about what others need to do or to input objections without repercussions to yourself. Therefore, I tend to invite as few people as possible and manage differently the sharing of outcomes or information gathering from others before the meeting.

In addition, if you invite too many people the meeting dynamics change:

- With 4 to 8 people, you have enough variety for a robust conversation. You also have fewer people so that everyone will engage in the meeting, as they are all likely to be interested in the whole discussion.
- 9 or 10 starts to become cumbersome.
- At 11, the dynamics really seem to change and it becomes more of a presentation, with people trying to take centre stage or make speeches. Talkative people become more talkative and quieter people withdraw.

When I was regularly facilitating production teams where the team size would change across the year depending on output required, I noticed how initially small teams that gained a lot from the facilitated session became very fractured and disruptive if they grew to 11 or more people. This was despite the initial team members being part of the larger team.

Now you have the people you believe are required to achieve the outcomes you want.

3. The agenda items

Now put together the agenda that you feel is required to work through and achieve the outcomes. It is probably easiest to begin with the most important outcome that you want from the meeting. The one you definitely want to achieve.

Usually agenda items are written as nouns: For example, Project A's Scope. A more useful way to write it is as the outcome. For example, "We are all clear about project A's scope and how it will affect our teams". This will keep people focussed on the conversation rather than just talking about Project A.

Now think about how to structure the conversation to achieve that agenda item. For the example of "We are all clear about project A's scope and how it will affect our teams" the structure may be:

1. Joe presents Project A's purpose, plan and scope
2. Questions about what Joe has presented
3. Give everyone 2 or 3mins to think about how this will affect their team
4. Go round each person and hear how they think it will affect their team. Ask, "How will this affect your team and how do you feel about that?"
5. Resolve any points of misunderstanding or conflict

Step 3 is important as it structures the conversations using questions to achieve the outcome you intend. Therefore, think about what questions you will ask and write them down on your notes.

4. Allocating time to the steps and overall agenda items

In thinking through exactly how each agenda outcome will be achieved gives you a good idea of the time required to complete it. For the example structure above, in Step 3, the timings for each part maybe:

1. Probably 15-20 minutes

2. Likely to be 15-30 mins
3. 3 mins
4. Probably 3-5mins per person - 8 people is 24-40 mins
5. Easily 15-30 mins

Therefore, the total time is likely to be between 1hr 15mins to 2hrs. In reality it is almost certainly closer to 2 hrs for 8 people but at the end there is a high probability of them all being clear about their own and other people's understanding of project A's scope and its effect on their team. This will save a lot of valuable time once they leave the meeting.

Whenever I get people to write down exactly how they think an outcome will be achieved they are surprised by two things: firstly, how much more time it will take and also how useful they found scoping it out as they can really see that what they have written will achieve the outcome. They are usually nervous about the time although once they do it that way they quickly understand that it was worth it as they actually achieve a more robust outcome rather than spending less time pretending to get one.

Interestingly in a number of cases when someone feels there is not enough time, they raise the topic without structuring the conversation, assuming this will be quicker. Then three hours later after a frustrating unstructured discussion, they move on either because they are fed up with the conversation or because they need to cover the next agenda item before all the time is used up. The result is, a lot of time spent not achieving the outcome and time lost afterwards due to people not being clear.

5. Closing the meeting

Whatever happens start to close a one-hour meeting with at least five minutes left and a longer meeting with at least 10 minutes left. Often we push on until people start to drift out to other meetings rather than reviewing actions and, if appropriate, allowing each person to comment on the meeting. Closing a meeting properly reminds people of the decisions made and actions required of them. It also sets the tone that this meeting has been professionally run.

As a minimum, I would recap on the outcome of each agenda item. Going through the agenda so people can clearly see the link between the discussions and the outcomes. In their minds, they can think about how they helped or hindered each outcome. They can also think about what they could have done differently if some agenda items were not covered. For example, they might have kept taking the meeting off track with side stories, or perhaps they knew the conversation was not relevant but did not say anything to the group.

If the meeting is two hours or longer then I ask for a quick thought about the meeting from each person: Just go round the room person by person. My question might be "How did you find the meeting?" or "What would you do differently next time?" or "What did you find most valuable about today's meeting?"

6. Invites and your notes

Send out the meeting invite to attendees and include:

- Purpose of the meeting
- Overall duration & location of the meeting
- Agenda using Outcomes required from each item.

(Refrain from putting any timings against the Agenda items as this can create the need to rush through them due to time rather than because the outcome has been achieved.)

Your agenda notes will look slightly different:	Covered in:
Meeting purpose	Step 1
Agenda item stated as the Outcome required	Step 1 & 3
○ how this agenda item will be structured & questions to ask	Step 3
○ timings for each part	Step 4
Closing the meeting: go through actions/ outcomes/ question to ask	Step 5

Meeting preparation template

Exercise: Think of your next meeting and use the template below to structure it.

Meeting Preparation Sheet	
Purpose of the meeting: What do you want to have happen/ be different / have decided by the end of the meeting?	
Agenda Item 1: Written as an outcome - what you want at the end of this part	
Structure: What steps will achieve the agenda outcome?	Times:

Agenda Item 2: Written as an outcome - what you want at the end of this part

Structure: What steps will achieve the agenda outcome?	Times:

Agenda Item 3: Written as an outcome - what you want at the end of this part

Structure: What steps will achieve the agenda outcome?	Times:

Agenda Item 4: Written as an outcome - what you want at the end of this part

Structure: What steps will achieve the agenda outcome?	Times:

Closing the meeting: Recap decisions / outcomes Recap actions - what, who & by when/ update by when For longer meetings, ask a review question: Q:

After you have run the meeting, reflect on how it went:

Meeting date/duration: Purpose: How did it go? What did you learn? (What went well? Less well?) Preparation: Meeting: What would you do differently next time? Preparation: Meeting:

Other thoughts

- 'Posters' on the wall remain visible for all to see therefore key messages have time to be read and absorbed throughout the meeting
- Keep agenda item timings to yourself so others are not worrying about how long discussions are taking
- Use flipcharts and sticky-notes as you can involve everyone which raises commitment and engagement rather than typing into a computer
- Get people to discuss things in pairs or smaller groups and then come back to share their thoughts with the whole group. This ensures that quieter people input and allows you to manage dominating people.
- Write up decisions as they are made so everyone can see the wording of them and what was decided. This makes it clear and allows you to review them at the end of the meeting.
- In "Sleights of mind", Susana Martinez-Conde demonstrates that if you are on your email you are not concentrating on the email or the meeting properly. She suggests that you should decide which you want to do and concentrate on that: Have the courage to put the email away or leave the meeting.

36. Monthly Team Meetings

What are the benefits of doing this?

Cascaded team meetings are the lifeblood of the organisation, feeding information upwards and downwards. They make information systemic rather than discreet points of news. In this way, there is a healthy exchange of views and messages rather than a fear of engaging with your team. Over time, the meetings become more about sharing rather than talking at people. Managers feel comfortable that they do not have all the answers and enlist everyone's helping in making the meetings successful. In this way, they become the team's team meeting rather than yours. This improves the involvement everyone feels and improves morale.

These meetings are a valuable use of time where people can reflect on how they are working, build relationships, ask for help, gain insights and broader contexts so decisions are made quicker and robustly. They become the equivalent of the monthly team 'pit stop' where things are refocused and refreshed for the month ahead.

Team meeting purpose:
- Bring people together to engage, to understand, to share
- Build a sense of community and belonging
- A routine face-to-face opportunity to talk together
- For people to hear and discuss important corporate and local business issues
- To take action, change behaviour, to know how something impacts on them and others
- Understand the business priorities and local priorities
- Improve their work and that of the business

They allow for:
- Having everyone in your direct team engaged in the conversation
- Debriefing relevant company items
- Talking about your team's performance with them and how you are collectively moving that forwards

- Time for the team to talk about what they feel it is important to discuss
- Progressing actions from last time

Possible pitfalls and concerns to consider

- Fearing people will just complain if they get a chance to talk: After many meetings of not being able to say much then initially people may vent their frustrations. If you think this may happen then discuss how you will handle that respectfully, by talking to an experienced line manager. Usually after one or two of the new style meetings people start to engage in conversation rather than just complaining.
- Large departmental monthly meetings: The tendency is to try to do everyone at once as senior managers feel that it is more efficient and that everyone hears the same messages although people rarely do. The down sides to this format are that people are not interested in everything, which affects their participation; they are less likely to feel it is relevant and messages are diluted to try to get everyone to understand them. So long term it is not an efficient method.
- Talking at people: Meetings in which you are 'talked at' are a struggle to remain engaged in even when you are interested in the subject so think about what questions you will ask after you have given some information. Also, think about how much to give before you stop and ask everyone some questions about it. A few easy questions are, 'What do you think about that?' or 'How do you feel about that?' or 'How do you think this will affect us/ you?'
- Cancelling because you cannot attend: This sends out the message that the meeting is all about you and is not relevant without you or, worse still, that you do not trust someone else to run it. Ask a volunteer to host the meeting if you know you cannot attend and you may be pleasantly surprised how well it goes. If you are involving your team in the meeting, then someone else hosting it will be easy.
- No consistent agenda or format: No format makes the meeting unpredictable which makes people nervous. In addition, it can mean that people prepare something for discussion and then there is no time to do that, which can be frustrating for them. A monthly rhythm allows people to physically and mentally prepare for it and creates predictability, which makes it safer for everyone to participate.
- Cancelling because you think there is nothing to discuss: Again, this sends out the message that what the team has to say is not important and creates frustration. Sometimes managers do this as they are uncertain how to create participative meetings or they feel no one will say anything. I find that is rarely the case and

the meeting can be ended sooner if there is genuinely less to discuss. Along with cancelling the meeting I have heard managers walk in and say 'this will be a short meeting as I have very little to share with you' which most participants take as, 'I am not interested in what you have to say'. It would be better to ask people what they want to discuss and listen to what they say.

Other relevant chapters

- Chapter 11   Questions That Invite Others to Contribute
- Chapter 15   Listening With Your Eyes, Ears and Intuition
- Chapter 17   Productive Language

How

Covers

> Three possible team meeting structures
>
> How to transition to cascaded team meetings

Team meeting structures

A team meeting of 1.5-2hrs allows enough time for it to add value. Although this may seem a lot, especially if you currently have poor meetings, when they are going well this will be quite a short amount of time in which to cover everything. Team meetings should happen every month, even if the manager is not able to attend as direct reports can run it. Monthly usually fits well into the wider business cycle with other monthly reports and briefings. The team meeting can happen shortly after a monthly business debrief. In this way, information can be cascaded down to everyone and still be relevant rather than being old news.

Having a regular agenda enables people to prepare properly and to know what to expect. This means they will listen to the information rather than trying to ensure that what they have to say is heard as they are worried the meeting may end before they get to say it. Therefore, having an agenda means people know when they can input the things they have to say.

You may have a slide template in a shared folder so people delivering each section can populate the slides for the next meeting when they want to. This helps to stop the last minute rush of needing to pull things together or worse, not being properly prepared because you run out of time. Start planning next month's meeting topics shortly after you have had this month's meeting as then everyone has enough time to prepare and find out the information required.

Team meetings work best if they are attended by the manager and their direct reports. This makes it safe enough for everyone to speak and the conversation is relevant to everyone. Each direct report then meets with their team and so on. If you have a team of ten or more people, then expect less participation initially as people are often nervous about speaking publically in such large groups.

The format of these meetings should be quite simple as the quality of discussion is important and over structured meetings stifle discussion. Here are some possible formats:

Option 1
1. Welcome everyone, link from last meeting and give the key message, theme or focus for this month
2. Complete the Business and local departmental briefings
3. Discuss ongoing topics from previous meetings (Items that need to be discussed over a number of meetings)
4. Discuss one-off items relevant for this month
5. Have an open session for people to ask questions and discuss what they want to

Option 2
1. Welcome
2. Discuss the Business performance: Key messages and metrics from the business
3. Discuss how are we performing? What do we need to focus on? etc.
4. What are the hot topics on our minds we want to talk about? Plus answer any questions or updates from the last meeting
5. News & Updates: Local things to share and do that are relevant this month
6. Have an open session for people to ask questions and discuss what they want to

Option 3
1. Welcome
2. Complete the Business and local departmental briefings
3. Have people give overviews from each of your main teams, sections, or departments

4. Looking forwards:
   o What's on the radar?
   o What concerns do you have?
   o What do you need help with?
5. Open floor forum:
   o What questions do you want to ask?
   o How is everybody getting on?
   o How are you feeling?
   o What problems or challenges do you have?
6. Feedback: "How did this meeting go today?"

In each of these options ask the main question and then let everyone speak by asking "What do you think about that?" Explore what people are saying by asking "Tell me a bit more about that?" or "What do you mean by that?" Read Chapter 11 on 'Questions That Invite Others to Contribute' to help you facilitate an open and free-flowing discussion. Remember that you do not need to answer or defend every comment made. Sometimes people can say something and you can just listen to it. Maybe you can ask them "What could you do about that?" or get the group to help by asking, "What do you think Fred could do about that?"

How to transition to cascaded team meetings

In many departments, it works well to use a cascade system. This is where the departmental manager has a team meeting with their direct reports. In this way, items relevant to the managers can be openly discussed and what needs to be debriefed to others is agreed. After this meeting, the managers then have meetings with their direct reports, tailoring the business information to their team and discussing items relevant to their team openly. Then those managers have a meeting with their direct reports and so on. In one company, I worked at, they found that the quality of discussion and questions being referred back to the management team from local team meetings were of a higher quality than from a departmental style meeting. The local teams could also fit their meeting around their work demands rather than having to attend larger meetings at a set time.

The downside to cascade meetings is that there is an uncertainty as to the quality of the meetings and their regularity unless there is a feedback mechanism. Having a plan for senior managers to rotate around the local team meetings across the year ensures they maintain visibility with the wider team as well as improving the quality and regularity of the meetings.

Town Hall meetings work well for presenting information once or twice a year. They are a good forum for other departments to 'showcase' their work to others and for the Director to share some common messages with everyone. They are not a replacement for local monthly team meetings.

Here are some useful steps for setting up local meetings: -

1. **Have a meeting with your direct reports to plan how this will happen successfully:**
   o Give yourself enough time to plan it and prepare for the first set of meetings
   o Ensure you have a plan to support the first three months of local meetings with extra feedback sought to see what is happening.

2. **Map out your division's family tree to see:**
   o Which direct reports will work with you to prepare and deliver your team meeting, if not all your direct reports.
   o Which Managers will attend your meeting, as it may be sensible to extend it to a few other managers.
   o Which Line Managers will complete their own local team meeting with their people and how will you support those that will not.

3. **Agree the format of your team meeting and the local team meetings.**
   o Plan in time to plan and prepare each month's meeting.
   o Agree on the meeting duration and dates for the year, usually monthly.
   o Create a meeting format template to use each month deciding what to put onto the agenda and who is doing what.
   o Create a template slide deck and think about if a different one is required for the local meetings. Agree where it will be located so people can populate it as they prepare their sections.

4. **Determine which Line Managers are able to run participative local team meetings, those currently less able and those are unlikely to be able to do so.**
   - Pair up or mentor less able line managers until they become competent enough to run the meeting on their own.
   - Permanently pair up line managers who are unlikely to run successful local meetings with a competent manager who will run the meeting or merge two meetings so the competent manager runs a larger meeting.

5. **Agree a schedule of the local meetings for you and your direct reports to attend so you maintain visibility and connection with the division.**

6. **Decide how you will gain feedback from the local team meetings so you know:**
   - The quality of the meetings and that they are happening
   - What messages and actions are being taken away

7. **Discuss running a meeting with all the Line Managers to gain their input and commitment to doing it.**

8. **Create the first meeting's content and run the meeting(s)**

9. **Get feedback and review how it went. Refine things as necessary.**
   - Simple feedback questions to ask are 'What do you like about the team meetings?', 'What would you like to see less of or do differently?' and 'What would you like to see us start doing?' If possible get a neutral third party to get feedback from all, or a good cross section of attendees. You can then share the feedback with your direct reports and the line managers.

37. Basic Kick-Off Meetings

What are the benefits of doing this?

Rarely is time spent at the beginning of a meeting to gain buy-in and clarity from the team as to what they need to deliver. Consequently, right from the beginning it becomes fragmented snippets and 'Chinese whispers' about who is doing what and what is required. Thus having an initial Kick Off meeting helps to start the project in a different way, one that gains buy-in and clarity for the team involved.

With clarity and buy-in comes commitment to delivering the required outcome and people look to solve problems rather than use them as reasons to slow down or stop. This makes it worth every valuable minute of time that it took to do.

Possible pitfalls and concerns to consider

- Inviting everyone involved no matter how small their contribution rather than just the core team tends to mean that the core team do not get enough time to ask the questions they need to and often there is a lot of conflicting information. I am not a great fan of inviting lots of people to the meeting: It may seem efficient in one way as everyone hears the same thing but it usually means that the core team do not have enough time together to form strong enough bonds to push their work through. They become easily distracted and struggle to maintain momentum. The core team needs to settle and then it needs to handle the other relationships.

- Making the meeting a one-way presentation of what needs to be done does not allow the team to buy into the objective. Usually the team cannot create its own outcome but it does need to discuss how it feels about that outcome and what it looks like for them. In this way, you create consistency and ownership.

- Rushing into' how will we do it' too soon often means that people are not clear about what they are doing and have not thought through any potential problems. Exploring these aspects early on may seem to slow the start of the project but overall the team will implement things quicker and more robustly.

Other relevant chapters
- Chapter 11   Questions That Invite Others to Contribute
- Chapter 15   Listening With Your Eyes, Ears and Intuition

- Chapter 35   Basic Meeting Outcomes, Structure and Tips

How

Covers meeting structures for

> Half-day kick-off session for small projects or tasks
>
> One-day kick-off session for larger projects

Simple half-day session timings to kick-off a small project or task

Time	Topic	Content	Notes
15mins (15)	Orientation	Team leader to welcome everyone and invite people to participate and create a successful meeting. Ask each person to introduce themselves: name, role, why they are here today. Tell them they have up to a minute to do this.	Use a watch to give everyone a minute to do this. This helps people feel part of the meeting
45mins (1hr)	Purpose	Get the Sponsor or a Senior Manager to tell the group what the project is, why it is so important to the company (what difference it will make to customers) and why he values their input. Allow Q&A session - ensure that everyone gets to ask their questions. If someone is dominating, then go round each person to balance participation.	Questions to ask the team to get input could be: What questions do you have? How do you feel about this project? What excites you about this project? What concerns do you have?
30mins (1.5hrs)	Why me?	Get the Team Leader to say why he values each person on the team. (10min) Then allow each person to say what they feel they bring to the team. (20min)	Ensure the Team Leader has prepared this. Q: What do you feel you bring to this project?'
15mins (1.75hrs)	Break		Ensure people keep to the time
45mins (2.5hrs)	Main Objectives to deliver the project	Split group into trios or pairs. Get each group to spend 10mins deciding on what they think the main objectives; phases or chunks are to deliver the required outcome. (10mins) Get each group to put up their sticky notes on the wall and talk through each one. (20min) Then finalise the clusters until you have 3 - 6 key objectives, phases, or chunks that deliver the project outcome. (10min) At this point these will be draft and can be finalised after the meeting: Agree who is doing which cluster (5min)	Clustering exercise Write each one on a sticky note. When the next group talks they can stick their objectives with previous objectives that are the same or very similar so the objectives get clustered. Remove any notes not required.

Time	Topic	Content	Notes
30min (3hrs)	What will help or hinder us?	Split group into different trios or pairs. Get each group to spend 10mins thinking about what will really help the team to be successful. They need to be a prerequisite for success rather than a 'nice to have'. Also get the groups to think about any known problems that need to be resolved otherwise, the project may struggle or fail. (10min) Get the groups to put up all their Help & Hinder sticky notes. Clarify any that are not clear. (5min) Then go through each one. If it is a duplicate discard it. If not decide: Are we going to do it? If yes, then who & by when. If not discard it. (20min)	Write each one on a sticky note. These are not the actual project tasks but team tasks that will make the project successful or cause it problems. For example: Weekly team meetings - helps. Make sure they are real and not just a wish list or possible issues.
15min (3.25hrs)	Close	Recap on actions: What, who and by when. Ask each person to briefly say how they now feel about delivering the project/task.	Q: How do you now feel about the project?

Simple one-day session timings to kick-off a larger project

Time	Topic	Content	Notes
8.30am 45mins	Orientation	Team leader to welcome everyone and invite people to participate and create a successful meeting. Ask each person to introduce themselves: name, role, why they are here today. Tell them they have up to 3 minutes to do this.	Use a watch to give everyone 3 minutes to do this.
9.15am 90mins	Purpose	Get the Sponsor or a Senior Manager to tell the group what the project is, why it is so important to the company (what difference it will make to customers) and why he values their input. (15mins) Allow Q&A session - ensure that everyone gets to ask their questions. If someone is dominating, then go round each person to balance participation. (20mins) Then split the group into pairs and get them to discuss these questions for 15min. What excites you about this project? What concerns do you have? What would make you feel truly proud about it? Get back together and ask each pair to share some of their thoughts. (40min)	
10.45am 15mins	Break		Ensure people keep to the time

Time	Topic	Content	Notes
11am 60mins	Why me?	Get the Team Leader to say why he values each person being on the team. (15min) Get each person (on their own) to create a time line of their life since they left school (flipchart paper or A3). Putting in their key career elements & highlights and their key personal highlights & interests. (15min) Get each person to present their time line to the group. (30min)	Ensure the Team Leader has prepared this. Need coloured pens and paper.
12pm 60mins	Lunch	Help people to mingle with each other.	
1pm 75mins	Main Objectives to deliver the project	Split group into trios or pairs. Get each group to spend 20mins deciding on what they think are the main objectives, phases or chunks that will deliver the required outcome. (20mins) Get each group to put up their sticky notes on the wall and talk through each one. (30min) Then cluster the ideas until you have 3 - 6 key objectives, phases, or chunks that deliver the project outcome. (25min)	Clustering exercise Write each one on a sticky note. When the next group talks they can stick their objectives with previous objectives that are the same or very similar so the objectives get clustered.
2.15pm 15mins	Break		Ensure people keep to the time
2.30pm 60mins	Main Objectives to deliver the project	In groups, write onto a flip chart what the objective is from those ideas. (1 or 2 clusters per group) (20min) Put up all the objectives and finalise what they are (40min).	Make ideas into a coherent objective. If one is tricky then resolve it outside of this meeting.
3.30pm 60min	What will help or hinder us?	Split group into different trios or pairs. Get each group to spend 15mins thinking about what will really help the team to be successful. They need to be key to success rather than a 'nice to have'. Also get the groups to think about any definite problems that need to be resolved otherwise, the project may struggle or fail. (15min) Get the groups to put up all their Helps & Hinders. (5min) Clarify any that are not clear. (10min) Then go through each one. If it is a duplicate discard it. If not decide: Are we going to do it? If yes, then who & by when. If not discard it. (30min)	Write each one on a sticky note. These are not the actual project tasks but team tasks that will make the project successful or cause it problems. For example: Weekly team meetings - helps. Make sure they are real and not just a wish list or possible issues.
4.30pm 30min	Wrap up meeting	Recap on actions: What, who and by when. Ask each person to briefly say how they now feel about delivering the project/task and what they felt about the meeting today.	Q: How do you now feel about the project? How do you feel about today's meeting?
5pm	Close		

38. Basic Review Meetings

What are the benefits of doing this?

Often, things tend to move off the path they were intended to be on, as things naturally evolve and the environment around them changes. Through regular reviews, your team and the work they are doing are less likely to wander off track. The other benefit of regular reviews is that the team feel that their work matters and remain engaged.

If the manager leaves it too long before the first review, the work can have major problems and the discussions are tough to have. The problems can no longer be ignored or hidden as they are out in the open. Therefore, some managers feel it is better not to complete reviews, keep their heads down and plough on. However, successful teams build the review process into their daily activities and do so early enough so that only a few alterations are needed to get things back on track. Then the focus on what needs to happen is easily maintained rather than finding someone to blame for the large problem that has occurred.

Possible pitfalls and concerns to consider

- People do not feel safe enough to be open: Inviting senior managers or everyone involved, no matter how small their contribution, rather than just the core team may mean that the core team feels unable to be fully open and honest about their progress so far. Valuable learning and progress becomes inhibited, therefore find a different way to involve or inform the extended team rather than compromise the review process.
- Not reviewing enough: Most team development exercises show how much improvement can be made from a regular review and yet we still tend to feel we do not have the time to do them. Often there is a feeling that we should keep going even though we know that we are not being fully effective, or worse, knowing that things are not really working very well. Therefore, getting into the habit of small regular reviews makes larger quarterly or annual reviews much easier to do.

Other relevant chapters

- Chapter 11   Questions That Invite Others to Contribute
- Chapter 15   Listening With Your Eyes, Ears and Intuition
- Chapter 35   Basic Meeting Outcomes, Structure and Tips

How

Covers the structures for

    A quick update meeting

    A review meeting

    A final review meeting

Quick update meeting

In the regular team meeting, allocate time for reviewing work or projects. It is an update with progress reported, key highlights given and any issues or concerns raised.

A simple 5min review format for an activity could be:

1. State the project/ activity and what should have been completed by this point
2. State what has been completed - thanking any one of note/ any highlights or challenges overcome (briefly)
3. State what has not been completed and what the reason is for this (keep it factual)
4. If the issue is small then discuss it there and then, otherwise agree with the relevant people when to meet about it.
5. Update the plans/ reports as appropriate

If an activity/ project has been completed, then thank everyone and congratulate the team.

Review meeting

The purpose of this session is to consolidate momentum and improve how they are working on their daily work/ projects/ activities.

A simple 1hr agenda could be:

1. How are we feeling about doing this? (Allow each person 2minutes to share their thoughts)
2. What are we doing that is working? (Allow people to input their thoughts)
3. What challenges are we having? (Allow people to input their thoughts)
4. Having heard how we feel about it, what is working and what challenges we are having:

a. What should we do differently, if anything?

b. Generate ideas onto a flipchart

c. Then get the team to agree which ones they will do

5. Anything else?

Write down any changes and review them during the monthly team meeting to check that the change has given the required benefit.

Final review meeting

The purpose of this one to two-hour meeting is mostly to recognise the effort and progress made by the team now the project/ activity is completed. They should leave the meeting feeling that their efforts have been valued and acknowledged. They should feel it was worthwhile. To ensure it meets this purpose it is useful to let the team do most of the input. In addition, this is a good meeting to invite a few senior people to so that they can congratulate the team: Make sure they understand the purpose of the meeting as well. Cakes or a team prize work well.

1. Highlights from the project/ activity – presented by the team

2. Differences made, including challenges overcome, and benefits delivered – presented by the team

3. Internal / external customer comments to indorse improvements made including senior managers

4. An insight or learning from each person (or pairs/trios if you feel that it would not work individually)

Building Teams

My experience is that a purpose without a team is just as bad as a team without a purpose. Each is important although in many cases we focus on developing, progressing and monitoring the task rather than the team. This frequently means that the tasks take longer to deliver the purpose they were meant to. Developing your team is just as simple as working with your projects and activities: It needs focus, a plan and to be done. I do not think we would get very far by running projects as we do teams. We would get better results for both the work and the people if we managed team development more in the way we manage projects and tasks.

Well-functioning teams rarely happen by themselves and within today's business environment you cannot really afford to hope that your team performs well. On the other hand, managers often think that team development is a black art that you need to bring a specialist in to do. The most effective and sustainable method is to develop your team through its work yourself by enhancing a few things that you are doing and stopping things that undermine a team being a team, such as individual objectives. 'What!' I hear you say, yes, I know everyone has their tasks and activities to do but collectively they all need to add up to the work your team or department needs to deliver.

Therefore, if you want people to be flexible, to collaborate and to help each other out, focus the outcome and measures on the team not individuals. If I have to make 50 items and you have to make 1000 items, if I am paid after 50 then I have little incentive to help you with your 1000. If, however, we are both paid when the 1050 items get made then I would have a very good incentive to help you and to care about your work too. Leading a team becomes much easier when the team care about each other's work as well as their own.

These chapters will help you to weave team development into daily work rather than specific and isolated team building events. I am not a great fan of 'team building events' as they are expected to achieve too much and are rarely followed up. However, they can be valuable as people get to see each other in a different environment, which usually strengthens relationships. Team events to allow people to build relationships by experiencing each other in a different environment can be many things, from a team lunch, a bowling evening to a charity day that is both useful for the team and the charity.

David Sibbet also has some interesting material on visual teams that is useful for team development ideas. His website is useful and he has written a number of books on the topic. Also, Paul Lencioni's model on the 'Five Dysfunctions of a Team' is very insightful as an alternative. The book is easy to read and there is a field guide with useful exercises in it, as well as website material.

Overall developing your team means that it handles problems from a better position where the focus is on the work to be resolved rather than worrying about the games people are playing for themselves. Team development creates trust, builds relationships and a commitment to doing the work.

The chapters that follow look to give you simple and pragmatic ways to develop a well-functioning team. For most managers that alone would be great.

Chapter 39 "The Yearly People Cycle" outlines the complete yearly cycle that a well-functioning team would go through. You can vary the elements in duration to suit your needs although in essence every event forms part of the jigsaw of a well-functioning team and business.

Chapter 40 "Team Deliverables for the Year" outlines how you share team deliverables and review progress against them.

Chapter 41 "How Well are We Working Together as a Team?" gives you four simple methods for the team to review how it is functioning. I feel that this is what many managers are missing, a method for having a structured conversation about the team's dynamics.

Chapter 42 "Implementing a Team Appraisal Approach" explores how you would complete a team appraisal, which is essential if you need your team to work together. It helps create collaboration and also acknowledges individual contributions.

39. The Yearly People Cycle

What are the benefits of doing this?

In companies, there is usually a yearly business rhythm that creates momentum for a business to grow and remain productive. The same is true for people management, there needs to be a yearly people rhythm as then people grow and become more productive.

This cycle is above and beyond the functional weekly operations meetings where the focus is on delivering the actions and tasks required in day to day business. This cycle puts the focus on allowing people to understand the wider business contexts, develop trusting relationships, develop themselves and maintain a longer-term focus on their collective work, improvement activities and team working.

The yearly people cycle is about creating, and engaging with, capable people so that they will chose to participate to the full extent of their ability, to deliver something that is mutually important to both them and the organisation. They will do this for managers and leaders who create and maintain an environment that enables this to happen. This cycle is about how you create that environment and make that happen.

This cycle creates the lifeblood of a team as well as creating emotional commitment in your people. This will result in faster decision-making, robust decisions, continuous improvement and a journey towards a high performing team where people feel proud of the work they do and valued for their contribution.

Possible pitfalls and concerns to consider

- This will take too much time: It does take time out of people's working year but overall it will save far more than it takes. Engaged and committed people are more productive and create an environment that raises others up with them. This means you will spend less time having unproductive meetings and conversations with them.
- I am uncomfortable running team or 1:1 meetings: Many managers do not like running team meetings or having development reviews with their people. If they are badly structured, then I cannot blame them as I would not like that either. However, the answer is not to stop doing them, the answer is to do them differently, and often more easily, so that people enjoy the meetings and get value from them, including you.

- Running meetings that are not participative and are a one-way monologue: When you are designing meeting formats think about how much the team members can do instead of you. It usually surprises most managers as to how little they really need to do. Or perhaps that concerns them as they feel that if they are not telling their people everything then they will have nothing to do and leadership will not be needed. That is seldom the case.
- In meetings, think about what questions you are going to ask people after you have given them some information. Allow as much time for questions as you did for your information giving. This will ensure that you do not overload people with too much information and that they have a chance to participate and have their say. This is how you get emotional commitment.

Other relevant chapters
- Chapter 4   Creating Meaningful Work and Sense of Community
- Chapter 36   Monthly Team Meetings
- Chapter 40   Team Deliverables for the Year

How

Outlined below are the key elements of the Yearly People Cycle shown in Fig 1 on page 233. I think it is useful to have an overview of meetings relating to your team and its work. The elements are referenced to the relevant chapters in this book, where appropriate, as they give you more detail and the ability to run that session.

The months

These could start at any point in the year to fit your business rhythm. Therefore, Month 1 could be January or April and for some companies it would be September. Write in what they are for your company, as people prefer to see that.

Team meetings

Business briefing

Usually each month a company issues a briefing pack to senior leaders and they may also attend a monthly briefing. From this, the senior leader can decide how to make the information relevant to their people.

Managers meeting (1hr) Chapters 35 & 36

Once the senior leader has attended the Business briefing they have a meeting with their direct reports. In effect, this is their 'local team meeting' or 'monthly management team meeting'. In essence, it covers this format:

- The leader discusses the Business Briefing, highlighting which aspects they expect to be cascaded to teams below and which are for discussion at that meeting only.
- The managers then present the department's top level performance information including actions, giving an update for those and including noteworthy points.
- Discuss items that need to be collectively talked about or shared. These items may be discussed at a number of meetings across the year or are one-off items that need to be covered. Again, from these discussions, agree what will be cascaded down to lower teams and what is not for discussion outside of the meeting.
- Finally, there is a 'round the room' session where each manager can talk about any concerns, challenges or highlights coming up in the next month.

Before the meeting closes it is agreed as to which topics are being cascaded down, who is generating the information for that and by when. In addition, the topics for the next management meeting are agreed and people allocated to prepare the information for it.

Local team meetings (1hr) Chapters 35 & 36

After the Managers' meeting, each manager has a meeting with their direct reports. The meeting covers information from the Business brief tailored for the team; how the team is collectively performing presented by individuals in the team; items carried over from previous meetings; updates or answers to questions raised at the last local team meeting. Finally, there is a 'round the room' session where each person can talk about any concerns, challenges or highlights coming up in the next month. In addition, the topics for the next meeting are agreed and people allocated to prepare the information for them.

Team performance improvement meeting (1hr) Chapters 35, 47/48

This is a meeting where the team either reviews the actions from its simple performance display boards (often called visual management boards) or where the team decides what small improvement projects it can do to improve how it is doing its work. These meetings then become reviews of those actions; adding in a new action when one has been completed. This meeting could be joined onto the end of a monthly team meeting, thus having an extended two-hour meeting every three months.

Daily/ weekly operations meetings or performance tracking boards Chapter 47

A number of teams have daily or weekly Operations Meetings. These sessions are focussed around task delivery and achieving the team deliverables. They provide valuable information and keep everyone focussed on the work at hand. The team may also use simple performance tracking boards. It is useful to feed this information into team meetings and team improvement sessions where there is a chance to spend more time to take a wider view, to reflect, to gain everyone's thoughts and to look at trends or patterns as well as actions.

Performance & Deliverables meetings

Sharing team deliverables (1hr) Chapters 35 & 40

This is a team meeting where the line manager shares with their team what the whole team needs to deliver that year. This is often the line manager's objectives. This is especially important if the team work together a lot. Also it can be valuable even if the team has a lot of individual work as it helps with creating flexibility between team members, creates a sense of community and helps people to share best practice. It is rare that teams are purely a collection of individuals as externally the team may be seen as one entity delivering a service or product and it is useful to think of it in this way when looking at the team's deliverable for the year. Yes, of course, people often do individual tasks but they need to collectively share the workload and feel committed to the outcome not just their aspect of it. If you don't talk to people collectively about the team's deliverables, then people will focus on their individual aspects. Getting them to help each other or be flexible will be difficult if they have no collective ownership or if your actions are not demonstrating a collective team approach.

How are we doing against our team deliverables? (1hr) Chapters 35 & 40

At least twice across the year it is good to get the team back together to review how they are collectively doing against their team objectives. This gives them plenty of time to make adjustments so they can deliver what is required and have a successful year. It also signals that you, as the manager, are committed to the objectives, which is important to do. Getting customer feedback as well grounds the session in reality and maintains the connection as to why they are doing the work and how valuable it is. Hopefully if the feedback is good it also helps them feel proud about what they are doing and maintains their commitment to it.

What did we deliver this year? (1.5-2hrs) Chapters 35 & 40

At the end of the year as the initial part of the appraisal process, the team should review what it actually delivered against its team objectives and reflect on how that went. It is also the time to celebrate successes and reflect so that the learning is taken forwards into the following year. Again, customer feedback is important to have as it grounds the session in reality and strengthens the feeling of how valuable their work is.

Agreeing individual deliverables (1hr)

Most companies have a process for agreeing individual objectives although how the conversation is actually conducted can often be unproductive. If you want people to feel committed to their work then allowing them to set as much of their own deliverables as possible works best. If this meeting takes place shortly after the session on 'Sharing team deliverables' then most people will be able to sensibly set their own work for the year ahead. Newer people or poor performers may need to work with you in doing this. Most managers fear that their people will set unrelated and easy objectives for themselves. I have found that the opposite is usually true and people tend to set themselves more challenging objectives than I would have done. The few that don't can easily be handled in the meeting but overall allowing people to set their own deliverables will improve commitment.

Reviewing individual deliverables (1hr)

At least quarterly, if not bi-monthly it is good to meet with each person and review how they are getting on with their deliverables: What's going well? What are they struggling with? What challenges have they overcome or are they having? What support do they need? It demonstrates to them your commitment to their work and their welfare. It also allows you to reflect on how they are coping with the work. It allows both of you to ensure that problems are surfaced early, and sorted out so that they have a successful year: Something you both want to happen.

Personal development plan creation (1-2hrs) Chapter 44

Now people know the work they have to do, it is time to look at what development they may need so they deliver that work successfully. Again, allow people to create their own development plans. Value-adding development plans link to making a difference to the person's actual work; something they need to do better or complete sooner. They also have action plans that make certain they become competent in new skills rather than just attending a course and doing little with their learning afterwards. Personal Development Plans (PDP) like these look to develop people in different ways such as using mentors, experienced managers, the Internet, webinars, as well as practicing and reviewing.

Personal development plan review (1hr) Chapter 44

Now people have sensible development plans with good action plans to work on, they will need to meet with you more often to review how those action plans are progressing. Also to check if they are becoming more competent and if that is making the required difference to their actual work. If you have a small team or a poor performer, you may choose to meet with them monthly as there will always be enough to discuss about their PDP, otherwise meeting quarterly is the minimum you should aim for. Regular meetings also signal to the person that you are serious about their development and you should be as it means they will do their work better, more easily or take on more responsibility.

Appraisal meeting (1-2hrs) Chapter 42

Each company has its own way of conducting appraisals. Often the process and the forms are not the problem. Problems usually occur for two reasons. Firstly, regular review sessions for both the person's deliverables and their PDPs have not been undertaken. This means that the manager has allowed problems to escalate and is not fully appraised with what has been happening for the person across the year. Secondly, the quality of 'how' the appraisal meeting is conducted is poor, usually by the meeting being a one-way monologue by the line manager. Within the yearly people cycle, appraisal meetings are just another 'Review of deliverables' meeting only this time it has to be documented on the company's appraisal system. The process is easier to complete if reviews have been held across the year, as well as being completed after the collective team meeting on 'What did we deliver this year?' The other various sessions across the year will also mean that the appraisal process is easier to complete for the individual and that they will be able to fully participate in the appraisal meeting.

Team development

Meaningful work & pride in what we do statements (1-2hrs) Chapters 4 & 5

This meeting is for the team to think about what work it is really doing and what makes each person care about the work they do. The outcome of the meeting might be that the team states how it really adds values to the customer and company as well as everyone stating what it is that makes them proud to be part of the team. These statements can be used as ways to develop the team working together across the year. It is worth revisiting this conversation at the start of each year to see if it is still relevant and how it has progressed.

How well are we working together as a team? Review meeting Chapter 41

To get a team to develop requires a way of having a conversation about that. This meeting will allow you to have a participative and structured format for allowing the team to think about how much of a team it is and how they would like to build on that. There are various methods for a team to review how it is functioning, such as its meaningful work and pride statements, or there are standard questions about team operations, or you can use a simple variation on Stop, Start, Continue. By regularly focussing on this aspect, you signal its importance to the team and your commitment to it. It also makes team development simple and productive so that across the months and years the team matures.

Departmental or divisional meeting (<1hr) Chapters 35 & 36

It is useful at least once a year for everyone in the department or division to hear directly and collectively from the Director or Departmental Head. The Director or Departmental Head can set the scene for the year ahead, talk about challenges and hopes for the year, talk about what they want everyone to focus on and accomplish that year. They can also celebrate successes and successful people or teams. These can also be useful places to invite one or two guest speakers, such as customers or for best practice sharing. Ensure you know they are good presenters by discussing their presentation beforehand. If they are not very good, either get them to redo their presentation or politely ask them not to do it. This is better than boring a lot of people and wasting their time because the presenter couldn't be bothered. Departmental Heads may wish to run these twice a year. Question and answer sessions are also a good idea.

39. The Yearly People Cycle

On-going People Cycle

	Month 1	Month 2	Month 3	Month 4	Month 5	Month 6	Month 7	Month 8	Month 9	Month 10	Month 11	Month 12
	Business Briefing	Business Briefing	Business Briefing	Business Briefing	Business Briefing	Business Briefing	Business Briefing	Business Briefing	Business Briefing	Business Briefing	Business Briefing	Business Briefing
	Managers meeting	Managers meeting	Managers meeting	Managers meeting	Managers meeting	Managers meeting	Managers meeting	Managers meeting	Managers meeting	Managers meeting	Managers meeting	Managers meeting
	Local Team meetings & Team Performance Improvement meeting	Local Team meetings	Local Team meetings	Local Team meetings & Team Performance Improvement meeting	Local Team meetings	Local Team meetings	Local Team meetings & Team Performance Improvement meeting	Local Team meetings	Local Team meetings	Local Team meetings & Team Performance Improvement meeting	Local Team meetings	Local Team meetings
	Daily or weekly VMB/ performance tracking boards/ information/ Operations meetings if relevant											
Share Team Deliverables for the year					How are we doing against our team deliverables?				How are we doing against our team deliverables?			What did we deliver this year?
Agree Individual Deliverables for the year				Progress Review			Progress Review					Appraisal
		Personal Development Plan: Set up / Review			PDP Review			PDP Review			PDP Review	
		'Meaningful work' & 'Pride in what we do' meeting				'How are we functioning as a team?' Review					Divisional / Departmental Meeting	

Fig 1: This diagram shows the main meetings across the year that help your team to be successful.

40. Team Deliverables for the Year

What are the benefits of doing this?

If you need your team to be flexible in sharing their work and helping each other to complete the team's work, then you are in a better place to achieve this if you use team objectives and conduct a team based appraisal.

Many managers treat their teams as individuals by focussing their attention on just what that person is doing. This creates an individualistic culture where everyone focuses on their own work and does not need to worry about how other people are doing. Despite the manager talking about being a team and needing to work together, if the reward incentives are individually based this is the overriding motivator. I know that people have individual pay but how they arrive at that can be team based rather than individually based and this is an important factor.

An individual focus often leads to one person working on lower priority work for the team whilst someone else is struggling with a higher priority task. It creates little incentive, beyond goodwill, for that person to help the other: "It is not in my objectives so why would I help them when this lower priority task is in my objectives?" If you would prefer that important team activities are completed above lower priority ones, then creating team deliverables will help. Once people's tasks need to come together then you create a reason for being flexible and collaborating therefore the team will drive that for itself rather than you having to force it.

Possible pitfalls and concerns to consider

- Creating team deliverables and then only talking to each person about their tasks: This is the main reason teamwork fails, as it needs a focussed effort to remain team-focussed. Therefore, remember when you are talking to people about their activities, which you need to do, connect them to the overall team deliverables. Another way to keep the team-focus is in team meetings where you get each person to own the review of a team deliverable as this demonstrates their need to focus on the collective outcomes of the team, not just what they have done.
- Not reviewing progress or the final outcome: The essence of developing a well-functioning team is consistency and maintaining a yearly cycle that fits together. With the work environment seemingly endorsing individualism, the message about team deliverables needs consistently and gently reinforcing across the year.

- Not telling people what and why: Managers spend of a lot of time telling people how to do their work and less time discussing what needs to be done overall and why. Telling competent people how to do their work is very demotivating. If you were to give them the bigger context for the work, what was needed and why, then, in many cases, they would be able to go away and deliver it themselves.
- People say very little in the team objective-setting meeting: This is often the case initially as they are not used to participative meetings or team deliverables. Logically they can see it makes sense and deep down they are worried that it will not last. Therefore, you will need to demonstrate that the meetings will be participative rather than just saying they will and that team deliverables are required.

Other relevant chapters
- Chapter 11   Questions That Invite Others to Contribute
- Chapters 14-16   Listening Productively
- Chapter 35   Basic Meeting Outcomes, Structures and Tips

How

Covers two different approaches to creating team deliverables depending on the type of team. It also covers each required meeting's purpose, preparation elements, meeting structure and post-meeting work.

Approach 1 for teams with clear team objectives and team members depend on each other's work
Meeting 1: Sharing the team deliverables	(Start of year)
Meeting 2: Reviewing the team deliverables	(Mid-year)
Meeting 3: 'What did we deliver this year?' review	(End of Year)

Approach 2 for teams with lots of activities the team needs to do and the team members do not necessarily have to work together but would benefit from doing so.
Meeting 1: Creating a team workload	(Start of year)
Meeting 2: Reviewing the team deliverables	(Mid-year)
Meeting 3: 'What did we deliver this year?' review	(End of Year)

Approach 1: Teams with clear team objectives and team members depend on each other's work

For example, in a production or operations team

Meeting 1: Sharing the team deliverables (Start of year)

Purpose

To share with the team what they need to deliver this year. It is important to gain participation in this meeting, as that will help create ownership for the work. Involve supervisors or competent people as much as possible right from the start to work with you on preparing and running the meeting. It is really good if you can get them, and other team members, to do as much of this meeting as possible. Although that will depend on the maturity of the team and whether they have been through a process like this before. Once they have become a mature team then they can prepare and run this meeting themselves. They can also prepare for and run the review meetings as well.

Preparation

Ensure you are clear about all the deliverables and that you can present them to the team in an easy to understand way: Posters and handouts are better than detailed slides. Think about what questions may come up and how you will answer those. Think about any issues that these deliverables pose and how you will discuss them. Finally, it is much better if team members present each deliverable as this includes them in the meeting. If possible, give each person a deliverable to present and to lead the discussion about it. This person can also present that deliverable at the review meetings as well. In this way, you create team ownership for them.

Running the meeting

Duration	Topic	Description
15-30 min	Orientation	Go through the purpose of the meeting: To set up this year's work and ensure everyone is clear about it and committed to it.
		Go through agenda: Overview of the year, going through each deliverable and what it means for us, wrap & close. (put up a copy of this on a flipchart)
		Also, allow everyone to speak before you start the formatted part of the meeting. Ask the team, "What do you think is important this year?" Go round every person and just listen to what they say. This helps to get everyone into the meeting and you will get some useful thoughts prior to working on the deliverables.

Duration	Topic	Description
30 min	Overview of deliverables	Show all the deliverables for the year including objectives for improvements so they can see everything that needs to take up their time in the next twelve months.
		Go through what you feel about them (include concerns you may have and things you are motivated about) and why they are important to achieve from a customer, business and team viewpoint. (10min maximum)
		Then ask the team what they feel about them. Allow everyone to say something. (20min)
20 min	Deliverable 1	Talk through the deliverable in more detail, highlighting potential issues or important aspects. Clearly show what the required outcome is.
		Ask the team:
		What questions do you have about it?
		What concerns do you have?
		What does this mean to us as a team?
		What is your role in this?
20 min each	Deliverable 2, 3, 4, etc…	Repeat as for Deliverable 1
		Repeat for each deliverable
30 min	Actions	Looking at all the Deliverables and taking into account the discussions about each one, what actions need to be taken, if any, beyond the normal business as usual?
		Ask the team and record them onto a flipchart. Until there are no more ideas.
		Then go through each one and either cross it off, note it for later or create a full action plan for it (What, Who, by When).
10-15 min	Wrap up	To close the meeting ask:
		"Briefly, what are your thoughts now about the year ahead?"
		Ensure everyone speaks and just listen to their comment.

After the meeting

Ensure that actions and outputs from the meeting are progressed and followed up: Use team meetings or improvement meetings for this.

Meeting 2: Reviewing the team deliverables (Mid-year)

Purpose

To keep the focus on the deliverables and the collective team effort required in achieving them. It also helps to address issues early and maintain a sense of pride and ownership for the work. Finally, it allows time for people to reflect and learn which raises performance over the longer term.

Preparation

Firstly, get customer feedback by getting everyone involved in interviewing customers for their feedback. These may be internal or external customers depending who your team does work for. Agree on a sensible number of customers to speak to and keep the questions simple. Three questions such as, "What are we doing well?", "What could we do differently or less of?" and "What would you like us to start doing?" will give you plenty of valuable information to work with. Collate all the feedback into a sensible format before the meeting and print off enough copies for everyone to read.

Second, prepare the review template below for each objective on separate flipchart sheets. Allocate the preparation of these sheets amongst the team and get them to complete sections 1, 2 and 4.

1. Deliverable: Completion date:	3. What has happened: What has worked well? What challenges have we overcome? What has hindered/ stopped us? What have we learned so far?
2. How far have we got so far: Date:	4. Specific customer feedback:

5. What are the implications for the full deliverable?
  A – continue as is
  B – change in effort required
  C – pull date forwards/ push date back
  D – change/ cancel deliverable	

6. Actions: What Who By when	

Running the meeting

The purpose of this meeting is for the team to do a full review of its progress so far and what needs to happen to deliver everything by the given dates. If everyone is involved in the discussions, then it re-energises people's commitment and motivation.

If you balance the review as shown below then the team are less likely to become defensive. If they do become defensive, then think about how you are engaging with them: Are you listening enough or being defensive yourself?

Duration	Topic	Description
5min	Orientation	Go through the purpose of the meeting: Track progress, review customer feedback, learn and take actions to ensure all the team deliverables are met. Go through agenda: Review deliverables, look at customer feedback, reflect on our learning and agree any actions required.
10-20min each	Review of Deliverables & Actions	Get the person who prepared the flipchart to lead the review of that deliverable: As a group, complete section 3 of the review sheet • either get people to write their thoughts onto sticky notes and put them up • or one person writes everyone's thoughts onto the flipchart. Next agree on 'What the implications are for the full deliverable' allocating it A, B, C or D. (Section 5) Finally agree on the required actions, if any (section 6). Review all the other deliverables in the same way.
15min	Overall customer feedback	Review any other customer feedback. Ask the team what they think about the feedback and allow or encourage everyone to speak.
20-30min	Overall learning	In groups of 2, 3 or 4 depending on the team size, ask people to discuss their learning from the year so far, using the questions below. (15min) Ask the groups to write their thoughts onto a flipchart: • What are we doing well? • How are we hindering ourselves? • What do we need to start doing? Then get each group to share their flipchart. (15min)
10-15min	Other actions	Finally, reflecting on everything, agree any other actions that need to be taken. Write them up on a flipchart (What, Who & By when).
10-15min	Wrap up	Review the outcome and actions for each Deliverable. Ask people what they thought about the meeting and allow or encourage everyone to say something.

After the meeting

Remember to feedback to the customers on what you did, or did not do, with their feedback. Also type up and issue out the agreed actions. Photograph, copy or store the

Review sheets for each Deliverable as they will be useful at the next review or End of Year meeting.

Meeting 3: 'What did we deliver this year?' review (End of year)

Purpose

There are three purposes for this meeting. Firstly, the team can see what it actually delivered that year. Second, you can celebrate your team's successes and thirdly, it is a chance to reflect, learn and improve. Therefore, it is also useful preparation for the yearly appraisal sessions and for the next year's work plan.

Think about how you are going to handle the meeting given the end of year result: If they have done well, are you going to have 'cakes' or a team dinner to celebrate? If they have struggled against adverse conditions, how will you make them feel good about what they were able to achieve? If they have not done well, how are you going to get a serious message across without demoralising them further?

Preparation

On a flipchart write up each deliverable the team had to complete that year and beside each one write up what was actually achieved. Also, get final feedback from a selection of customers using the team to gather the answers to the three questions: What did you like about what we did for you this year? What do you want us to start doing more of? What do they want you to start doing or do more of next year? Get all the answers collated ready for the meeting.

Running the meeting

Duration	Topic	Description
15-30min	Orientation 5min	Go through the purpose of the meeting: Celebrate, review what we actually did and learn from it.
	10-25min	Go through agenda: Review actual deliverables; celebrate key achievements; discuss major challenges; reflect on what we have learned this year; review customer feedback and decide what to take forward into next year or do differently.
		Also, allow everyone to speak before you start the formatted part of the meeting. Ask the team, "How do you think this year has gone?" Go round every person and just listen to what they say. This helps to get everyone into the meeting. It also helps you understand how people feel which will affect how the meeting goes.

Duration	Topic	Description
20min	What did we actually deliver?	Put up the flipchart of what the team had to do that year versus what they actually did. Ask them, what they think about it and have a group discussion on how they feel the year went.
15min	Celebrate Key Achievements	Get the group to tell you what they think their key achievements were and put them up on the flipchart. Once you have them all, stick the sheets onto the wall so they can be seen throughout the meeting. Then ask the team, how they feel about achieving them. Ensure that you congratulate them on their achievements.
15min	Discuss Major Challenges	Ask the team what their major challenges have been and put them up on a flipchart. Once you have them all, stick the sheets onto the wall so they can be seen throughout the meeting. Then ask the team, what they would do differently to avoid them happening again next year, if possible.
30min	Review customer feedback.	Break the team into groups of 2, 3 or 4. Give each person a copy of the collated customer feedback. Ask them to discuss what they think about the feedback and possible actions arising from it. Get each group to write proposed actions onto a flipchart sheet. (15min) After 15min, get each group to share its thoughts and proposed actions.
30min	What have we learned this year?	In the same groups, ask each group to discuss what they have learned from this year. Ask them to decide on their collective top 3 learning points and to write them on a flipchart. (15min) After 15min, get each group to share its top 3 learning points. Finally, discuss with the team overall how well they think they did so that you can use this as part of their formal yearly appraisal. (10min)
45min	Next Year	In different groups of 4, get them to reflect on everything covered so far. From this discussion, get each group to propose its top 3 actions and write them onto a flipchart. (15min) After 15min, get each group to share its top 3 actions. Put them all up on the wall. Then agree the first 3 actions that the team will do from all those proposed. Type the others up and review them at subsequent team meetings.
10-15min	Wrap up	To close the meeting, ask each person to say one thing that they are 'taking away' from the meeting: Something that was an insight, thought provoking or that they enjoyed. Ensure everyone speaks and just listen to their comment. Collect in all the information you need to keep. Ensure that actions are followed up at subsequent meetings.

After the meeting

Remember to feedback to the customers on what you did, or did not do, with their feedback.

Approach 2: Teams with lots of activities the team needs to do although the team members do not necessarily have to work together but would benefit from doing so.

Meeting 1: Creating a team workload (Start of year)
Purpose

To create a collective workload priority for all the team's work rather than having each person with their own priorities. This changes how people will help each other and allows you to complete a team appraisal, both of which encourage collaboration and flexibility. This method is harder to do with more than eight people, as the meeting dynamics are more complicated. Getting an external (to the team) facilitator would be a good idea if you have more than eight people so you can contribute and they can manage the meeting process separately.

This session is enhanced if the team have discussed and formulated their work purpose; the meaningful work they do which they are proud of. This allows you to evaluate each activity against the purpose and to stop doing work that does not come under the team's remit. It is good to do this once a year as extra work can accidentally be picked-up during the year. If the team has not created a meaningful work purpose, then use the scope of work that your team was given.

Preparation

Before the meeting, get everyone to write all their activities onto sticky notes. Everything they are working on or have to work on this year: One activity per sticky note. You will need at least nine sheets of flipchart-sized paper, some glue and some masking tape as well as an A3 size copy of the team's work purpose or remit.

In this approach, you are going to prioritise everyone's work collectively on a 3 by 3 grid. One axis will be Red, Orange, Green.

Where:

Red = needs a lot of attention due to being out of control, high risk, high profile etc.

Orange = needs some attention due to becoming more out of control or was red and is now becoming more in control but still needs attention.

Green = in control, low profile, easy to do, ticking-over, 'may not do' or 'nice to have'.

	X	Y	Z
Red			
Orange			
Green			

Now you need to decide what would be the best three categories for the other axis: X, Y & Z. How would you split your team's work purpose? For my Operations Learning & Development team, we split it as: Corporate & Director needs; Our internal Customer needs, and Our team needs.

	Corporate & Director needs	Our internal Customer needs	Our team needs
Red			
Orange			
Green			

Corporate & Director' were things we needed to do for their requirements. The majority of our work came from our internal customer's requirements. 'Our Team needs' were things that we felt needed doing to enable us to do the other work, such as improving our training database and exploring e-learning. Notice that we split the work from a customer perspective not by 'who did what in our team'. In essence, it was 'high profile work', 'customer' work, and 'internal to us' work. It might be that you have:

	Regulatory	Internal Customer	Our team needs
Red			
Orange			
Green			

	Steady-state customer work	Change Projects	Large Projects
Red			
Orange			
Green			

For overall team priority, I chose to prioritise the activities in this way.

	X	Y	Z
Red	1	2	3
Orange	2	3	4
Green	3	4	5

This can be used to make decisions about the team's workload and need to be flexible when problems occur. Also, it often this means the priority 5 activities do not get completed or must take up exceedingly little time.

Not all your people need to have something in every category (box) as this is about workload shifting. For example, if there is a problem with a Red activity some people will need to drop Green activities in order to pick up a larger part of their Orange activities so that the person with the Red issue can focus more on that and do less Orange activities. If you need to create time to work on a Red or Orange issue, that time needs to ripple through the team's priorities and a green activity or two needs to be dropped or paused. Sometimes an Orange activity may need to be halted to create more time for a Red activity. Once you have the activities categorised it will be easy to see how to shift the workload around if required. Also it helps the team understand their collective priorities and progress.

For example:

Sam is doing Green Task A and working with Mary to do Orange task B. Mary also has Red Task C and Orange task D.

	Regulatory	Internal Customer	Our team needs
Red	C - Mary		
Orange	B – Mary & Sam	D - Mary	
Green			A - Sam

If Mary has a problem with Red Task C and needs to give it more attention. She could stop doing Orange task D but Sam could stop Green Task A and take on all of Orange task B. This allows Mary to spend more time on Red Task C and still work on the other Orange activity D.

	Regulatory	Internal Customer	Our team needs
Red	C - Mary		
Orange	B – Sam	D - Mary	
Green			

In this way, the team's important work is completed. In many cases, what would happen would be that Sam continued with Green Task A and Orange task B but Mary stopped Orange task D to spend more time on her Red Task C issue. In that scenario, the Green task is completed and a higher priority Orange task is not.

Running the meeting

Duration	Topic	Description
20 min	Orientation	Go through the purpose of the meeting: To set up this year's work and ensure everyone is clear about it and committed to it.
		Go through agenda: Look at all our activities in the context of our team's work purpose; prioritise the activities against that remit; understand what it means for each of us; wrap & close.
		Also, allow everyone to speak before you start the formatted part of the meeting. Ask the team, "What do you think is important this year?" Go round every person and just listen to what they say. This helps to get everyone into the meeting and you will get some useful thoughts prior to working on the deliverables.
5 min	Setting up the information	Get out all the activities so everyone can see them all - either stick them on the wall or lay them out on a table.
		Get everyone to help, stick nine pieces of flipchart paper onto the wall in a 3x3 grid. Label the column headings with what you decided X, Y & Z were for your team and label each row as Red, Orange & Green
				X	Y	Z
			Red			
			Orange			
			Green			
		Put up the definitions of Red, Orange & Green and your Team's Purpose/ Remit
		Then number the flipcharts in this way:
				X	Y	Z
			Red	1	2	3
			Orange	2	3	4
			Green	3	4	5
		From the team's perspective, this is the order of priority that each box has. Therefore, Red X (1) activities are top priority. Also tell the team that Green Z (5) activities either need no time at all or realistically are not going to get done. This may also be true for some of the activities in boxes labelled 4.

Duration	Topic	Description
60 - 120 mins (or as long as it takes)	Placing the team's activities onto the grid	Start with the first sticky-note (activity) Decide if this activity should be done at all – does this activity fall under our work purpose/ remit or is it helping us to deliver what our team's purpose/ remit is? If no, put it to one side. If yes, then agree as a team which column, X, Y or Z, it should go in. Then agree whether it is a Red, Orange or Green activity. Repeat this for each of the sticky-notes (activities). Take a break from time to time, as it is quite intense work. Definitely have a break after 2 hours. If an activity causes a long discussion and a place for it cannot be agreed, then put it back and go on to another one. Often when that activity is discussed for a second time the conversation is easier to resolve or the issue has gone away. If most work is in the Red row then you need to be more realistic about splitting the work into Red, Orange & Green categories otherwise you will not be able to get people to do the workload rebalancing if that needs to happen.
30 - 60 mins (or as long as it takes)	Who does what?	Now go through each sticky note (activity) and write on it who is completing that activity. It may be more than one person. Once you have done that, get everyone to stand back and check that no one person is overloaded or has too many priority 1 or 2 activities. People do not need to have an equal number of activities but they do need a workload that is appropriate for their level of seniority
5 min	Checking the 'not doing' activities	Finally, have a look at the sticky notes (activities) that you put to one side and check that that is still appropriate. Resist the temptation to add them back just because they have been discarded.
10 min	Wrap up	To close the meeting ask: "Briefly, what are your thoughts now about the year ahead?" Ensure everyone speaks and just listen to their comment.

After the meeting

Glue the sticky-notes on properly and get the grid typed up so everyone has access to it. Store the flipcharts as you will need them for the quarterly and end-of-year reviews unless you can print off each typed up box, A2 size.

Meeting 2: Reviewing the team deliverables (Mid-year)

Purpose

This meeting is to keep the focus on the deliverables and the collective team effort required in delivering them. It also helps to address issues early and maintain a sense of pride and ownership for the work. Finally, it allows time for people to reflect and learn which raises performance over the longer term.

Preparation

Firstly, get some customer feedback: Get everyone involved in interviewing customers to get their feedback. Agree on a sensible number of customers to speak to and keep the questions simple. Three questions such as, "What are we doing well?", "What could we do differently or less of?" and "What would you like us to start doing?" will give you plenty of information to work with. Collate all the feedback into a sensible format before the meeting, and print enough copies for everyone in the meeting.

Second, get everyone to prepare to talk about their activities:

- What percentage of the work is complete?
- What challenges has the work had?
- What are the implications of that?

For example, an activity could be 50% complete with few problems and be on track. Another activity could be 75% complete, as it has had a major problem and is behind schedule. For joint activities, people will need to agree on the answers together.

Running the meeting

The purpose of this meeting is for the team to complete a full review of its progress so far and what needs to happen to deliver what is required by the given dates. If everyone is involved in the discussions, then it will re-energise people's commitment and motivation.

If you balance the review as shown below then the team are less likely to become defensive. If they do become defensive, then think about how you are engaging with them: Are you listening enough or being defensive yourself?

Duration	Topic	Description
5min	Orientation	Get the original flipcharts, or have a large print out of the typed up version, put up on the wall: Ideally A2 printouts of each box.
		Go through the purpose of the meeting: Track progress, review customer feedback, learn and take actions to ensure all the team deliverables are met.
		Go through agenda: Review deliverables, look at customer feedback, reflect on our learning and agree any actions required. (put up on a flipchart or the wall)
15 mins per box (135 mins)	Review of Activities	Take the Priority 1 box (Red X) and review each of the activities in it. Tell people to quickly cover the ones that are ok and on track so that you can discuss the ones that are behind or have a problem properly.
		Once you have reviewed the Red X box (1), now review the Orange X box (2) activities followed by: Red Y (2) box, Green X (3), Orange Y (3), Red Z (3), Green Y (4), Orange Z (4) and finally Green Z (5).
		Take a break after two hours.
		If any actions are agreed, then quickly record these onto a flipchart. Later in the meeting, once everything has been reviewed, you can decide which actions need to be taken as by then everyone understands the total work picture for the team.
30 min	Customer feedback	Break the team into groups of 3 or 4.
		Give each person a copy of the collated customer feedback. Ask them to discuss what they think about the feedback and propose any required actions arising from it. Get each group to write those actions onto a flipchart sheet. (20min)
		After 20min, get each group to share its thoughts and proposed actions.
20-30min	Overall learning	In the same groups, ask people to discuss their learning from their experience so far this year, using the questions below. (15min) Ask the groups to write their collective answers onto a flipchart:
		• What are we doing well?
		• How are we hindering ourselves?
		• What do we need to start doing?
		After 15 minutes, get each group to share their thoughts using their flipchart. (15min)
10-15min	Actions	Finally, reflecting on everything:
		Decide if any work activities need to move into a different box: red to orange, orange to green, green to orange or orange to red
		Look at the actions listed from the Review of Activities, the Customer feedback discussion and the Overall learning questions: Agree what actions to take. Write then up on a flipchart agreeing: What, Who & By when
10-15min	Wrap up	Ask people what they thought about the meeting and the rest of the year ahead. Allow or encourage everyone to say something.

After the meeting

Remember to tell the customers what you did, or did not do, with their feedback. Also type up and issue out the agreed actions. Photograph, copy or store the nine sheets as they will be useful at the End of Year review meeting.

Meeting 3: 'What did we deliver this year?' review (End of year)
Purpose

There are three purposes for this meeting. Firstly, the team can see what it actually delivered that year. Second, you can celebrate your team's successes and thirdly, it is a chance to reflect, learn and improve. This is useful preparation for the yearly appraisal sessions and for next year's work plan.

Think about how you are going to handle the meeting given the end of year result: If they have done well, how are you going to celebrate? If they have struggled against adverse conditions, how will you make them feel good about what they were able to achieve? If they have not done well, how are you going to get a serious message across without demoralising them further?

Preparation

Firstly, get some customer feedback: Get everyone involved in interviewing customers to get their feedback. Agree on a sensible number of customers to speak to and keep the questions simple. Three questions such as, "What did we do well this year?", "What could we have done differently or less of this year?" and "What would you like us to start doing next year?" will give you plenty of information to work with. Collate all the feedback into a sensible format before the meeting and print off enough copies for everyone in the meeting.

Second, get everyone to prepare to talk about their activities: What percentage of the work was completed, what challenges has the work had and what are the implications of that? For example, an activity could be 60% complete but had major problems so getting 60% completed was excellent. Another activity could be 85% complete, as it had a problem but it could have been completed if the team had spoken about the issue earlier. For joint activities, people will need to agree on the answers together.

Running the meeting

Duration	Topic	Description
15-30min	Orientation	Go through the purpose of the meeting: Celebrate, review what we actually did and learn from it. Go through agenda: Review actual deliverables; celebrate key achievements, discuss major challenges, review customer feedback, reflect on what we have learned this year and decide what to take forward into next year or do differently. (put on a flipchart on the wall). Also, allow everyone to speak before you start the formatted part of the meeting. Ask the team, "How do you think this year has gone?" Go round every person and just listen to what they say. This helps to get everyone into the meeting. It also helps you understand how people feel which will affect how the meeting goes.
20min	What did we actually deliver?	Get the original flipcharts put up or have a large print out of the typed up version and put up on the wall. Preferably A2 print-outs of each box. Get everyone to write on the sticky-note or next to the activity, what percentage of the work was delivered. (Ideally, everything is 100% or close to that.) For the ones that are less than 95% get the team to share with each other what challenges prevented it from being 100% Ask them, what they think about the team's overall result. Have a group discussion on how they feel the year went. How would they rate it?
15min	Celebrate Key Achievements	Get the group to tell you what they think their key achievements were and write them onto the flipchart. Once you have them all, stick the sheets onto the wall so they can be seen. Then ask the team, how they feel about achieving them. Ensure that you congratulate them on their achievements.
15min	Discuss Major Challenges	Ask the team what their major challenges were and write them onto a flipchart. Once you have them all, stick the sheets onto the wall so they can be seen. Then ask the team, • what they would do differently to avoid them happening again next year, if possible • what they learned from tackling the challenges
30min	Review customer feedback.	Break the team into groups of 2, 3 or 4. Give each person a copy of the collated customer feedback. Ask them to discuss what they think about the feedback and propose any actions required. Get each group to write them on a flipchart. (15min) After 15min, get each group to share its thoughts and proposed actions.

Duration	Topic	Description
40min	What have we learned this year?	Keep in the same groups. Ask each group to discuss what they have learned from this year. Also, ask each group to decide on its collective top 3 learning points and to write them onto a flipchart. (15min)
		After 15min, get each group to share its top 3 learning points.
		Finally, discuss with the team how well they think they did overall so that you can use this as part of their formal yearly appraisal. (10min)
45min	Next Year	In different groups of 3 or 4, get them to reflect on everything covered so far. From this discussion, get each group to propose its top 3 actions and write them onto a flipchart. (15min)
		After 15min, get each group to share its top 3 actions.
		Put them all up on the wall. Then agree the first 3 actions that the team will do from all those proposed. Type the others up and review them at subsequent team meetings.
	Wrap up	To close the meeting, ask each person to say one thing that they are 'taking away' from the meeting: Something that was an insight, thought provoking or that they enjoyed. Ensure everyone speaks and just listen to their comment.
		Collect in all the information you need to keep. Ensure that actions are followed-up at subsequent meetings.

After the meeting

Remember to tell the customers on what you did, or did not do, with their feedback.

41. How Well are We Working Together as a Team?

What are the benefits of doing this?

When it comes to projects, we monitor progress and review how things are going. When it comes to developing teams and people we seem to think that it will somehow happen without much reviewing. Conversely, I have found that applying reviews to team development makes a difference. It allows you, and importantly the team themselves, to have a systematic way of improving how you work together. The benefit is a simple and ongoing way of teams developing themselves within their daily work so that their business outcomes improve as well.

Possible pitfalls and concerns to consider

- This is not meant to be an onerous or formal review reporting back to anyone. It is meant to be a simple and yet effective way for the team to think about how they are working together and what they might choose to do differently after that conversation. It helps to enable a healthy and productive conversation that ultimately improves team morale.

- Answering the questions beforehand: I have found that getting people to come to the meeting with their rating makes them more nervous and makes it feel more arduous than it needs to be. I prefer to make it simple and of minimal effort so I just get people to do it there and then. As many questionnaires say, 'don't spend too long thinking about your answers; go with what first comes to mind'. These are often more intuitive and not over analysed.

- These are superficial meetings: Initially people may feel concerned about being open and may prefer to not say things. That's alright, I have found that over time people will engage more and this is a sign that your team has progressed and is more mature. As the manager it is useful to think about what needs to happen over time for people to feel safe enough to fully participate in these meetings so that they become as valuable as possible.

- Making people feel that their input is wrong: If one person has a different view to most other people then that person can quickly be made to feel that they are somehow in the wrong. As the manager it is good to have a meeting where people feel safe to be open and share how they feel about something. It does not mean that you agree with them. So help maintain a 'sharing of thoughts' atmosphere rather than a 'who is right or wrong' atmosphere.

- Too many actions: In many meetings it seems that creating lots of actions makes people feel good. In these meetings the focus is on long-term change so it is better to focus on actions that get completed and make a difference. Therefore, fewer actions that are progressed and monitored is good. You can always add a new one when one is completed.

Other relevant chapters
- Chapter 1   Understanding Their Perspective
- Chapters 14-16 Listening Productively
- Chapter 35   Basic Meeting Outcomes, Structure and Tips

How

Covers four possible ways of reviewing how well your team is working together, using

> Stop, Start & Continue
>
> "How are we operating as a team?" questions
>
> Meaningful work and pride statements
>
> Reputation and customer satisfaction feedback

Stop, Start & Continue

This is a simple method where the team decides what it will continue doing, stop doing and start doing. These can be things for the team members or collective things the team can do. For example, team members can continue being on time for meetings, the team could start doing a weekly operations meeting or the team could stop creating a weekly blog.

This session takes about 45-60mins depending on the team size.

1. Briefly discuss the team's purpose, how it fits into the business objectives and who its customers are. (10mins)
    a. Display or hand out feedback on the team's performance
    b. If possible, have some customer feedback for the team to read

2. Split the team into trios (pairs are a bit too small)
3. Get the trio to write down (on sticky notes) what they think the team should do to improve itself by: -
   a. Continue doing
   b. Stop doing
   c. Start doing

   Ask people to be realistic about the suggestions and to think of ideas that they really believe should be done. This will help to limit the quantity generated.
4. Get each trio to share their 'Continue to do' by sticking them on the wall or laying them on the table. Put duplicate ideas together and group similar ideas. Get people to clarify any ideas that are not clear.
5. Get each trio to share their 'Stop doing' by sticking them on the wall or laying them on the table. Put duplicate ideas together and group similar ideas. Get people to clarify any ideas that are not clear.
6. Get each trio to share their 'Start doing' by sticking them on the wall or laying them on the table. Put duplicate ideas together and group similar ideas. Get people to clarify any ideas that are not clear.
7. Count the number of clusters of ideas and divide by three, rounding down to the nearest whole number. This becomes the number of votes each person has. For example, 20 ideas mean each person has 6 votes.
8. Now get each person to vote on the ideas they feel most committed to doing. Tell people that you will work on the top two or three that get the most votes. Then allow people to vote by putting a clear mark by each group of ideas. (Only one vote per cluster of ideas.)
9. Once everyone has voted, count the marks and write down the number of votes that each cluster has. In this way everyone can see which are the top two or three ideas that people voted for.
10. Write up the two or three ideas selected.

"How are we operating as a team?" questions

The main objective here is to get the team to focus on developing itself so the conversation is the important aspect.

Put up the following questions, or some of your own, onto a flipchart. You could also use questions from a different team or leadership model you have come across.

1. We are clear about our own and each others' objectives?
2. We listen well to each other?
3. We are good at planning our work?
4. We are happy to discuss new ideas and changes we need to make?
5. We are happy to be open and honest?
6. We are good at celebrating small wins/ our achievements?
7. We are good at learning and improving?
8. We give each other useful feedback?
9. We discuss problems and work on solving them effectively?
10. We handle conflict well?

Get each person in the team to rate their answer from 0 to 10 on where they think the team is. (0 = rarely true, 10= true on a daily basis.) Then everyone puts up their scores for each question.

The team's collective ratings for each question (everyone has marked on where their rating is for each question) might have one of four patterns:

Pattern 1: 0 ---------------------- 5 --------------xxxx-----xx-------- 10

Here the whole team agrees that they are doing well for this question. Ask what made them score it highly? This will help consolidate good practice so they do more of it.

Pattern 2: 0 -----xxx-----x--x------x------ 5 ------------------------- 10

Here all the team agree things are not working very well for this question. Ask them 'what is working?' as they have not scored it as 0. Then ask them what needs to be different to score it higher.

Pattern 3: 0 ----x-----x--------x------ 5 ---x-------x--------x-------- 10

Here there is a real difference in perception on this question. This could mean people have different views and once aired they are more in agreement. First start with the people that scored it 7 or above and ask them what they think is working – why did they score it highly? Then ask the other people, firstly what is working for them as they did not score it as zero? Then ask them what needs to be different for them to score it higher?

Pattern 4:   0 ----x---x--------------- 5 --------------x-x--x-x------------- 10

Here there is a split on perception for this question, with just a few people feeling it is not working. It will be easy for the larger group to make those 2 people feel 'wrong' and yet they probably have valuable insights. So firstly start with the higher group and ask them what they think is working – why did they score it higher? Then ask the lower group, what is working for them as they did not score it as zero? Then ask them what needs to be different for them to score it higher?

As you discuss each question, write down the possible actions next to the rating scale or on a separate flipchart sheet. Once all the questions have been reviewed ask the team to vote on their top three actions: Which actions do they want to do to help them improve the scores?

Allow each person to put up their three votes. Count the votes for each action and write it next to that action. Clarify the top three actions. If there are four clear winners, you may choose to do all four although you may take only two of them. Be careful not to overload the team with lots of actions. It is better to do less and then once an action is completed, add in another one.

Review the actions regularly across the year and redo this exercise once a year.

Meaningful work and pride statements

With this method you take the Team's Meaningful Work and Pride Statement created in Part I of this book. Use the 0 to 10 scoring system in Method 2 above by breaking the statements into their smaller elements and rate each of these.

For example, if this is your Meaningful Work and Pride statement:

- We are passionate about customer service; committed and motivated to deliver first class expertise to our clients and stakeholders
- We are known for being a talented and trusted team who can be relied upon to take ownership of our responsibilities and always get the job done.
- We work efficiently and proactively, through sharing our knowledge and skills within the team, which allows us to integrate with our customer teams to deliver an exceptional customer experience

Then you break it up like this:

1. We are passionate about customer service
2. Committed and motivated to deliver first class expertise to our clients and stakeholders

3. We are known for being a talented and trusted team
4. who can be relied upon to take ownership of our responsibilities
5. and always get the job done.
6. We work efficiently and proactively,
7. through sharing our knowledge and skills within the team,
8. which allows us to integrate with our customer teams
9. to deliver an exceptional customer experience

Then ask people to rate each statement from 0 (this is rarely true) to 10 (this is true on a daily basis)

We are passionate about customer service

0 ------------------------------------ 5 ------------------------------------ 10

We are committed and motivated to deliver first class expertise to our clients and stakeholders

0 ------------------------------------ 5 ------------------------------------ 10

We are known for being a talented and trusted team

0 ------------------------------------ 5 ------------------------------------ 10

We can be relied upon to take ownership of our responsibilities

0 ------------------------------------ 5 ------------------------------------ 10

We always get the job done.

0 ------------------------------------ 5 ------------------------------------ 10

We work efficiently and proactively,

0 ------------------------------------ 5 ------------------------------------ 10

We share our knowledge and skills within the team,

0 ------------------------------------ 5 ------------------------------------ 10

We integrate with our customer teams

0 ------------------------------------ 5 ------------------------------------ 10

We deliver an exceptional customer experience

0 ------------------------------------ 5 ------------------------------------ 10

Follow the structure in Method 2 for reviewing the scores generated and creating actions.

Reputation and customer satisfaction

In this method, you get feedback from your internal or external customers as to how the team is doing and perceived. Firstly, in a team meeting decide what three or four questions to ask your customers. This is enough, as you will get a lot of information from just three or four questions. Then agree who will talk to which customer. Allocate four customers per person maximum and get people to talk to customers they would not usually interact with. When I did this with my team we inverted who we spoke to so I spoke to four production workers and people in my team spoke to the directors, departmental heads and managers.

The questions we used were very simple:

o What do you think we are doing well?

o What is our reputation – what are we known for?

o What would you like us to do that we are not doing?

o Any other comment?

Everyone types up their answers for each person interviewed. Do not delete duplicate answers as the number of similar answers tells you how strongly people felt about something. For example, when nine people say you are doing well and one person says you are doing badly. Then deleting the duplicate answers would give equal weighting to doing well and doing badly whereas this does not represent that ninety percent of your customers feel you are doing well.

Next have a meeting to review the information. Put all the answers to question 1 together, to question 2 together and so on. Then take each question one by one and review the feedback.

1. Look at the feedback for question 1: What do you think we are doing well?

Ask the team: -

a. How do you feel about the feedback?

b. What does it mean for us going forwards?

c. What actions need to be taken, if any?

2. **Look at the feedback for question 2: What is our reputation – what are we known for?**

   Ask the team: -

   a. How do you feel about the feedback?

   b. What does it mean for us going forwards?

   c. What actions need to be taken, if any?

3. **Look at the feedback for question 3: What would you like us to do that we are not doing?**

   Ask the team: -

   a. How do you feel about the feedback?

   Look at the suggestions and get the team to sort them into two groups: 'Not going to do' and 'might do'. Then ask: -

   b. What actions need to be taken, if any?

4. **Look at the feedback for question 4: Any other comment?**

   Ask the team: -

   a. What are your thoughts on these comments?

   b. What does it mean for us going forwards?

   c. What actions need to be taken, if any?

5. **Action Plan**

   Now look at all the possible actions the team has generated. Collectively decide which actions are definitely going to be worked on and which are not. Then create an action plan for those actions being taken forwards. Ensure they get reviewed at monthly team meetings or specific improvement review meetings.

42. Implementing a Team Appraisal Approach

What are the benefits of doing this?

In a busy world people need a method that makes them work together: Team objectives along with a team appraisal approach achieve this. Many appraisal processes can unintentionally reward people for individual contribution without consideration for how that affected the team's overall work. It can encourage people to focus on delivering their results at the expenses of the team's results through lack of flexibility and cooperation. This undermines a team environment especially if the members are dependent on each other for their collective output. Therefore, implementing a team appraisal approach will enhance your team's performance. The appraisal is based on the team's collective performance and the contribution of the individual to that so that a balance between the two is achieved. This focuses team members on how they work together and makes them feel more accountable for the actions of their colleagues. In this way, the team starts to manage its own performance rather than you having to manage it all.

Possible pitfalls and concerns to consider

- Our Appraisal system is different and people are paid individually: That was true when I implemented team appraisals so I designed this more as an approach building up to completing the individual form. It is mainly the focus of the discussion about the person's contribution that changes. The team appraisal approach is designed to help structure the appraisal conversation between the manager and team members towards a collective team effort and how everyone is contributing to that. The actual information you need to submit remains the similar although should be of higher quality by having undertaken a team appraisal. Although about an individual, ultimately, you want to focus on a team effort, so the appraisal conversation is tempered by how well the team did overall and how much that person contributed to that success.

- The team will not like the process: When I introduced the team appraisal approach into our factories, the people really liked it as it helped them to complete their appraisal form as they generated a lot of usable information from the end of year team results review and the feedback from their peers. They particularly liked the feedback from their peers, which I had not expected. The team performance review meeting gave them the structure for part of their forms. The rest was specific to their contribution although they also found that easier to complete when positioned against the team results.

- Poor performers: In our team appraisal approach, we exempted poor performers and those in any disciplinary process from benefiting from a team result that was little to do with them. It was felt that true poor performers should not benefit from being carried by their teammates' efforts to deliver a quality result. Although they participated in the full process and completed the appraisal paperwork, when it came to the individual rating, the team element was discounted or not taken into account.

Other relevant chapters
- Chapter 12   Questions to Help Overcome Unhelpful Perceptions and Thinking
- Chapter 15   Listening With Your Eyes, Ears and Intuition
- Chapter 40   Team Deliverables for the Year

How

Covers four steps within a team appraisal
1. Team Performance Review Meeting
2. Feedback Interviews
3. Individual Contribution Meeting
4. Organisational Requirements

This is the analogy I use: If the team were a company then the profit to be shared comes from how well the company performed. How you share it out depends on how much each person contributed to the creation of that profit. Although sounding fair, sharing out the profit equally creates unrest with those that have worked harder and complacency with those who worked less.

Therefore, a team Appraisal can be very simple and it helps people complete their yearly appraisal form as well as understand how they have contributed to the team's work. In essence, an individual's appraisal rating is a combination of the team's performance and their contribution to that. For a production team, usually 50% comes from the team's performance and 50% comes from their contribution. In this way, the team-working and individual contribution are equally valued. Hence, if the team performed well and a person contributed a lot, overall they would get a high appraisal rating. If team members contributed less to the team's success, then their rating would be lower.

The basic process is:

1. Team Performance Review Meeting
2. Feedback Interviews
3. Individual Contribution Meeting
4. Organisation's Appraisal Process

1. Team performance review meeting

For this meeting, follow one of the two formats for Meeting 3 in Chapter 40 'Team Deliverables for the Year':

Meeting 3: 'What did we deliver this year?' review   (End of year)

This gives the first part of the individual appraisal rating by agreeing how well the team performed overall that year.

2. Feedback interviews

An independent person interviews each of the team members for their feedback about the other team members. The feedback covers:

- Technical ability/ Role competency
- Contribution to the team deliverables
- Ease to work with
- The questions are:
- What do you think about this person's ability to do their work, their technical ability/ competency?
- How do you feel this person has contributed to the team's deliverables this year?
- What is this person like to work with?

The interviewer writes down all the responses to each question. They ask that person about each of their colleagues using a separate answer sheet for each person. Afterwards they type up the notes and collate the relevant feedback for each person regarding each question. Finally, they tidy-up the information, removing duplication and maintaining anonymity. Give the completed feedback to the line manager ready for the one to one meeting.

I am not in favour of using an online survey as I believe the quality of the feedback is higher from an interactive interview. Partly this is because an interviewer can probe for examples and understanding. Partly on-line surveys are 'faceless' and there is research that indicates that we tend to become more negative because we have fewer consequences when there is no one to hold us accountable. Also, I didn't want this to become an onerous process so I just kept it simple and asked for the personal opinions of their colleagues.

3. Individual contribution meeting

Preparation: Go through the person's feedback and ensure you are comfortable with the conversation you need to have. If you are not, then work with an experienced colleague or your manager until you are comfortable. Ensure you have evidence for your thoughts on their contribution that year.

It would be useful to read the chapters on questions and listening to ensure this is a productive meeting where both of you understands how that year has gone and what they have learned from it.

The meeting: The line manager runs this meeting with each of their people and covers what the individual has done that year. The basic format is:

- Initially ask, 'Overall, how do you feel this year has been?' (This allows you to gauge their expectations against yours so you can adjust the meeting if required.)
- For each deliverable ask,
  - What was the team deliverable?
  - How have you contributed to it? (With evidence)
  - What challenges did you face?
  - What more could you have done?
  - If required, add in your thoughts with your evidence
- Discuss the feedback from the team by
  - Allow them to read the feedback (give the feedback to them in the meeting rather than beforehand in case it is misinterpreted)
  - Ask them what they think about the feedback – what are they pleased about, what are they surprised about.
- Ask, 'What have you learned from this year?'

- Agree the level of overall individual contribution having discussed it thoroughly

This gives the second part of the individual appraisal rating.

After the meeting: Write up your notes from the conversation.

4. Organisational requirements

Combine the Team rating and the Individual Contribution rating to give the overall Individual Appraisal rating. Use this information to complete any formal Appraisal Process requirements from your organisation.

Developing Individuals

This book is about bringing out the best in people in many different ways. In these chapters, I focus on individual considerations as well as how to handle some of the more challenging aspects of line management. Inductions and Personal Development plans often add little value as they are poorly handled or 'paid lip service' to, so I have covered those comprehensively.

Chapters 43 "Inductions That Build a Good Foundation for Work" looks at how to complete inductions that enable new people to develop a solid business foundation for their role. This will put them in good stead for understanding the context and stakeholders of their work enabling them to work soundly.

Chapter 44 "Personal Development Plans That Add Value" will take you through, step by step, on how to create and complete development plans that enable the individual to become more competent at their work on an on-going basis.

Chapter 45 "Having Difficult Conversations" looks at how to have difficult conversations around unsuitable behaviour, poor performance and unexpected situations such as redundancy. It will help you to thoroughly prepare for the meetings, give you a proposed structure for the actual meeting and help you reflect upon it afterwards.

Chapter 46 "Taking Individuals Through Change" discusses three key change models, that will help you understand how people emotionally go through change and your role in helping them navigate that smoothly and quickly. It looks at the steps to get personal change in behaviour to happen such as changing to a new process or modern technology. It also looks at a 3-phase model of change from a psychological point of view with a fundamental aspect being that of 'letting go of what you are losing'. In any change, these three models will give you insights into how your people are responding and some thoughts on what you can do as a manager to help them navigate that change successfully.

43. Inductions That Build a Good Foundation for Work

What are the benefits of doing this?

When people join a company or a team it is the time when they can easily ask questions that may appear naive and yet can be very thought provoking. As managers, we can be quick to get our new people doing their jobs as we have probably already waited a long time to get the person but in many ways, this means that a few more days will not hurt either. It will be time well spent as over the coming months these people will fit into the team quicker and have a good understanding of the context that their work fits into. This often means they make faster and better decisions.

Possible pitfalls and concerns to consider

- I cannot afford the time for them to do it: In many ways, you cannot not afford the time to do it. It is a question of short-term verses long term. Invariably looking back, time spent on even a simple induction would have paid for itself repeatedly; as many problems would not have occurred or would have been resolved quicker if the person had had an induction.
- They waste time: This is a very real concern and can happen if an Induction is not well structured and supported, so ensure yours adds value.
- It is not structured/ prepared: You need to put effort into a good Induction although they can be structured so that once designed the Inductee does it for themselves. I also found that talking with the people the Inductees are going to meet and helping them prepare for the meeting, made a significant difference to the quality of the induction as both parties understood what was expected.

Other relevant chapters

- Chapter 6   What is the Added Value Your Team Delivers?
- Chapter 11   Questions That Invite Others to Contribute
- Chapter 33   Delegating and Holding Others Accountable

How

Covers three aspects and an example

Their role

Their team

The Company

Induction Plan Example

Their role

This is usually the main area that is already taken care of through their job description. Here are some things to think about during the Induction:

- Are all the basics in place for them: desk, tools, computer, information they need, lunch and refreshment arrangements.
- Have you discussed their job description with them?
  - Do they know what success looks like for them in 3 months, 6 months and 12 months? What do you expect from them?
- Have they been told about all the meetings they need to attend and the purpose of each meeting?
- What does their Personal Development Plan look like for the next 12 months?

The team

- Introduce them to everyone in the team. People will get to know everyone eventually but they will feel more at ease and ask for help sooner if everyone is introduced to them within the first few days.
- Take them through team aspects such as:
  - purpose & work objectives
  - what makes the team proud and how their work adds value to the customer/company
  - how the team operates together
  - the way the team reviews the way it works together and the current information on this
  - team meetings and their purpose
  - improvement projects
  - how the team measures its performance

- Get them to spend time with each person, including you, the Team Leader, to help build relationships and find out information such as: -
    - the person's role
    - how the newcomer & team member interface
    - how their work affects each other
    - share career history
    - issues/ concerns the team member has and why they like working in the team
- If it is a functional role and team, then 15mins with each person to get an understanding of their work and how the new person's work may affect them is probably enough. It would also be useful if during that conversation the team member gave the newcomer a short career history as this helps to build better relationships. If the newcomer is joining a project team, then I would expect the newcomer to spend an hour with each person understanding the team member's role and how they might interact with them. In addition, the team member can give the newcomer some thoughts as to the culture and norms of the team.

The company

The purpose of this induction area is twofold. Firstly, so that the newcomer can find out about the company they have joined - what its real drivers and vision are. Secondly to understand the context that their work fits into which will enable them to make more robust decisions.

The Inductee could meet with: -

- Directors/ Departmental Heads: Questions to ask -
    - What does your role encompass?
    - How do you see the company evolving over the next one and five years?
    - What challenges do you feel that the company has in the next year and in the longer term?
    - What would you really like to see happen in the next year and in the longer term?
    - What makes you proud to work for the company?
    - How does my (the newcomer) role affect the company and your department?
    - How can I help you/ the company through my role?

- Managers and/or Counterparts in related Departments. For example, someone in Production may meet with Maintenance, Quality, Planning and Logistics. Someone in Finance might meet with various people in the teams that they do the finances for. Someone in Sales might meet with people from all Customer facing roles such as the delivery team, the aftercare team, the logistics team and the customer invoicing team.

Questions to ask -
  - What does your role encompass?
  - How does my work affect your work?
  - How does your work affect my work?
  - What problems do you have short term and long term?
  - What makes you proud about the work you do?
  - What would you really like to see happen in the next year and in the longer term?
  - How is your area developing/ changing in the next few years?
  - How can I help you through my role?
- Visits to sister factories/ companies: Things to find out -
  - What is your role?
  - How does my work affect your work?
  - How does your work affect my work?
  - What problems do you have short term and long term?
  - What makes you proud about the work you do?
  - How is your area developing/ changing in the next few years?
- Short placements such as in a Factory, in a Call Centre, out in the Field or at a Customer's Site. These might be one-two day placements or a week's duration.

Induction plan example

It is easiest for the Inductee if they get an Induction Pack or Sheet. This pack would lay out the people they needed to meet with, how they would book those meetings if they were not already booked for them, the purpose of each meeting and any questions they might ask to achieve that outcome.

This could be a simple table:

Person, role & contact details	Purpose of meeting (What you need to know)	Suggested questions to ask	Date booked for	Completed
Andy Jones, Head of Service (t:01234 456789)	To understand the Service Department as it is a key customer of yours.	What does your role encompass? How do you see the company evolving over the next 5 years? What challenges do you feel that the company has in the next year and in the longer term? What would you really like to see happen in the next year and in the longer term? What makes you proud to work for the company? How does my (the newcomer) role affect the company and your department? How can I help you/ the company through my role?	25th May	
Teresa Holiday, Service Centre Manager (t:01234 445566)	Experience what the Service centre people do	Two-day placement in Service Centre	3rd – 4th June	
Philip Connaut, Head of HR (t:01234 567899)	Relationship building as you have a lot of people to manage. To understand how HR works with you.	Philip has a structured Induction meeting	6th June	

If you have a regular number of Inductees that tend to meet with the same people, then it would be worth speaking with those people to develop a format for those meetings and agree a standard presentation for it. This means that you get some consistency for all Inductees and it is less time consuming for the other person.

44. Personal Development Plans (PDP) That Add Value

What are the benefits of doing this?

I am intrigued by the fact that at university most students take ownership for their work and what needs to be done. Yet often when these same people come into an organisation they seem to wait for development to 'be done' to them and go on training courses without much understanding of why they are attending it or what they are supposed to do differently when they return. When they get back to work they get on with their jobs with little visible or focussed consolidation of what they have learned. In addition, managers send people on some training courses without defining what need this is addressing or with little attention on the learning being used afterwards. Maybe it is something to do with consequences, or rather the lack of them. What is worse is that most managers and workers know this and still do it. As at least they can say they did as they were told or that they did something.

The Burnham Rosen Group suggest that only 15-33% of people on training courses make a difference back in their role, which is the same as people that had no training and who just make changes throughout the course of their job. In these economic times and with a different attitude towards development, personal development plans (PDP) at work need to, and should, add value. It is a simple case of refocusing the conversation onto the business objective rather than looking at which training course someone wants to attend.

Often PDPs are completed because you are told to do them once a year and then they are put in a drawer and forgotten. At best, they may just be a list of courses so the Training Department knows which courses to book for the year ahead. This is useful but it would be good if PDPs really did add value to the person's work. Unless all your people are achieving their deliverables every year then PDPs are valuable to you as well as them. Little and often, regularly reviewed is a more sustainable approach that over time delivers quite a shift in ability. With this approach, you will reduce the time people spend on training courses and increase the time they spend learning something required and applying it to their work.

Also if you notice I use 'development' rather than 'training' as I feel that there are numerous ways to learn things; lots of them are free and more pertinent to the requirement.

When I was a young shift manager on a production line, some of the best development I had was talking with experienced shift managers about issues.

The other benefit of a PDP like this is that it is much easier to keep the ownership with the person as their end of year appraisal is affected by their development and they will be able to demonstrate that. So overall, you both have a real interest in continuous personal development. In addition, they will become more creative about the way they learn and develop, as there is so much easy access free learning on the internet and within your own company.

Possible pitfalls and concerns to consider

- Our company's development plan has a different format: That is ok. You have a number of options. Maybe once you have read this chapter you can use this approach in completing the format you currently use. Or you can use this format (it only uses blank sheets of paper with columns on) and then take off what you need to complete the official paperwork.

- Showing the full PDP to someone else: When I was getting my people to do these PDPs I wanted them to be honest about the development they needed and what it would take to become competent. I found that knowing that the whole of the PDP was not going to HR meant they were able to do this. I also discussed this with HR so that they understood the situation as well and were happy that they got what they required.

- Focussing on training courses: Trained does not necessarily mean competent. Usually after training, the new skill or knowledge needs to be applied for someone to become competent in it. In addition, it is easy for people to say that none of the courses are useful and that may be true although it does not mean that development is not required. Training courses have their place as one method of development; it is just that they are not the only method.

- Poorly written PDPs: Often development plans are written as "I need to facilitate meetings better therefore I'll go on a facilitation course. I have been on the course so the development is complete and I'll mark it as successfully completed." 90% of PDPs I see are written like this and stand little chance of being valuable. This is not a PDP it is an action list that is not focussed on becoming competent.

- Not having regular PDP reviews: Development Plans need to be reviewed regularly, as with other projects and tasks, as this keeps the momentum going and says that as a line manager you think this development is important. If you have development linked to a business outcome being improved, then it will be important.

- Too much on the PDP: Work on 2-3 Desired Outcomes, adding new ones once one has been achieved. 'Do less better' and it will be more effective. If there is too much, then the person will feel overloaded and is likely to stop doing anything.
- No ownership or need or consequences: If you cannot connect the personal development to some form of business benefit then don't do it. Stop kidding yourself that it will be helpful in some way as it is a waste of valuable time and you have plenty of other development that does have a business need. Business needs can of course be about retention, promotion, etc.

Other relevant chapters
- Chapter 8   Making People Feel Stronger
- Chapter 11   Questions That Invite Others to Contribute
- Chapters 14-16 Listening Productively

How
Covers the steps for creating and reviewing PDPs using a worked example

Creating the PDP
1. Creating a 'List of Possible Development for (year e.g. 2017)'
2. The first item to work on
3. Focussing on the Business benefit and measures
4. Creating the personal development objective(s)
5. Adding in 'evidence statements' for the personal objective
6. Creating an Action Plan to achieve the personal objective
7. The Development Plan

Reviewing the PDP

A good place to start is with the deliverables or tasks for the year rather than what training or development someone might like. Asking, "Looking at what you need to achieve this year, what do you need to do differently?" works well and delivers real improvements in business outcomes.

Therefore, this is a different way of thinking about and doing PDPs. The ones I am about to show you are better kept between you and your people as you really want them to be honest about what they need to be doing differently to achieve their deliverables that year. Your people need to be honest with you so that you can help them develop where they need to. If all of it is shown to HR, then I might shy away from being too honest and that is partly why we get the PDPs we do. If required, you can put high level details onto the official appraisal with any courses that need to be booked; that way everyone is happy.

Initially your people will probably need help in working through this method and after a few times of at creating development plans together they will be able to write them for themselves. This means that your longer-term goal is for your people to come to their initial PDP meeting with a draft PDP.

Creating the PDP

Once someone knows what they have to deliver for the year then they are ready to do their development plan. Book a 1:1 meeting with them to discuss that year's personal development plan. There are seven steps.

1. Creating a 'List of possible development for (year e.g. 2017)'

The first question to ask is:

"Looking at what you have to do this year, what do you personally need to do differently to deliver that?"

Get them to write down all their answers on a piece of paper. It will be a mixture of:

- actions (I need to get the person on long term sick back to work)
- business deliverables (75% of my business case presentations do not get the green light first time which wastes a lot of time)
- personal development, which may be: -
  - knowledge (I need to technically understand what work my team can and can't undertake)
  - skills (I need to be able to handle difficult conversations with my team)
  - judgement (I can ask the correct questions of a customer requiring our services).

All of these are valid so get the person to write them all down. This becomes their 'List of Possible Development for (year)'.

List of Possible Development for (year)
• Item
• Item
• Item

Worked example:

> **Q:** "Looking at what you have to do this year, what do you personally need to do differently to deliver that?"
>
> **List of Possible Development for 2017**
> - I need to get the person on long term sick back to work
> - 75% of my business case presentations do not get the green light first time which wastes a lot of time
> - I need to technically understand what work my team can and can't undertake
> - I need to be able to handle difficult conversations with my team
> - I can ask the correct questions of a customer requiring our services

2. The first item to work on

Taking what they need to deliver that year into account and their List of Possible Development, ask the person:

"Given your deliverables for this year, which item from the list you just created, do you feel would be the most valuable to work on first?"

Let them choose and now they have the first item to work on.

Worked example continued:

> List of Possible Development for 2017
> 1. I need to get the person on long term sick back to work
> 2. 75% of my business case presentations do not get the green light first time which wastes a lot of time
> 3. I need to technically understand what work my team can and can't undertake
> 4. I need to be able to handle difficult conversations with my team
> 5. I can ask the correct questions of a customer requiring our services
>
> **Q:** "Given your deliverables this year which item from the list, you just created, do you feel would be the most valuable to work on first?"
>
> They may say, "I need to get the person on long term sick back to work ".
>
> Now you have the first item to work on.

3. Focussing on the business benefit and measures

Next link the item back to a business benefit or need connected to their deliverables for that year. If it is already stated as a business need then that's ok. If it is not stated as a business benefit, such as "I need to technically understand what work my team can and can't undertake", then ask them,

"If you do this then what will be the benefit to your deliverables this year? (What will this help you to do or do better?)"

Get them to write that down.

Once you have the Business need, check that it is tangible and make sure it is measurable. To get the measures ask them,

"How will you measure that or prove to me that you have made that difference?"

Write down their answers. Now you have the business need/ benefit and measure.

Business Need/Benefit & Measure for development	Person Objective & Measure for development	Action Plan for development
Item 1 1. Measure 2. Measure 3. Measure		

Make sure the measures are robust for example, 'the report will be written by 22nd March and to the same standard as Joe's reports' is much more robust than "the report will be written by the 22nd March". The latter report could be of poor quality. The business need and measures mean that there are consequences to doing or not doing the personal development. This makes a big difference to how things are progressed and reviewed throughout the year as you both have a need for the development to happen.

Worked example continued:

> **Question if you already have the business need:** "For 'getting the person on long term sick back to work', how will you measure that or prove to me that you have made that difference?"
>
> The measures they give could be: -
>
> - Improved team output by 15%
> - Person back full time and back up to productivity by 30th July
>
> **
>
> **Question if it is not given as a business need,** such as 'I need to technically understand what work my team can and can't undertake'. Then ask:
>
> **Q:** "If you do this then what will be the benefit to your deliverables this year? (What will this help you to do or do better?)"
>
> The Business need they give could be:
>
> "I would be able to effectively take on work from customers to agreed timescales."
>
> **Q:** When do you need this to happen by?
>
> They may say: "31st Oct""
>
> Then ask:
>
> **Q:** "How will you measure that or prove to me that you have made that difference?"
>
> The Business measures they give could be:
>
> - Can go to 3 business meetings without needing to take an extra person with me. (Saves 8 hrs per month)
> - Do not have to go back to customer to amend requirements or decline work. (50% at moment)
> - Team can complete work to agreed timescales and quality. (50% incorrect at moment)

4. Creating the personal development objective(s)

Next you are going to develop the personal development objective that the person needs to focus on becoming competent in.

Now looking at the business need & measure, ask:

"What is it that you want to be able to do or do differently so you can achieve this business need?"

You may need to discuss this so that they can think about what that might be. Once they are certain then get them to write it down. Ensure the statement is written in the affirmative, by that I mean rather than writing 'I don't want to feel so nervous when I meet my clients', write it as 'I want to feel calm and confident when I meet my clients'. Get them to write down what they want rather than what they want to avoid or stop doing.

There are two reasons for this: Firstly, I believe you get what you focus on and the first statement has nervous as its theme. Secondly there are many different things that you might want to be instead of 'nervous'. You might want to be calm or confident or assertive or outspoken. These might need quite different action plans so it is useful to be clear about which one you are working on. In the second statement the focus is on 'calm and confident' and it is clear that that is what is being worked on.

Next, get a date for when they want to do this by. Usually within 6 months is good, otherwise it feels too far away and is therefore likely to get put off. This may mean that a larger objective needs to be split into several milestones over shorter time frames.

Worked example continued:

Business need: Improve team output by resolving long term sickness.
- Improved team output by 15%
- Person back full time and back up to productivity

By 31st July

Q: "What is it that you want to be able to do or do differently so you can achieve this business need?"

They may say:

"I need to be able to apply the sick procedure to the current situation and to be assertive when handling difficult situations."

Q: "Which one do you want to work on first?"

They may say: "Being able to apply the sick procedure to current the situation as that comes first".

Q: When do you need this to happen by?"

They may say: "1st Mar"

5. Adding in 'evidence statements' for the personal objective

Now you have a personal development objective and a date. Next, you want the person to give you statements of how it will be different once they have achieved their objective. This helps them to really understand what they want and the aspects that might need to be worked on.

To do this I usually say to them, "so if we met the day after you said you would have achieved this, so on the (date plus one day), then what would you say to me to demonstrate that things were different and you had achieved your objective?"

I list these bullet points down and keep the statements flowing by asking "Anything else?" if they pause. Eventually they say 'no nothing else.'

This list of evidence statements may contain some actions but it is really about showing the difference between the situation now and how it will be once the personal objective has been achieved. So in the example about being calm and confident rather than nervous, once the person is calm and confident with clients, they may describe the new situation as – feeling calm and confident; speaking in my usual voice; looking at the person as I would usually in a conversation; nodding & gesturing appropriately. Rather than an action that might be 'I will read about how to improve eye contact'.

Now you can make the statements as measurable as possible. For some using a 0-10 rating scale works well.

So for 'feeling calm' you can ask:

"How calm would you feel at the moment?" They may say "5/10".

Then ask: "How calm would you like to feel when you have completed this objective?"

They may say "8/10". By putting in those numbers they tend to be clearer about what needs to be done to move them from 5 to 6, then 6 to 7 etc.

Now you have: -

- a business need & measure(s)
- a personal development objective with evidence statements (measures).

Business Need/Benefit & Measure for development	Person Objective & Measure for development	Action Plan for development
Item 1 • Measure • Measure	Objective 1 (date) • Evidence • Evidence • Evidence	

Worked example continued:

Personal Development Objective 1:

"Being able to apply sick procedure to the current situation by 1st Mar".

Q: "If we met the day after you said you would have achieved this, so on the 2nd Mar, then what would you say to me to demonstrate that things were different and you had achieved your objective?"

The evidence statements they give could be:

- State all elements of procedure.
- Be confident to use procedure (2/10 -> 8/10)
- Can tell you which aspects relate to the person I have off sick and why.

Q: "Anything else?"

Further evidence statements they give could be:

- Can tell you what possible outcomes are for this person.

Or they may say "no that's it."

6. Creating an action plan to achieve the personal objective

Take another blank sheet of paper and ask them:

"Looking at this personal development objective and its evidence statements, what are all the things that you could do to learn how to do this?"

Get all the possible options written down. Then ask:

"Out of these what are the things that you need to do so that you become competent in this and can apply it to your situation?"

Get all the possible options written down.

Possible actions
• Action
• Action
• Action

Now ask the person to create an action plan that will get them from where they are now to the point where they can say 'yes I can do that/ be like that' to all the evidence statements and the overall development objective.

Business Need/Benefit & Measure for development	Person Objective & Measure for development	Action Plan for development
Item 1 • Measure • Measure • Measure	Objective 1 (date) • Evidence • Evidence • Evidence • Evidence	1. Action 2. Action 3. Action 4. Action 5. Action 6. Repeat actions 3-5

Ensure that you have thoroughly discussed the action plan so that it is robust and will ensure they are successful in developing through it. The action plan will probably start with the person gaining some new knowledge or skill. Next, they can work with someone to apply it to their situation. Then they can give it a go and then review what happened with the same person. They can adjust something if they need to, give it a second go and review again. They can repeat this until they are competent.

For example, if they are learning how to be more engaging when giving a presentation.

- First, they may go on a presentation skills workshop or talk with a colleague who is very good at giving presentations. This gives them some new knowledge and skills.
- Next, they could prepare their presentation and then discuss it with that colleague, make a few changes and then run through it with the colleague again. The colleague could give some feedback that the person can use to adjust the presentation.
- Then they give the presentation to the intended audience. Afterwards they can get feedback from the audience and maybe the colleague attended as well.
- Then they can meet with the colleague again, review the feedback and adjust the presentation from this feedback.
- Then they could give the presentation again to a new audience with the colleague attending.
- They can repeat this plan, do and review cycle until they feel they have met their objective with either the same presentation or a variety of presentations.
- It is this cycle that creates competency and is important for consolidating the development into their work.

Worked example continued:

Personal Development Objective 1:

Be able to apply sick procedure to current situation. (1st Mar)

- State all elements of procedure.
- Be confident to use procedure (2/10 -> 8/10)
- Can tell you which aspects relate to the person I have off sick and why.
- Can tell you what possible outcomes are for this person.

Q: "Looking at this personal development objective and its evidence statements, what are all the things that you could do to learn how to do this?"

The actions they give could be:

- Read the sick procedure and talk to HR about the sick procedure
- Talk to an experienced line manager about the sick procedure
- Test myself on the sick procedure
- Apply the sick procedure to my situation.
- Look on the Internet for case studies
- Talk to my line manager/ an experienced line manager about how it applies to my situation – create an action plan
- Discuss with a line manager who has been successful in getting a long term sick person back to work
- Use the experienced line manager as a mentor throughout getting the person back to work
- Tell someone else how the sick procedure applies to their case
- Do a presentation on the sick procedure

Q: "Out of these what are the things that you need to do so that you become competent in this and can apply it to your situation?"

The action plan they create could be:

- Read Sick Policy; check understanding with HR Manager. 7th Feb
- Describe to LM how procedure applies to my case. 11th Feb
- Meet with 'expert' Manager at handling long-term sick and discuss options. 16th Feb
- Create plan of action with LM 20th Feb
- Implement & review with LM. 23rd Feb

The development plan

Now you have written down:

- A business need/benefit and measure for development
- A personal objective and measures for the development
- An action plan for the development

44. Personal Development Plans (PDP) That Add Value

To fully achieve the business need and measure, more than one personal objective and its action plan may be required. Ask the person, "For this business need is there any other personal development objective you need to work on?"

Worked example continued:

> **Business need:** Improve team output by resolving long term sickness.
> - Improved team output by 15%
> - Person back full time and back up to productivity
>
> By 31st July
>
> **Q:** "For this business need is there any other personal development objective you need to work on?"
>
> They may say:
>
> "Apart from being able to apply sick procedure to current situation, I also need to be assertive when handling difficult situations."
>
> (work on this objective using Steps 4-6)

Overall the Personal Development Plan may look like

Business Need / Benefit & Measure for development	Person Objective & Measure for development	Action Plan for development
Item 2 • Measure • Measure • Measure	Objective 1 (date) • Evidence • Evidence • Evidence • Evidence	1. Action 2. Action 3. Action 4. Action 5. Action 6. Repeat actions 3-5
Item 1 • Measure • Measure	Objective 1 (date) • Evidence • Evidence • Evidence • Evidence • Evidence Objective 2 (date) • Evidence • Evidence • Evidence	1. Action 2. Action 3. Action 4. Repeat actions 2-3 5. Action 1. Action 2. Action 3. Action

Be careful not to overload the person: Usually no more than three personal development objectives or less if they are large ones. It is better to have fewer, complete them and then add another one from the initial list.

An example PDP

Business Need/Benefit & measure (Why do I need development?)	Personal Development Objective(s) (What do I want to become competent in?)	Action Plan(s) (How will I become competent?)
1. Improve team output by resolving long term sickness. • Improved team output by 15% • Person back full time and back up to productivity By 31st July	Be able to apply sick procedure to current situation. (1st Mar) • State all elements of procedure. • Be confident to use procedure (2/10 -> 8/10) • Can tell you which aspects relate to the person I have off sick and why. • Can tell you what possible outcomes are for this person.	Read Sick Policy; check understanding with HR Manager. 7th Feb Describe to LM how procedure applies to my case. 11th Feb Meet with 'expert' Manager at handling long term sick and discuss options. 16th Feb Create plan of action with LM 20th Feb Implement & review with LM. 23rd Feb
	Be assertive when handling difficult situations. (30th Apr) • Remain calm with normal breathing. • Maintain good body posture and eye contact. • Ask questions to gain information. • Summarise and clarify. • State what is required. • Create plan of action to move forward.	Go on Assertiveness workshop to learn how to remain calm; good body posture. 10th Mar Practice in situations and review with coach. 19th Mar Improve eye contact through exercise and check with coach. 1st Apr Work with LM on good questions to ask during meeting – produce format for meeting. 17th Apr Have meeting and review with LM. 23rd Apr
2. Be able to effectively take on work from customers to agreed timescales by 31st Oct • Can go to 3 business meetings without needing to take an extra person with me. (Saves 8 hrs per month) • Do not have to go back to customer to amend requirements or decline work. (50% at moment) • Team can complete work to agreed timescales and quality. (50% incorrect at moment)	To be competent in the technical aspects of my team's work. • Can state all the acronyms and their meanings. • Can state correctly all the services we can offer and the timescales, information etc. required. • Feel confident in meetings (4 ->8) • Can ask the correct questions of a customer requiring our services.	Generate list of acronyms used during meetings – find meanings – learn – get tested. 12th Feb Sit down with team and create sheet of services we offer and all relevant information – learn – get tested. 19th Feb Generate template of questions to ask at meetings. 21st Feb Get team member to role-play customer meeting - review afterwards. 26th Feb Take colleague to meeting as back-up if required. Review with colleague after meeting. 5th Mar Repeat 5. until feel 8/10 confident and competent.

Business Need/Benefit & measure (Why do I need development?)	Personal Development Objective(s) (What do I want to become competent in?)	Action Plan(s) (How will I become competent?)
3. Put together business case presentations that achieve their intended purpose. Date: 3rd April 80% of presentations do not have to be re-presented. Currently 75% are re-presented.	To deliver credible business presentations. • Create a fit for purpose and well-structured presentation. • Use value-add Powerpoint. • Have confident body language – voice tone steady and audible, good eye contact, well-paced delivery, comfortable gestures. • Handle mistakes well.	Attend presentation skills workshop. 9th Mar Apply new skills to next presentation and discuss with LM and with a co-workshop participant. 23rd Mar Deliver presentation. 30th Mar Review with LM and workshop colleague. 5th Apr Repeat steps 2-4 until competent.

Reviewing the PDP

Now you have a business need with measures, appropriate personal development objective(s) and action plans to become competent. This means that monthly development meetings become crucial and there is a useful conversation to be had.

Each month you meet with the person for 30-60minutes and find out what actions they should have completed on their plans, what actually happened, what they have learned, what they need to do differently if the action was not completed.

Once the action plan is completed you can ask them if they feel that they have completed the personal development objective: Are they competent as described? Most of the time they will be able to say yes although sometimes the action plan may not have fully addressed all that was needed. This is not surprising as there may be another area that needs working on now they have a better understanding. So create a new action plan, as above, to be able to complete the development objective fully.

Once you have completed all the development objectives related to the business benefit/ need, check to see if that business need has been met; have the business measures been achieved? If yes, then this whole aspect is completed. This item can be removed from the PDP and you can return to the person's initial list and add a new item using the Steps above.

It may be that, although having addressed the development objective, the Business Need has not been achieved. This is ok. Ask the person, with their new knowledge what they think they need to do differently to achieve the whole business benefit and its measures. Again, create personal objectives and associated action plans as above. In this way, the development of the person is continued until the tangible business benefit is gained. This keeps the focus of development plans on business benefits and competency rather than just going on training courses.

A structure for monthly personal development plan meetings

Each month meet with the person for 30-60minutes

1. For each action, review: -
- What worked?
- What didn't work so well?
- What needs to be completed, if anything?
- What did you learn?
- How far did this advance you towards achieving your objective?

2. Once all actions for a particular personal development objective have been reviewed: Then ask - has this objective been met?
- If not, then what further actions need to be taken?
- If yes, then the personal objective is complete.

3. As personal development objectives are completed, review if the Business Need & Measures have been achieved: -
- If they have, then the development has been successful and this section can be removed from the PDP.
- If not, then a further personal development objective may need to be set, with an action plan.

45. Having Difficult Conversations

What are the benefits of doing this?

Most feedback as described in Chapters 21 to 23 is simple and easy to give. In this chapter, I want to cover more difficult conversations such as giving people difficult news or feedback, as I think this is different to giving on-going feedback. The feedback described earlier gives on-going nudges to keep the person on track or get them back on track. If given throughout the year, then these more difficult conversations may not arise. However even with regular reviews and feedback there are situations that occur when the conversation is more challenging. The situations I am covering here are for Performance problems, Behavioural issues and Difficult or Unexpected situations. In each case, preparation and focus is vital. It makes a real difference to achieving a positive outcome. Of course, a positive outcome may be where the person feels treated with respect even though they are not happy about the situation.

Sorting out issues swiftly means that things do not escalate, which is harder to handle. In addition, you do not over analyse the issue or get overly anxious about it. One main areas of concern is that the person will get emotional during the meeting so I am also covering how you can gracefully handle that.

Sometimes we avoid handling a difficult situation due to the nature of the person. In these situations, the message we are signalling to the rest of the team is that if you play up you will get away with it or I am scared to handle this. Eventually the rest of the team start to wonder why they should bother so much and overall performance can start to fall. In one case, I was coaching a manager who was worried that by confronting the problem person he would upset her. I asked him if it was ok that this person caused eight other people to feel intimidated and anxious on a daily basis. He said he had not thought about that before and realised that by not wanting to upset one person he was allowing eight other people to be upset. Once he realised how much that affected the team, we worked on how he would have the conversation with the problem person.

Possible pitfalls and concerns to consider

- Lack of preparation/ Facts that are not true: Before any meeting, prepare really well. Gather information and cross check it thoroughly. Understand for yourself what needs to happen or is going to happen. Decide what you are focussing on and do not bring in other things that are not related as it dilutes the conversation. Invariably not remaining factual will cause problems that you will later regret. When describing issues or situations, remain factual, objective and non-judgemental so that people feel respected. Usually thorough preparation improves the meeting enormously.

- You do not listen well enough: It is important in these meetings to listen to the person's view on what is happening, as there may be mitigating circumstances that you need to understand.
- No follow up reviews: Nearly every one of these situations will need more than one meeting. It needs the initial meeting and then a second discussion once the person has had time to think about it. Regular reviews are often needed especially if there is an agreed action plan.
- They shift the conversation onto someone else / Getting side tracked: This is where your preparation counts as you will have thought about how this might happen. The simplest way to deal with it is not to engage in the conversation but to remind them that this meeting is about them and how it relates to them.
- The action plan is not specific enough: It is very easy to assume that because you understand what needs to happen that they also understand it. Get them to write their action plan and ask questions to check they understand what it means for them.
- Avoid condoning or colluding: Even if you think, "I know how you feel, that person is annoying and makes me feel angry" do not say it. It is not the time to do that. As a line manager, it is important to stand firm on this point and act as a role model.
- Being defensive/ aggressive: Talk through with a colleague until you can remain calm and assertive otherwise get another manager to have the meeting.
- What beliefs do you have about the situation that could compromise your handling of it? Ensure that when you have the meeting you have the ability to put these to one side. If, for example, you disagree with how the redundancies overall have been managed, when you meet the person you need to focus on handling their meeting well rather than discussing with them the issue you have with HR. The best way to do this is to talk it through with your line manager, a mentor or a colleague beforehand.
- You are not clear about how to handle the conversation: At this point you should gracefully curtail the meeting rather than getting stuck. Graceful ways to end the meeting early could be: Needing to get information; Needing to think about what

you have heard; Needing to think about or consult with someone on that point. The other way is to write down the point that you are not sure how to handle and then continue with other things.

- Not pausing or stopping the meeting: At any stage, be prepared to pause the meeting for 5-10 minutes or to stop the meeting and book a future one.

Other relevant chapters

- Chapters 11-13   Questioning for Robustness
- Chapters 14-16   Listening Productively
- Chapter 17   Productive Language

How

Covers

    Preparation (for any of the meetings)

    Difficult conversation meeting formats

        Performance issues

        Behavioural issues

        Difficult / Unexpected news

    What to do next

    Handling emotions

Preparation

1. Get all the facts and ensure you understand them thoroughly.
    - Get factual evidence and examples. First-hand is best, if it is second-hand information then cross check it with others to ensure that it is true.
    - If appropriate, ensure you are able to give clear examples of the difference between their current performance and what you require. Be clear about what you expect.
    - Ensure your description of any behaviour is not judgmental and that it states observable behaviour: For example, "When you raise your voice to shouting level, people in the meeting feel intimidated" rather than "you intimidate people by shouting". Also, avoid labelling people – "a person who shouts in this situation" rather than "an angry person".

- Ensure you have a very clear understanding of what happened/ is happening and the effect it had/ is having.

2. Lay out your facts and evidence so that they are logical and clear for the other person: Check this with a colleague.

3. Get someone to ask you questions about it. Otherwise, think about the questions the person is likely to ask and work out what you need to know to answer them.

4. What outcomes are possible from your point of view – what do you want/ need to have happen? What needs to happen to get each of those outcomes? How can you ensure you get the outcome you want?

5. How might they react? What outcomes might they want? How will you handle this?

6. Ensure that the implications, consequences, what will happen or needs to happen are very clear and that you are certain of them. Also, be sure that you have the backing of your line manager and HR. Take both of them through the situation and what you are going to do about it. It is better to resolve any differences before you talk to the person than to have to go back and change your position.

7. Think about what questions you do not want to be asked during the meeting: The ones you are nervous or concerned about being asked. Once you have written these down you need to get an answer for them and check those with a colleague. Make sure that when you answer the question you sound congruent with it rather than sounding that you are uncertain or do not believe it yourself.

8. Book a private room for the conversation. Book it 15mins before your meeting so you can get there and mentally prepare beforehand rather than rushing in at the last moment, as that tends to put you in the wrong frame of mind. Also, book it for at least 30mins longer than you think you'll need as these meetings often take longer than you think.

Difficult conversation formats: Performance issues

The bottom line is that you need them to deliver; to do the work they are being paid to do rather than not doing it or having others do it for them. Sometimes I get a manager to stand back and look at how much more time they would have if they were not having to compensate for a poor performer. It can be quite enlightening. Also it is not fair on other hard working team members. Longer term you may find that your best workers find other roles where they feel their effort is appreciated and poor performance is dealt with.

In addition, handling poor performance creates an environment where people realise that performance is taken seriously and there is pride in doing a good job. Often team members report that they feel their line manager is strong because they handle poor performers. Also people tend to put more effort into ensuring that they don't underperform so they don't have to have any conversations about it.

Overall having an expectation about performance and how poor performance is handled creates a healthy environment where people feel accountable for their standard of work.

I came across the 'Gap framework' for having performance conversations during my training at Mars UK and it has proven to be a sound way to keep the conversation focussed.

The basic meeting flow for performance issues
Establish the gap,

First, you need to be able to demonstrate the difference between their performance and the required performance. You need to have enough examples so that you and they are very certain about the gap in performance. The purpose of this part of the meeting is to establish the gap in one of two ways: -

- o You tell them this is the standard and this is where they are; therefore, this is the gap.

"Initially we would expect new starters to handle 10 customer complaints per day on average. After 3 months, we would expect that to rise to 30 complaints a day. After 4 months you are handling 20, which is 10 less."

- o You tell them this is what you expect and this is what you saw/ heard; therefore, this is the gap.

"When you answer the phone, I would expect you to give your name and ask how you can help in a pleasant tone. Yesterday, I heard you answer the phone 5 times by just saying "yes" in a flat tone."

Explore the gap

Next, you need to explore the gap and establish if the performance issue is getting worse, is steady or has been improving slightly.

Once you have established the gap, you can ask them: -

- o What are your thoughts on this?

This is the time to get their thoughts and to start to explore what they feel about it. It maybe that there are circumstance you are not aware of, therefore this is a good time to ask probing questions and to listen well.

Probing questions are useful to help explore and clarify: -

- o Tell me more about that?
- o What do you mean by (that)?
- o How is ...... affecting ...?

The purpose of this part of the meeting is to get the person to tell you everything that is affecting their performance so that you both understand how it has happened. Keep exploring until both of you understand how the gap has happened. You may also need to give them information to help them understand. Take notes if you feel comfortable to do so although it makes it a more formal meeting, which may not be helpful initially. If this conversation is part of a formal company process, then you will be taking notes.

Eliminate the gap

Finally, you need to work with the person so that they have a plan for eliminating the gap.

1. Ensure they are very clear about what you have told them, the implications, the consequences and what will happen or needs to happen.
2. Ask them if they have any questions.
3. Be thorough and straight forward about what happens next – create a plan together. It needs to be a plan that they own so allow them to decide how they want to close the gap whilst ensuring that it delivers the required improvement. There also needs to be regular reviews, weekly or monthly probably, to help keep the focus on the situation and raise any concerns on progress as early as possible.
4. Book in regular reviews to check progress and consolidate the change at the end so it does not reoccur in a few months. The purpose of this part is to ensure that the gap is eliminated and does not happen again.

Difficult conversation formats: Behavioural issues

As a line manager, you need to demonstrate that poor behaviour is not tolerated as it may escalate into a larger problem. Despite how much you dread the actual meeting it is not fair on others and tackling this is part of a line manager's role.

Sometimes people do not realise how they are affecting others and are grateful to be told. Maybe they do not know how to handle a situation and that is causing the poor behaviour. Other people simply need help with having a different way to handle their frustrations or to understand how people do things differently. Overall handling behavioural issues improves the working environment and leads to better performance.

The basic meeting flow for behavioural issues

1. Firstly, you need to be able to state the behaviour that is unacceptable, why it is unacceptable and what behaviour you expect. You need to have enough clear examples so that they understand the situation.
   - Tell them what is and is not acceptable.
2. Next, get their thoughts and start to explore what they feel about it and what is happening for them. It maybe that there are circumstance you are not aware of and therefore this is a good time to ask probing questions and to listen well.

Ask them what they think, feel or want to say
   - Tell me more about that?
   - How do you feel about ……?
   - What do you mean by (that)?
   - How is …… affecting …?

Sometimes people try to shift the problem. For example, if people say, "well I don't intend to intimidate people, they shouldn't take it that way" then say "You may not mean to intimidate them and I need to let you know that you do, as that is how they feel; they feel intimidated". If they say, "well that's their problem" then you need to set the limit on what is acceptable behaviour. "Actually I need to tell you as your line manager that your behaviour is not acceptable. It is not acceptable to raise your voice to a level where people in the room feel intimidated."

3. Ask questions so that you can check if they have understood the conversation so far. Be clear and factual in talking about what needs to happen next and the consequences of not addressing the issue.
   - Ask them frequently if they have any questions
4. Finally, you need to work with the person so that they have a plan for changing or managing their behaviour or the situation. It needs to be a plan that they own so allow them to decide how they will address the issue whilst ensuring that it will deliver the required improvement. Regular reviews also need to happen to help keep the focus on the situation and raise any concerns on progress as early as possible.

- Be thorough and straight forward about what happens next – create a plan together
- Book in regular reviews to check progress and consolidate the change at the end so it does not reoccur in a few months.

Difficult conversation formats: Difficult/ unexpected news

Difficult situations such as redundancies are part of a line mangers' role. I have found that treating people with respect and being professional is important: We do not have to agree with what needs doing but we need to manage it professionally. As line managers, we sometimes have to do things we are not whole-heartedly behind and although these situations are rarely ideal, minimising the overall impact is within our gift.

The basic meeting flow for difficult/ unexpected news

1. Tell them the unexpected/ difficult news.

With these meetings, it is easy to spend too long at the start talking about things that are not relevant to the conversation to make yourself feel comfortable. It is much better to keep it cleaner by quickly telling them the news, keeping it as straightforward as possible. With difficult news, people tend to forget things so having less to remember at this point is good.

2. Next, simply, ask them what they think, feel or want to say and listen to them. Be patient if they do not speak at first. Allow the silence and wait for them to respond.

Gently go through each point, carefully ensuring that they understand everything they need to. Having simple notes or handouts to give them is useful. Ask them frequently if they have any questions.

3. Ensure they are very clear about what you have told them, the implications, the consequences and what will happen or needs to happen.
4. Finally, work with them on the next steps. If appropriate, create a plan together or ensure they have relevant dates.
    - Be thorough and straight forward about what happens next – create a plan together.

Book in follow up meetings, at least one more to check how things are, after they have had time to reflect. Step 4 may be better completed once they have had time to think. Ensure you book it in before you leave the meeting.

What to do next

Immediately afterwards

Write up your notes on how the meeting went; what was agreed; keys things you said or they said. Do it immediately as you will lose the clarity quite quickly. Every time I thought I would be ok to do it later, I regretted not writing my notes immediately afterwards as I found things were not that clear any more. It can be useful to write notes even if you do not think you will need them. I always do it, just in case. You can always shred them later if they are not needed but you cannot write them if you have forgotten.

Ensure you complete any post meeting requirements that are required by your company.

Shortly afterwards

Reflect on the meeting with a colleague:
- What had you expected to happen?
- What did happen?
- How do you feel about that?
- How did the other person feel about the meeting?
- What worked well?
    - In your preparation
    - In the meeting
- What would you do differently?
    - In your preparation
    - In the meeting
- What affected the outcome of the meeting the most?
- What have you learned from this?
- What do you need to do now?

Prepare for the follow-up/ review meetings

- Although it might have been a successful conversation given the circumstances, think about what might have changed since then: What might have changed now they have thought about it and spoken with someone else?
- Do you have responses to everything that the person raised in the first meeting? If not, get them.

- Read through your initial notes and the notes you wrote up afterwards. Read any further correspondence that is relevant. What has changed from your point of view and what are the implications of that?
- Go back through Preparation Steps 1 to 8 above and repeat the ones which are relevant for a follow up session.

Follow-up/ review meeting key points

- Start by asking them what their thoughts are since you last met and listen to what they say as it may change the meeting.
  - If you feel that this has significantly changed the meeting, it is ok to postpone it whilst you get more information or think about how to handle what has been said. The worst idea is to keep going because 'you've booked the time'.
- Go through any actions from the last meeting thoroughly.
- Be clear with any new information and check they understand any implications.
- Update the action plan appropriately.
- Afterwards, write up your notes and reflect afterwards with a colleague.

Handling emotions

Most managers fear people becoming emotional and are surprised when it doesn't happen as most people will remain calm and composed. Also good preparation will mean that you handle the meeting better, which reduces the emotional reactions managers are concerned about.

However, a few people will react emotionally and as a line manager, you need to take this in your stride: Being professional and respectful of that other person in a difficult situation has the best chance of allowing them to feel dignified and well treated. They will appreciate this.

If the news is difficult or unexpected then how much they react emotionally will depend on the severity of the news, how unexpected it is and the person's emotional control. Reactions could be:

Crying

Anger

Withdrawal

Joking / not taking it seriously

If you think they may react emotionally then during your preparation, talk with an experienced line manager who has successfully handled such situations before.

Over the years, I have found that emotions mean different things to different people. Therefore, it is useful not to assume that they are feeling how you would feel. For example:

- Anger can be self-directed so the person could actually be angry with themselves for not seeing the situation arising although they may sound angry towards you or others.
- Anger can also be a reaction when someone is fearful or embarrassed. In this case, you need to address their fear or embarrassment rather than respond to their anger.
- Joking can be a way of distracting attention when someone feels nervous or is hiding the fact they are nervous. A good way to handle this is to refrain from joining in and gently bringing it back to what needs to be discussed.
- Sometimes a witticism is another way of expressing anger and it can be useful to keep the conversation focussed on what needs to be discussed.
- Crying can be a short emotional release and once composed they can continue.
- If someone goes quiet, then it may be useful to allow them time to think about what they have heard. In this case, sit quietly yourself rather than talking to fill the silence. When the conversation starts again take it slowly and be pragmatic about what needs to happen next.

In every case, if the person gets angry, tearful or withdrawn then stop the conversation until they regain control.

- I usually allow someone crying a bit of space to regain their composure by getting a glass of water or just sitting quietly until they are ready to continue. Usually a tissue is appreciated if they do not have one. I feel that they do not want you to make a fuss, be uncomfortable or overreact to them crying as that emphasises the situation. I feel that they would prefer it if you calmly let them regain control and then continued as if that was part of everyday life.
- If they cannot stop crying or are very withdrawn, then I would handle it differently as it is a deeper response. They may need a friend to be with them or to go home.
- If someone gets a bit angry then I let them speak until they have calmed themselves down. I find that I can usually hear the difference in their voice and they may even eventually laugh a bit or smile.
- If they are very angry then I will stop the meeting and either give them 15-30minutes to calm down or rebook it for later. I feel that there is no point talking to some-

one who is very angry, as they are too emotional to be able to function reasonably. They are reacting from our more basic 'fight/ flight' threat response.

If you feel that their emotional state is affecting you then stop the meeting and excuse yourself from the room. Only continue the meeting when you are calm and can remain in control. The most common examples of this are:

- Becoming tearful when they get upset and cry
- Becoming angry when they get angry

By becoming emotional yourself, you are less able to think clearly as well as being less detached from the situation. Both of these will affect your ability to act professionally and handle the situation as required. Overall, remain supportive and professional. If you know that you are likely to get tearful if they cry or angry if they get angry then discuss the meeting with a colleague or HR until you are able to remain detached from the situation. The exercises in chapters 25 'Detach to Get Things in Perspective' and 28 'Looking at the Situation From Different Perspectives' are useful for doing that.

46. Taking Individuals Through Change

What are the benefits of doing this?

People handle change in different ways depending on how they have experienced change previously and how resilient they are. As a manager, understanding something about how people go through change will help you support them so that they navigate the change as smoothly as possible given the circumstances; be those corporate change or individual change.

Helping people get through the change and ensuring that the new situation is consolidated is a valuable role for you to play. Not acknowledging how people feel and forcing people to accept change usually results in change that does not deliver the promised results, is not sustained or that creates poor performance and low morale.

The three models outlined below will give you a good insight in how to take people through change in a constructive way and with the best chance of delivering the required benefits. These are not about managing a whole change project. If you are doing that then I would recommend looking at John Kotter's website or book "Leading Change" as it is an excellent eight step framework to follow.

The final short section is focussed on how people can alleviated stress in times of change rather than accidentally adding to it.

Possible pitfalls and concerns to consider

- Doing these things slows the change down: Initially time will be required to close out the old ways and to plan and communicate the new world. Overall, this saves you time later and in many cases is the difference between the change working or not.
- The conversations will be difficult so I would rather not face that: At some time, you will have to have these conversations and they are usually easier at the start before people get entrenched in their views. Many of the chapters in this book will help make those meetings as constructive as possible.
- Communication is lacking: This must be the most common reason that changes fail and people become disenchanted. However much communication you think you are doing it is likely to be too little. Maintain regular team meetings during change even if you think you have nothing to say and tell people as much as you

can. If you cannot tell people about decisions, then tell them about the process or when decisions might happen. Be comfortable about telling people that dates have changed and decisions were not made when you said they would be: that's life. Help people understand that in times of change no one is ever really prepared and things are in a state of flux. If you react calmly to things shifting, then so will your team.

- Managers showing their anxiety and frustration: It is during change when your team need to see you being consistent and calm even if there is a lot of chaos around them. Acknowledging how you feel is useful, displaying it is rarely helpful and often fuels the anxiety within the team.

- Letting everything go – why bother? Maintaining as much normality as you can, no matter how little, gives people something that is familiar to them and something to focus on. It helps them have something they can control when they are feeling very out of control. Explorer, Ernest Shackleton's leadership mantra was about focussing on the goal, having structure and being social. His policy was that if one drops, the other two need to be increased. In times of change often the goal is unclear at the start therefore maintaining some structure (routine) and social (team meetings, social activities) improves people's resilience.

Other relevant chapters
- Chapters 11-13   Questioning for Robustness
- Chapters 14-16   Listening Productively
- Chapter 45   Having Difficult Conversations

How

Covers three change models with some implementation thoughts

Transition model	(three main phases of change)
Five steps	(practical pathway for personal change)
Change curve	(emotional journey)

How to be good to yourself in times of change

Across the years I have come across three models related to change that I find very useful. These are William Bridge's 'Transition Model', Prochaska & DiClemente's Five steps to change and the Kubler-Ross 'Change Curve'. These models will help you and your team to handle the changes you face and need to make with each covering a different aspect. Each aspect needs to be worked through rather than skipped and this is why most changes fail to deliver the required benefits. They miss out elements rather than focus on enabling people to get through each one promptly.

The Bridge's Transition Model looks at change from a psychological point of view. In essence it gives you an overview of change and the three phases that need to be dealt with for successful change to happen. These are about formally letting go of the past, navigating the period of uncertainty and then consolidating the new ways until they are habits.

The Five Steps to change give you a framework to plan how a change needs to happen for someone and the steps they usually go through from a practical point of view. This allows you to understand what support they require in a practical sense.

The Kubler-Ross Change Curve helps you understand how people are feeling and what support enables them to work their way smoothly and quickly through the change curve. It helps you work with what is driving their actions rather than just responding to what might be considered as poor behaviour.

Transition model

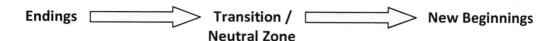

I only came across William Bridge's Transition Model recently and it is one of those books that I wish I had read years ago. It is an easy book to read with helpful examples and checklists at the end of each chapter. The basic premise is that change is physical, we move buildings, we get new equipment or we have a new process, whereas transition is psychological and goes on within a person. His model has three stages and it is the first stage that I was particularly taken with.

The three stages are:
- The Endings stage is about acknowledging what will be lost and not done again so that people get closure on those.
- The Neutral Zone, or Transition Stage, is about transitioning from the old to the new often involving a period of uncertainty and chaos although this can allow innovation to happen.

- The New Beginnings stage is what most managers talk about in change as it is the outcome that is hoped for.

For me, the big learning was that a lot of changes fail to fully deliver because of the Endings stage as people are not helped to accept what they have lost and then encouraged to close out those things. Emotionally they are attached to what they have lost. So whilst most managers describe how wonderful it will be once the change has happened, which is good to do, they also need to allow people to formally let go of what they will not have happen anymore.

The Endings stage can be quite simple. For example, as a manager you can run a team meeting to get people to think about what will be different for them. This can be as small as not taking a report to someone anymore and thus not spending a few minutes talking to that person, therefore a relationship is lost. Or it can be larger. If people are moving locations, they will lose colleagues or only now talk to them on the phone. In both these cases having a 'final meeting' and marking it in some way as an end would be good. Maybe have a coffee with the colleague you take the report to, as a final chat with them and have lunch with the colleagues to say farewell before you move locations. In whatever form it takes, emotionally people need to acknowledge an ending, acknowledge it in some way and close it out.

The Neutral zone, or Transition stage, can be the more challenging stage as often there is uncertainty or periods where people feel little can be done. Thus keeping people focussed and motivated takes thought and effort. On the other side, it can be quite creative as things need to be done differently which forces people to be more innovative and break old habits. In this stage help people feel more in control by focussing on what can be done and involve them in things as much as possible. In yourself it is good to be comfortable with uncertainty and know that maintaining as much stability and focus on certain tasks as you can, is helpful. Even getting people to meet to come up with possible new ideas is useful and helps them feel in control. It also involves them in the change itself which means they have more commitment and ownership for the outcome.

The final stage is about New Beginnings. This is about building the new way and consolidating it so it is an equally important stage. Although the final part of it is about celebrating the success of the change there is more to it than that. This stage is about implementing the new way, making it yours and then consolidating it until it becomes the norm. Involving people as much as possible ensures that this stage happens thoroughly. There are many chapters in this book that will help with this stage depending on what it is. In my experience, managers make this stage too short and take their focus off of the change before it is fully consolidated: They see winning one battle as having won the war. Thus when there is a slight problem things revert a long way back or the change gets derailed. It is often when this happens that you find out that you did not complete the Endings stage as well as you thought you had.

Overall, put thought and effort into each stage and complete each stage thoroughly although neither of these means that you have to take a long time to do it: Do it appropriately, once, as in the long term that is always quicker and more value-adding.

Five steps to change

```
                                              Maintenance
                                    Action
                          Ready
              Getting Ready
Not Ready
```

This model, also called The Transtheoretical model, has its background in behavioral change, such as giving up smoking, and was developed by Prochaska & DiClemente. As with all models it is not perfect although it does provide a useful practical framework from which to plan what needs to happen to implement a change. It also helps you understand where your people are in that process.

The model has five steps:

Step 1 is "Not ready" where the person is not aware that they need to change either because the change has not arrived yet, they have not realized they need to change or because they really haven't understood that they personally need to change. Think about what they need to know, understand or experience for them to realize that they need to change. This is not about 'how' it is about 'why'. They need powerful information or experience to 'get it'. This might be seeing customer complaints, working within the team they provide services to, getting information on how bad a situation the company is in or what the consequences of not changing are.

Step 2 is "Getting ready" where the person realizes they need to make a change and starts to explore what this means for them. Therefore, they need information about the change, what is expected of them, what will be different at the end and what the consequences of various alternative actions could be. In this step, team meetings or 1:1 sessions will be important as people attempt to make sense of what the options and consequences mean for them. Encourage people to ask questions and find answers to their questions and concerns as information will help them make sense and move forwards. A relapse back to Step 1 might happen if they feel the change does not fit with them, it changes who they feel they are or they find information that indicates to them that the change is not needed after all.

Step 3 is "Ready" where the person develops a plan for how they are going to change. Therefore, people need to understand how they might go about changing. This is the time to discuss what communication meetings are happening, what information is available, how they could find out more and what training workshops or development options are available. It is the point to talk with other people who have experienced a similar change or who helped others make these changes. Get people to think about how they have successfully made previous changes and share these in team meetings if appropriate. At the end of this step the person has a plan or knows the plan for changing. A person may relapse back to early steps for various reasons including the change process feeling too large or too vague, they cannot find a way to do it or they try something and it goes badly wrong.

Step 4 is "Action" where the person starts to try new things out and learns from this experience. During this step, encouragement and feedback are vital otherwise the person or your team may become discouraged and give up. Help them to have small wins and acknowledge them. Help them to work through mistakes and review their learning from them. Ensure that the change is being consolidated and the focus is on becoming competent in the new ways rather than rushing too quickly onto the next thing. A person may relapse back to early steps for various reasons including: Something they try fails or goes badly wrong; they feel no one notices their efforts or cares about them changing or they feel circumstances mean they no longer need to change.

Step 5 is "Maintenance" where the change has taken place and new habits have been adopted. In this step ensure that the change is fully embedded so encouragement and feedback are still vital. Also check out how robust the change is by seeing what happens in a more challenging situation. Many managers take their focus off of change too soon and people may relapse back to earlier steps because the change has not been properly embedded and doesn't stand up to daily use.

Throughout the five steps there is also the possibility of a relapse where people go back to previous steps. Think about how you will notice that and how you will handle it. Remember that when you handle it, you want the person to feel re-motivated to keep with the change so think about how your actions will make them feel: Talk to them about what is happening by asking good questions and listening well to what they say. Help maintain their ownership by asking them what they plan to do and also ask them what needs to be different going forwards to help prevent them from relapsing again.

Change curve

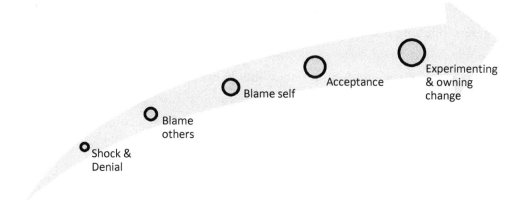

The classic change curve most commonly taught was devised by Kubler-Ross. Their change curve explains the emotional journey that people go through when they are bereaved and now it is commonly used as a framework to explain change in a broader context. I found it useful to help me understand, as a manager, what emotions could be driving the behaviour I was seeing in my team. It also helped me to understand my own feelings and that they were perfectly normal to have. Thirdly, it helped me to think about how I could support individuals in my team to get through the early stages of Shock, Denial, Anger, Blaming Others, Despondency and Blaming themselves to the stages of Accepting the Change and Experimenting with the new way. People need to go through each stage, although as a manager, you can help them to do this quicker and get them to the final stage of Integration sooner. There is a lot of literature on the Kubler-Ross Change Curve that is very easy to read and work through. I would recommend having a look at some of it to help you really understand the stages as they allow you to work on what is causing the behaviour you see rather than reacting directly to it.

Shock will depend on how much the person has realised that a change might happen and on how resilient that person is. For some people this will be a moment of surprise and for others it will paralyse them with fear. If they react heavily with shock, then they may need to go home or have counselling support. Overall, allow people time and space to absorb what they have just heard.

Denial can be fleeting or enduring. Often people stuck in denial continue trying to use old processes or equipment long after it has changed. They may also look for ways to stall the change by holding on to the old ways or just acting as if it is not going to happen. If you think you have people in Denial then you need to be very clear with them that the change is going to happen, what the timeline of change is and when training is going to happen. Ask them what they think will be different for them and start to get them involved in what is happening so they can really see the change is happening. Overall be clear and consistent about the change happening.

Anger or 'blaming others' comes from our natural resistance to change. As a manager, allow people to feel heard although do not allow their behaviour to become disruptive. Sometimes anger is a way of hiding fear. With change, people can be fearful of looking silly or awkward, especially if they are very competent in what they do. Some people get angry to cover up the feeling of inadequacy, thinking they could have headed off the change by having made a different decision at some earlier stage. I find it helpful to think of anger as misdirected energy and once it becomes usefully directed it becomes a powerful driving force. I find it helpful with people who are angry to be respectful that it is how they feel and to get them to think about how their angry behaviour is impacting themselves and those around them. My overall thought is that long term anger is not good for the person's health.

Despondency or 'blaming themselves' is a stage to watch carefully because if it is left unchecked it can become more serious and turn into depression. If you think one of your people is becoming depressed, then urge them to seek professional advice. Many companies have a healthcare helpline that may be a good first step. For most people, this stage is about a moment or two of self-doubt. Often they think about what they should have done differently and how that would mean this would not have happened to them. In this stage people feel out of control and at the whim of others so it is important to find something that they can control. Get them to focus on what they can do rather than how they should have done something different to have avoided the change happening to them. What they can do may be to find information or to focus on the part of their work which at the moment is still required.

The stage of **Acceptance** is what you have been helping your people to get to as quickly as possible whilst respecting the need to go through all the previous stages. Once you start to hear signs of acceptance gently get the person to explore those and build on them as this helps them consolidate their view that this could work out. Using questions to explore their thinking and getting them to talk is really important. Chapter 11 on Questions can help you do this. Be careful not to take signs of Acceptance as an invitation to rush ahead with the change as these are early days.

As the acceptance grows stronger, get the person to take actions to experiment with the new ways. **Experimenting and making the change their own** is very important although do not assume that the change is fully over. Think about how you might handle setbacks or days when the person feels more despondent again. Be comfortable yourself with the fact that the person will have times where they may go backwards along the change curve. How you react to that will facilitate them coming back to experimenting or entrench them back in an earlier stage. Planning how to progressively take on more and more change will help, especially if the person creates that plan for themselves. If possible, get people in the team to help others so that everyone is involved in consolidating the change.

At the point where the new situation is the new 'business as usual' then the change is fully implemented. The real signifier for this point is when the new situation or ways have a momentum of their own and people naturally do them. It takes no effort, it just happens and reinforces itself.

How to be good to yourself in times of change

We all have times when our lives are stressful therefore it is likely we cannot avoid being stressed at some point. What we can do is refrain from adding to that stress and therefore be in the best possible state to endure the period when we are stressed. There is a lot of information on wellbeing and mindfulness and I would encourage you to understand something around this either through reading, taking a course or talking with others.

There are also some easy things to consider so that someone is not adding to their already stressful situation. Here are a few simple things to think about:

- Eat healthily rather than grabbing junk food because you have a lot to do, because it's easy or because you can't be bothered.
- Talk to people: others going through the change or a good friend. It helps to talk to a good listener as you start to make sense of how you are feeling and what you are thinking. Conversely avoid being with others who are just moaning or being pessimistic about the situation.
- Have a lunch break even if it is a short one and take breaks when you can't think properly. Stand up and get some fresh air or at least walk away from your desk as it will help you think better when you return.
- Give yourself time elsewhere: Think about what you can stop doing whilst you are stressed and stop it. This maybe something at home or at work but it helps give you some mental or emotional space. Also don't add in anything extra until you are comfortable to handle it once the stressful period has ended.
- Be careful about having too much coffee or alcohol. Short term they might feel as if they are giving relief but overall it is not helpful.
- Have enough rest and sleep.
- Exercise in some way even if it is a walk.

Getting Your Team to Improve its Own Work

In the absence of, or alongside any company initiatives, it is quite simple to engage your people in small and numerous improvements to their daily work. Over time, these can add up to significant improvements both for the business bottom line, and for the satisfaction and pride of your people. Most people come to work to feel valued and satisfied. Despite appearances, people mostly come to work to be engaged. Waiting and completing non-value adding or wasteful work tends to lead to boredom and frustration, neither of which is good for the individual or the company.

These next two chapters give simple ways to engage people in improving their work, often with surprising results. The knack with both of these is to keep things simple, in all aspects. They need to be formal in a pragmatic way that the team develops for itself. The focus here is that it is about the team helping itself. Therefore, any information and data collected should be useful to the team in the short and long term. This keeps it relevant and engaging for them. People can get quite frustrated collecting information for someone else, especially if they are not certain whether it makes a difference to the business or not.

Chapter 47 "Making it Easy to Understand What Work is and is not Being Completed" looks at how your team can use simple displays to make it easy to understand how things are going. It looks at the full process from setting them up, to using the displays and annually reviewing how effective they are.

Chapter 48 "Little and Often Improvements" looks at how to get your team to complete continuous improvement activities across the year so that they deliver a change in performance. It gives you a step-by-step process for doing this in a sustainable way.

47. Making it Easy to Understand What Work is or is not Being Completed

What are the benefits of doing this?

If your team has lots of daily or weekly tasks such as a production line, maintenance, IT Help Desk, orders to fulfil or repairs to be done, reports to be checked, calls to be made, clients to be seen, etc., then this chapter will be useful to you. It will allow your team to take more ownership of its work and be continuously focussed on how they can improve things so that it is less problematical and more satisfying.

The important aspect of this chapter is that the team take ownership for improving itself and to do that they need to clearly see and understand what is working and what is not. A simple way to do this is to create a visual display of the daily or weekly requirements, what actually happened and why something didn't happen the way it should have: This is often called 'Managing Visually'. It is this 'self-improvement ownership' element that really delivers the value that you are looking for both in terms of engagement and improvements as they are doing it to and for themselves. The knock-on effect for the company is usually pretty good as well. It is not something to do overnight though where one day you are telling everyone what to do and the next day you are leaving it up to them. It is something to aim towards over time so plan how it will become implemented and embedded. Let them take the reins as much as they are willing to and sometimes you will need to nudge them along into doing it.

Another benefit is that it helps them to understand the value their work adds to the company as well as some of the company's reasons for doing or not doing certain things. It often gets them involved with the wider business as their problem solving starts to require them to connect and work with other areas. Invariably it creates energy and drive within the team as they start to feel more in control of their work and help to shape it. Overall, that has a high chance of improving performance levels across the team.

Possible pitfalls and concerns to consider

- Managers are often concerned that their people will come up with outrageous or untenable ideas and that means that they will constantly have to say, "We can't do that". Usually the opposite is true at the start. Getting people to create ideas to solve problems can be daunting for many people so they are reticent to do it and will need encouragement.

- People will not want to participate. That's ok. Focus on the people who want to get involved although everyone should attend the meetings. Gradually more and more people will become involved. In some respects, you can't blame people who think that it is just another management initiative and that it won't live up to expectations. The most enduring way to change these people's view is to demonstrate over time that it is here to stay and that it is worth getting involved. Defending your position just entrenches them further so demonstrate the difference.

- People will just moan. Again sometimes people have not had the chance to really get involved so they don't always know how to participate, strange as that may seem. Their benchmark to date is often one-way meetings that may not encourage true open debate. In these cases, people have built up frustrations that tend to need to be voiced first before they can fully engage. So it maybe that you need to let that happen. Usually after three or four meetings people understand that this is different and settle down into focussed problem solving.

- Keep the daily/ weekly work boards simple and then they will maintain themselves. Marker pens, handwritten notes are much easier for everyone to keep up to date than computer printouts. In addition, handwritten notes mean that you minimise what needs to go up whereas it is so easy to create numerous sheets of paper from a computer that overload the boards.

Other relevant chapters
- Chapter 12   Questions to Help Overcome Unhelpful Perceptions and Thinking
- Chapters 14-16 Listening Productively
- Chapter 33   Delegating and Holding Others Accountable

How

Covers seven steps that help to make this successful
1. Talking with your team
2. Get the board designed
3. Getting the team to complete the boards
4. Running the meeting
5. Managing escalated actions

6. Review meeting

7. Full review meeting held once a year.

Implementing managing in a visual way is relatively simple. It only becomes burdensome if it is being done for the wrong reasons and is not focussed on the team helping itself. Managing visually is exactly what it says, it is about managing using boards to visually and simply display information or status, etc. such that everyone can see and understand what is going on. It should take around 15-20 seconds for anyone to understand a team's board.

In true managing visually there are different levels of boards that can go from frontline up to the director level, in this book we will look at the first level of board aimed at teams managing themselves. It is easy to get the idea of them. If it starts to feel too onerous, and that it may not be adding value, then STOP and review what is actually being gained. Strip it back down until it becomes simple and effective.

These are the basic steps that you probably need to do to implement managing visually within your team:

1. Talk with your team about what it is, why you want to do it and how it will help them. Weave in their thoughts and ideas as much as possible.

2. Design the boards as a team: layout, headings, how things are recorded. The layout on page 279 gives you a simple starter layout, which well works for most teams.

3. Get the boards up and initially populated then agree a first meeting date but go live sooner rather than waiting for everything.

4. Have the daily/ weekly meetings: Start to collect and collate the data and generate actions as required.

5. Manage escalated actions that need people outside of the team to complete them.

6. Every month/ 6-8 weeks have a review meeting where you discuss how it is working and how the actions are progressing (or not). Also discuss what you are learning and any improvements required to the board or meeting: remember to keep it simple.

7. Once a year hold a full review meeting: Celebrate the difference made by the team and the improvements achieved. What has been learned across the year? What has each person got from it?

1. Talking with your team

Go through the purpose of managing visually and how the boards work in principle. Then ask them what they think about it. Have a general discussion about how it could work and what may stop it working. How could it be simple to operate and also be helpful to people? What do they really need to know?

Purpose of the boards: They are for your team to help improve their work productivity through identifying and removing waste and inefficiencies. They also give you data to put forwards as a business case for getting things sorted.

How do they work: Basically it displays what you did yesterday and how that went (what did and didn't get completed or took longer); it displays today's work and what can be completed or not; it displays on-going actions, feedback from escalated actions; it displays important issues for today and new successes they've had. It also displays the required verses actual performance levels across the year and a 'year to date' bar chart of the issues hindering the work.

Over time, you would expect the efficiency of your team to improve by continuously removing the waste that stops or hinders work each day. In turn you would expect morale to rise as people prefer to come in and get on with the work they need to do. Also as they are sorting out some of the issues that helps them feel more in control and therefore more satisfied and proud with their work.

2. Get the board designed

The boards can be relatively small, say 1m by 2m or perhaps 2m by 2m. Only have a board large enough for the information you need to display as otherwise the blank space gets filled up with irrelevant information that clutters the board so it loses focus.

- If you already have work schedules printed out, can you use them? Perhaps print them larger or just add a 'completed/not completed' column to the print out.
- Green, red, black and blue marker pens work very well on a wipe-board. Stickers on sheets of paper also work well. Anything that clearly shows how things are going.
- Charts can be hand completed and maybe computerised once every month or 3 months if required.
- Agree the Meeting Rules with the team and put these above the board. For example, 'arrive on time for the meeting'.

Fig 2: A simple board layout

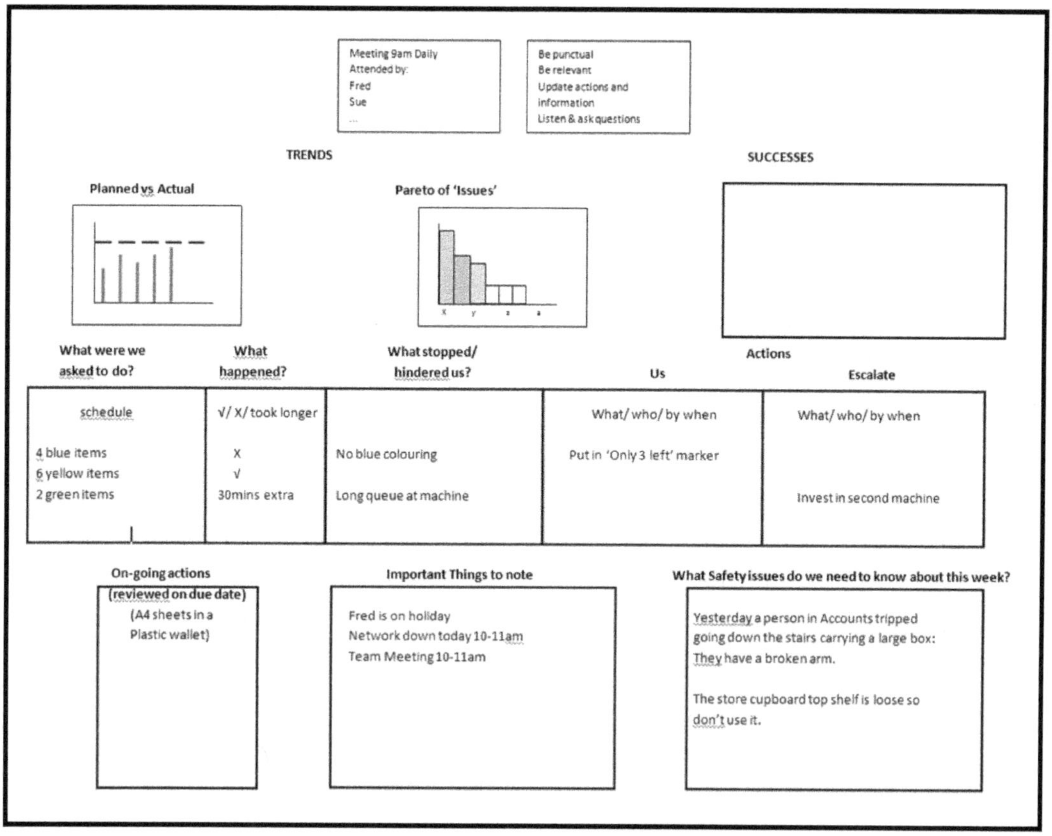

[Board diagram showing sections: Meeting 9am Daily (Attended by: Fred, Sue); Be punctual, Be relevant, Update actions and information, Listen & ask questions; TRENDS with Planned vs Actual and Pareto of 'Issues' charts; SUCCESSES; columns labeled: What were we asked to do? / What happened? / What stopped/hindered us? / Actions Us / Escalate, with entries: schedule, 4 blue items, 6 yellow items, 2 green items / √/ X/ took longer, X, √, 30mins extra / No blue colouring, Long queue at machine / What/ who/ by when, Put in 'Only 3 left' marker / What/ who/ by when, Invest in second machine; On-going actions (reviewed on due date) (A4 sheets in a Plastic wallet); Important Things to note: Fred is on holiday, Network down today 10-11am, Team Meeting 10-11am; What Safety issues do we need to know about this week?: Yesterday a person in Accounts tripped going down the stairs carrying a large box: They have a broken arm. The store cupboard top shelf is loose so don't use it.]

3. Getting the team to complete the boards

Agree with the team how they will keep the boards up to date. Little and often works best.

- For tasks, usually the easiest way is to go to the board after each task has been completed.
- For items to be produced, delivered or despatched, it is useful to update the board once or twice a day at set times.

Colours

- Red for things that did not happen, did not get completed or delivered, etc.
- Orange for things that were delayed or that took longer, etc.
- Green for things that went as planned.

Successes and Issues important to the team that day

Agree with the team how these should be completed. It usually works best if there is some spontaneity so adding things by hand as they happen, works well. Just ensure that they are covered at each meeting and old items are removed.

Trends

Agree how the trends graphs are to be updated. The Bar Chart can be designed so that it is updated by the person putting that issue down in the "What stopped / hindered us" section: For example, by the person colouring in the next segment up on the bar chart. In this way no one person has to do a large updating task every week.

On-going actions

Actions need to be recorded so it may be easier to write them on separate sheets. At the bottom of the board hang an A4 plastic folder to put the on-going action sheets in so they do not clutter up the board. Also agree when and how completed actions are going to be stored.

4. Running the meeting (15-20mins):

As the Team Leader: View the board 15mins before the start time so you can have a good look at it and understand what is and isn't happening both work-wise and with the board.

- Ensure it is up to date and tidy, remove any old items and get people to update it if needed
- Actions past their end date should be highlighted. Maybe highlight the date with a highlighter pen or use a red sticker. In this way you can see if Actions keep going beyond their completion date by the number of red stickers on it.
- Ensure you have the actions that need to be reviewed ready. These may be in the A4 wallet
- Ensure everyone arrives on time and keep the session focussed
- If new people are attending for the first time, remind everyone of the reason for the session:
- Looking at what happened yesterday and how that went,
- Review of on-going actions and feedback/ updates from escalated actions,
- Important notes for today and new Successes to be recognised.

- Quick look at today's work and any comments

Now review the main section of the board, looking at the actual work. Review by exception (red or orange items) otherwise the meeting will take too long. This is an example of how the meeting may go: -

a. Overall yesterday 8/11 tasks were successfully completed.

b. Task X couldn't be started because …. The action to stop this happening again/ sort it out is ……. and Fred is doing that by Friday 12 noon. (If there is no action assigned, ask the team what they think needs to happen and who is going to do it, by when. If an action is going to take some time to complete, then put in a date for that person to give the team an update rather than allow it to get forgotten.)

c. The reason that stopped Task Z being completed / took longer to do is … What could we do to stop that happening again? / What do we need to do to sort that out? Who is going to do that? (Or escalate it – be careful of ending up with all the actions being escalated as they are then out of your control. Also let people offer before you allocate the action as they will have more ownership that way.)

d. Looking at today's work: Today there are 12 tasks to complete and one of these cannot be done because ……… (give reason and create the action for it).

e. Then review any 'Important Things to Note' for today. Draw people's attention to any note and only talk about it if it is not self-explanatory otherwise this section can become unnecessarily long.

f. Now we will review the actions due today. Ask each person for their update on their action and discuss any problems or delays with it. Agree a new completion date for it if required. Also thank them if they have completed it on time so that you reinforce this success. Include in this section any updates from the Escalated actions.

g. Acknowledge any New Successes and those involved.

h. Thank everyone for their time and remind them to update the boards and work on their actions as appropriate.

i. Clear the appropriate sections and set up the board for today's/ this week's work.

5. Managing escalated actions

The problem with Escalated Actions is that they can vanish into a 'black hole' and become outside of the team's control which can be very disheartening. So be careful about how many actions get escalated and to manage the expectations of the team as well.

The more facts these actions have to back them up, the more likely they are to get the attention of a person outside of the team. Also these facts can be used to enlist the support of senior managers so that the action does get resolved or at least improved to some degree. If the action is not going to be addressed, then you need to bring the reasons back to the team. If possible it would be good if the manager who is not going to progress it, for sound business reasons, could come and explain those reasons to the team themselves. In this way both parties get to understand the issues faced by each other and relationships get built.

As Escalated Actions are likely to be larger actions then it is useful to put in a number of Review dates. Wherever possible spread the managing of Escalated Actions around the team. This is good development for the team as well.

6. Review meeting

Each daily / weekly meeting at the board is 'in the moment', working with what is happening and getting things resolved with respect to the team's work. Every couple of months it is worth holding a separate meeting, for an hour, where the team can stand back and look at the managing visually process itself.

A simple agenda could be:

- Go through actions from the last Review Meeting (Skip if this is the first Review Meeting).
- How many actions are closed out by their completion date? Do we have a backlog problem?
    - What can we learn from this: what is working and what is not working?
    - What do we need to do differently? For example, many teams put unrealistic end dates on their actions so they take longer than expected. A simple solution would be to extend the end date by an amount each time.
- How many actions are we generating and how many do we have open at the moment?
    - What can we learn from this?
- Too many actions may suggest that the team is being unrealistic about what it can handle.
- Too few actions may suggest that issues are not being highlighted or that the team is not really being stretched.
- What does the Performance Trend graph tell us?
    - What should we do differently, if anything?

- What can we learn from our Success?
  - What should we do differently, if anything?
- How are the Escalated Actions progressing?
  - What should we do differently, if anything?
- How do we feel about the board layout and processes we are using?
  - What can we learn from this: what is working and what is not working?
  - What should we do differently, if anything?
- Anything else?

Any actions should be written down and reviewed at the start of the next Review meeting.

7. Full review meeting held once a year

The purpose of this one to two-hour meeting is predominantly to recognise the effort and progress made by the team. They should leave the meeting feeling that their efforts have been valued and acknowledged. It should consolidate their desire to continue making improvements within their daily work. To ensure it meets this purpose it is useful to let the team do most of the input. Also this would be a good meeting to invite a few senior people to such that they could also congratulate the team but make sure they understand the purpose of the meeting as well. Cakes or a team prize would also work well. A simple agenda could be:

- Highlights from the year – presented by the team
- Improvements made, including challenges overcome, and savings created – presented by the team
- An insight or learning from each person or pairs/trios if you feel that it would not work individually
- If possible, internal / external customer comments to indorse improvements made.

48. Little and Often Improvements

What are the benefits of doing this?

In some cases, managing visually as described in the previous chapter does not fit with the team's work. When I was managing my Training Team, managing visually in that way would have been cumbersome and it would have lost momentum very quickly. However, you can get many of the engagement and improvement results by getting your team involved by continuously working on 'little and often' improvements. I have chosen not to call it anything more officious so that once again it is kept simple, pragmatic and sustainable.

So if you would like your team to take more ownership of its work and be continually focussed on how they can improve things so that work is less problematical and more satisfying then completing 'little and often' improvements would be beneficial. These easily fit into monthly meetings and you can enable your team to start working on different things that over time will add up to more satisfying work and better productivity. As they are working on these things for themselves they will have greater ownership and commitment to do them. So let them take the reins as much as they are willing to although sometimes you'll need to nudge them along into doing it as well.

As with managing visually, another benefit is that it helps them to understand the value their work adds to the company as well as some of the company's reasons for doing or not doing certain things. It often gets them involved with the wider business as their problem solving starts to require them to connect and work with other areas. Invariably it creates energy and drive within the team as they start to feel more in control of their work and help to shape it.

Overall that has a high chance of improving performance levels across the team.

Possible pitfalls and concerns to consider

- Start with improvements that will be successfully completed and yet will give the team satisfaction. This helps to build the thought that this can be done and is worth doing. Often teams take on too much or managers are impatient and start with large projects. These can easily lose momentum and the team loses confidence in themselves and undertaking small improvements. Build up slowly and the momentum will grow and be sustainable.

- Managers are often concerned that their people will come up with outrageous or untenable ideas and that means that they will constantly have to say, "we can't do that". Usually the opposite is true at the start. Getting people to create ideas to solve problems can be daunting for a lot of people so they are reticent to do it and will need encouragement.

- People will not want to participate. That's ok. Focus on the people who want to get involved although everyone should attend the meetings. Gradually more and more people will become involved. In some respects, you can't blame people who think that it is just another management initiative and that it won't live up to expectations. The most enduring way to change these people's view is to demonstrate over time that it is here to stay and that it is worth getting involved.

- People will just moan. Again sometimes people have not had the chance to really get involved so they don't always know how to participate, strange as that may seem. Their bench mark to date is often one way meetings which may not encourage true open debate. In these cases, people have built up frustrations that tend to need to be voiced first before they can fully engage. So it maybe that you need to let that happen. Usually after three or four meetings people understand that this is different and settle down into focussed problem solving.

Other relevant chapters
- Chapters 8-10   Inspiring People
- Chapter 12   Questions to Help Overcome Unhelpful Perceptions and Thinking
- Chapters 14-16   Listening Productively

How

Covers seven steps that help to make this successful

1. Discuss and agree with your team about doing this
2. Generate possible improvements, refine and choose first three items
3. Complete simple Improvement sheets: Who does what by when
4. Review actions regularly
5. Process review: How it is working and are the actions happening
6. Yearly full review meeting: Celebrate successes and learn

The simplest and most effective way at ensuring that this is sustainable is to make it part of your monthly team meetings. Once underway it would only require 30mins per month as the meeting is for progress reporting not for completing or working on the improvement.

1. Discuss and agree with your team about doing this

At the first team meeting talk to your team about the concept of 'Little and Often' Improvements. Ask them what they think about doing it. Discuss how to make it sustainable.

Purpose: To work on small improvement projects across the year such that a variety of things improve enabling the team to productively spend its time on more satisfying and value add work.

How: Initially projects are proposed and further ones added to the list at subsequent meetings. Three projects are chosen to be worked upon and once one is completed then the team decides which one to work on next. Use the monthly meeting to review progress, celebrate successes and assign the next improvement.

Over time, you would expect the efficiency of your team to improve by continuously removing the waste that stops or hinders work each day. In turn you would expect morale to rise as people prefer to come in and get on with the work they need to do. Also as they are sorting out some of the issues that helps them feel more in control and therefore more satisfied and proud with their work.

2. Generate possible improvements, refine and choose first three items

Using post-it notes, get the team to write down all the simple improvement projects that could improve their work (One idea per post it note). At this point it does not matter what they are. Now sort the ideas:

1. For identical ideas, just keep one post-it note and remove the duplicates

2. Merge any similar ideas onto one new post-it note. Be careful only to merge very similar ones otherwise they get too generic.

3. Remove any 'non-starters' for whatever reason, as agreed by the team.

4. Now sort them into four groups: A - Simple and we can do ourselves; B - simple and we can get others to do; C - less simple and will take longer; and D - larger and more complex to get done.

5. To start with pick 3 ideas from group A. This means that in the early stages, when

the team is learning, they are in control. Any mistakes can be sorted and the learning is taken on board. As the team's confidence grows it can pick items from group B and then from group C. It may be that items from group D are left or they may be taken by very confident and competent team members to run in parallel with the other improvements across the year.

6. Agree how the full A-D list will be kept and how items get added to it which could be through the monthly team meetings. It is a good idea that items are added when people think of them although they are only formally added once the team has vetted them during a team meeting.

3. Complete simple Improvement sheets: Who does what by when

For the three items being worked on it is useful to agree and highlight a few facts. A simple A4 sheet can be used for this. The advantage of using a sheet is that they could be display on the team's notice board or in the team's work area. This means that they are on view and people can read about the project in their own time or at their own pace after the meeting.

It is useful to agree:

- Project title
- Who are the people in the team working on it and who is the main champion
- What is being fixed or improved
- What will be the difference or benefit when this work has been completed? This is useful to put in as time or money saved or quality improved etc.
- When is it due to be completed
- If the completion date is longer than one month, then agree what milestone(s) will be completed each month so that these are reviewed at the monthly team meetings. This means that they will get progressed rather than forgotten about.

4. Review actions regularly

In the regular team meeting allocate about 30minutes for reviewing the projects. It should only take up to 30minutes as it is an update with progress being reported, key highlights given and any issues or concerns raised. Any changes to dates or outputs can be amended on the sheet.

A simple review 10min format could be:

- State the project title and what should have been completed by this point

- State what has been completed. Thanking any one of note and stating any highlights or challenges overcome (briefly)
- State what has not been completed and what the reason is for this (keep it factual)
- If the issue is small then discuss it there and then, otherwise agree with the relevant people when to meet about it.
- Update the sheet as appropriate

If a project has been completed, then thank everyone and acknowledge the success of the team. Then get the team to agree the next item from the full list to work on. Create a sheet for this one. File the completed sheet so that a record of progress is kept. If appropriate inform others of the project's success. For a significant project it may valuable for a senior manager to thank the team formally or informally: Keep it simple.

5. Process review: how it is working and are the actions happening

Every 6 months it is worth holding a separate meeting, for an hour, where the team can stand back and look at 'how' they are working on the projects. The purpose of this session is to consolidate the momentum and improve how they are working on the 'little and often' improvements.

A simple agenda could be:
- How are we feeling about doing these little and often projects?
    (Just allow each person 2minutes to share their thoughts)
- What are we doing that's working with the projects?
- (Allow people to input their thoughts)
- What challenges are we having with the projects?
- (Allow people to input their thoughts)
- Having heard how we feel about it, what is working and what challenges we are having:
    o What should we do differently, if anything?
    o Generate ideas onto a flipchart
    o Then get the team to agree which ones they will do
- Anything else?

Any changes should be written down and reviewed during the monthly team meeting to check that the change worked and gave the desired benefit.

6. Yearly full review meeting: Celebrate successes and learn

The purpose of this one to two-hour meeting is predominantly to recognise the effort and progress made by the team. They should leave the meeting feeling that their efforts have been valued and acknowledged. It should consolidate their desire to continue making improvements. To ensure it meets this purpose it is useful to let the team do most of the input. Also this would be a good meeting to invite a few senior people to such that they could also congratulate the team but make sure they understand the purpose of the meeting as well. Cakes or a team prize would also work well.

A simple agenda could be:

- Highlights from the year – presented by the team
- Improvements made, including challenges overcome, and savings created – presented by the team
- An insight or learning from each person or pairs/trios if you feel that it would not work individually
- If possible, internal / external customer comments to indorse improvements made.

Connecting With Others to Enable Your Team's Work to Happen

In our busy working lives with the focus on delivering tasks it can easily become about what we and our team are doing rather than who we know and how our relationships are helping or hindering the work. If we really are doing independent tasks, then not worrying about how we are perceived or how you are affecting others is ok. For most of us, we need to lift our heads and look at those around us whilst asking ourselves, "Where is help if I need it? Who would support me?"

Chapter 49 "Developing Appropriate Inter-Team Relationships" outlines a simple model that looks at the inter-relationships between various teams within a project or piece of work. It helps you think about how to manage the relationships between them rather than involving everyone to in everything.

Chapter 50 "Analysing Required Business Relationships" gives you a simple template to help you analyse your relationships and appraise how that affects your work. Overall, it looks to align your efforts in building relationships with your work deliverables. It is surprising how much people gravitate towards comfortable relationships rather than the ones that would be most valuable.

Chapter 51 "Internal Networking to Improve Your Team's Work" lays out simple steps to creating a useful and workable internal network.

Chapter 52 "External Networking to Improve Your Team's Work" looks at how to create a worthwhile external network.

49. Developing Appropriate Inter-Team Relationships

What are the benefits of doing this?

I have found when working with teams to help them focus and perform, that there is a fear that the team will become insular and will do things for itself that will cause problems for others and the company. Often the solution to this is to insist that everyone remotely connected to the work is invited to every meeting. Therefore, the meetings have numerous people in them, which causes problems with participation and feeling safe enough to contribute openly. Also various people have ideas about what they think should be done, knowing that others will have to do it and it is very easy to come up with ideas when you do not have to implement them. Both these issues waste a lot of time and energy and impact heavily on the team and their work especially in the early stages of setting up a new team.

The Team Systems Model in Fig 3. helps you consider the dynamics between different groups involved in a project or daily work and gets you to think about how to manage those relationships. This keeps meetings, decisions and work focussed whilst addressing the relationship and communication issues.

Possible pitfalls and concerns to consider

- Not everyone will like being excluded: True and these situations will need to be handled. Involving everyone can be a way of avoiding those conversations rather than what you would really prefer to do which is not to involve them. In my experience, it is less uncomfortable long term to have those conversations.
- I should involve everyone: although ideal, that approach is rarely practical and the strength of a high performing team is that it knows when not to involve everybody: It builds trust and appropriate relationships to be more agile and flexible. Mature teams are very pragmatic about this.
- Shouldn't the dedicated sub teams shown in the model be in all meetings? No, not all of them. Inviting people to meetings because they are part of the team is not a valuable use of their time or the meeting's time. Understand who needs to be at the meeting to deliver the outcomes for it and invite those people. I know that people will get something from attending the meeting but given they are a valuable resource is that the most useful thing they could be doing?

Other relevant chapters
- Chapter 6   What is the Added Value Your Team Delivers?
- Chapter 11   Questions That Invite Others to Contribute
- Chapter 35   Basic Meeting Outcomes, Structure and Tips

How

Covers the model and how to use it.

The Model

Fig 3, on the next page, shows the Team Systems Model. When a team is asked to do some work there is usually a Core Team of people who are dedicated to the work and need to be involved in all the key decisions. There may be some other people who are also dedicated full time to the work but are mainly involved in a particular aspect, a sub section (for example, design or programming), and do not need to be involved in all the decisions. They form a Dedicated Sub Team.

Then there is the Champion or Supporter of the work. They help clear problems at a higher level and champion the work within the larger business arena. Often they will be the person who asked you to do the work in the first place. This element also includes strong advocates of the work your team is doing.

Many teams will also have Part Time (Satellite) Members: Members who are vital but cannot be fully released from their day jobs, for example procurement, or who are a scarce resource and need to be shared. Often these people link your team directly to other teams (satellite teams) and may become that team's representative in this work.

Finally, we have Experts: Experts may be needed by the team for a short period of time at some stage or they may join the team briefly as and when required.

The Team Systems Model is a diagnostic tool that helps prevent the fear those other managers have about the team and allow the Core Team to be in control of the situation. It gives you a simple framework to look at the different relationships you have with people and how to successfully manage those.

Using the model
- Understand who you have in each of the elements and put their initials on a copy of the diagram on the next page.
- With the core team:

o Understand the type of relationship each person has with the work (satellite, expert, sub team, champion, etc.), their commitment to it, what you need from them and what they need from you.
o Decide how to manage that relationship, and any communication, so that it delivers what is required in a sensible way.
o Decide how to monitor the effectiveness of that relationship and how well you are managing it.

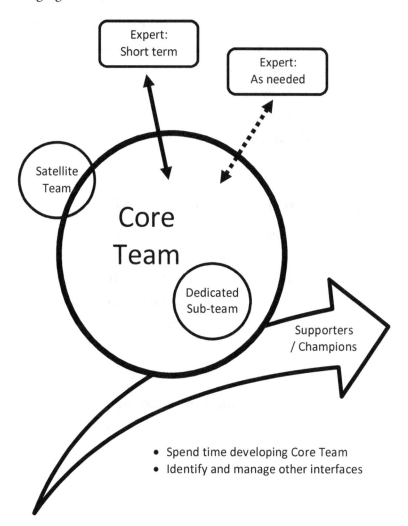

Fig 3: The Team Systems Model

50. Analysing Required Business Relationships

What are the benefits of doing this?

I have found that most managers need a simple way of thinking about the relationships they have or do not have with various people. This can mean that they gravitate towards the easiest relationships rather than the ones that will be helpful to them and their team in getting the work done. On the other hand, I have seen projects with cumbersome stakeholder analyses that are swiftly forgotten. Neither of these situations is useful and spending some time every four months thinking about the state of your relationships will have benefits for the work you are doing in many ways. The table templates, on the next page, can help you do that.

Possible pitfalls and concerns to consider

- This will create extra work for me: It may or it may not, as it helps you to make as many relationships as possible beneficial to your work. Therefore, you may reduce your time with some people and increase it with others. Alternatively, you may gain time because the new relationships speed up getting things approved. At least you will have an informed view by doing this.

Other relevant chapters

- Chapter 2   What is Driving Their Behaviour?
- Chapter 28   Looking at the Situation From Different Perspectives
- Chapter 49   Developing Appropriate Inter-Team Relationships

How

Covers the five steps for this review

1. "Who is relevant to your work?"
2. Table A "Who are you currently working with?"
3. Table B "Who are you currently not connecting with where you should be?"
4. Table C "In the future, who should you be connecting with?"

5. Review

1. "Who is relevant to your work?"

On a blank sheet, draw three columns, headed:

Should ✓   **Should** ✗   **In Future**

Which stand for:

Should ✓ = people you should be connecting with to ensure good delivery of your work and where you <u>are</u> working on the relationship. (Have some form of relationship)

Should ✗ = people you should be connecting with to ensure good delivery of your work and where you are <u>not</u> working on the relationship. (Have no relationship)

In Future = these are people who you will need help from/to work with in the near future.

In the three columns write down all the relevant people for your work: Choosing a column most appropriate for that person. If you work on multiple projects, then it is probably easier to focus on one project at a time. Occasionally, a team name is more appropriate than listing each individual person. You could also get a colleague to check it and ensure it is a robust list.

Now transfer the names to the relevant table on the template:

Should	✓	Table A
Should	✗	Table B
In Future		Table C

2. Table A "Who are you currently working with?"

Name	Activity	0 - 5	What makes this a 4 or 5? If 4 or 5	Actions to get 4 or 5: If 0 - 3

"Activity" Column

For each name/team write down how you are connecting with that person, Such as: -

- Creating initial prototype
- Weekly project review meetings (1 hour)
- Monthly update meeting (30 minutes)
- Leadership forum project

- Design reviews
- Developing operating schedules

"0 – 5" Column

Rate each activity from 0 – 5.

0 = Relationship poor and activity not working well.

5 = Strong relationship and activity adding value.

"What makes this 4 or 5?" column.

For those relationships scored 4 or 5, complete this column. In this column, distil out what is really making this relationship successful. Then you can share this best practice with others or use it to enhance other relationships. Really articulate the tangible aspects that can be replicated, such as: -

- "Make time every Friday morning to go over to marketing to see what releases they are making the following week; therefore, I know what to expect" rather than "good relationship".
- "New person met with all nine team members for 30 minutes within the first two days" instead of "good induction".

"Actions to get 4 or 5" column

In this column write down possible actions to get 0 -3 ratings up to 4 or 5. Pick actions that you are going to complete and put together a sensible action plan for them.

3. Table B "Who are you currently not connecting with where you should be?"

Name	Decide to do something OR actively decide not to engage	If doing something - what is your action plan for getting there OR if not - why have you decided this? What are the consequences and are you happy to accept them?

"Decide to do something OR actively decide not to" column

In this column either write down what you are going to do to build the relationship or write down that you are deciding not to engage with them. Although this may appear strange, Section B is about being pragmatic rather than putting something off with no underlying intention of doing it. There are many reasons why it may not be practical to engage with someone, so be honest and reduce your 'to do' list.

"If doing something - what is your action plan for getting there? OR, if not why have you decided this - what are the consequences and are you happy to accept?" column

In this column

- If you are going to do something: Pick actions that you are going to complete and put together a sensible action plan for them.
- If you decided not to engage with them, then write down what you think the consequences will be of that. Talk with a colleague about this decision so that it is robust.

5. Table C "In the future, who should you be connecting with?"

Name	On what activities?	How could you 'warm up' the working relationship?	Start date

"On what activities?" column

In this column write down the activity that you will eventually be doing with that person.

"How to 'warm up' the working relationship?" column

In this column, think about ways in which you could "warm up" the relationship so that when you need to engage fully with them they are receptive. Such as: -

- Monthly updates on progress and expected timings.
- Visits to the new site, talks from the sponsor or early demonstrations of the new equipment/interfaces.

"Start Date" column

Write a date by when you will have started each activity.

7. Review

At least, every 4 or 6 months review the tables using the steps above and make the appropriate changes.

51. Internal Networking to Improve Your Team's Work

What are the benefits of doing this?

Despite processes and procedures much of working life depends on the quality of our relationships with others. Think for a moment about the difference in your attitude and helpfulness towards someone you are friends with versus someone who you don't know very well. As managers rise through the company these relationships become more and more important, as they become a key ingredient to getting work done smoothly. Therefore, it is important that you have good relationships with all your key stakeholders and influencers, as decisions happen quicker and the path is less turbulent.

In addition, you will find that you are well informed in a broader context so you are able to make decisions more aligned to the business needs. A good internal network is a great source of quality information that can be quickly accessed thus saving hours of research. Also, there is so much information available these days with much of it being of variable quality but you can quickly identify good quality information using your network.

Possible pitfalls and concerns to consider

- Takes too much time / I have more important things to do/ Quicker to do it myself: In the short term it appears to take time but as a way of life, networking takes much less time as you will know things quicker and get decisions accepted easier. When people say "I don't know why he got promoted as he doesn't do very much" what they often mean is that the person doesn't do lots of tasks themselves. Often the point missed is that this person is more effective at ensuring his team's work is effective through building strong relationships with stakeholders.
- It is manipulative/ Wasting other people's time/ They will not be able to help: If you are asking for advice or information then people love to help especially if you also let them know how you benefitted from it. As adults, let them decide if they want to spend some of their valuable time helping you and whether they feel they can help you, rather than you deciding for them. Think about how you would respond if someone asked you for some advice on a topic you knew a lot about?
- Not preparing for the meeting: If you don't prepare for the networking meeting then

you are probably wasting the other person's time and your own. Think of networking as a purposeful conversation rather than just a chat. By preparing you will come out of the meeting with something useful which is why networking is so powerful.

- I shouldn't have to do this to get work done: May be this should be true but often it isn't. On a practical point it is difficult for someone to know what you are doing and how well you are doing it if you don't share this information with them. Sometimes not all networking appears valuable but overall there will be a number of very useful connections and insights that come from it, which makes it worthwhile.

- With people who you know well there may be a reluctance for you to declare that you need some help. Be careful your pride does not get in the way and remember that most effective managers network in some form.

Other relevant chapters
- Chapter 11   Questions That Invite Others to Contribute
- Chapter 15   Listening With Your Eyes, Ears and Intuition
- Chapter 27   Building Rapport

How

Covers five steps that make this valuable

1. Who are your stakeholders?
2. What opportunities do you already have?
3. Create a simple plan
4. The Networking meeting
5. Reviewing

Some of your internal networking will be opportunistic and some of it needs to be methodically planned. For those internal people who you need to have a good relationship with these steps will help you work through how to network effectively.

1. Who are your stakeholders?
(The people you affect and the people who affect you)

List down all the people that are affected by your work or who affect your work: Rank their ability to influence your work, positively or negatively, into three categories: Low (not much), Medium and High (a lot).

Start your internal networking with the people ranked as High. This can be as simple as a quarterly meeting to catch up with the person and to find out what may be different for them since the last meeting. These questions might be useful to discuss: How do they feel your work is going? What might they be doing differently if it was them? Do they have any concerns about it? Has anything changed with their work that would be useful for you to understand?

Other useful questions could be:

o How do our roles interact? How could they help or hinder each other?

o How do you see the company evolving over the next one to five years?

o What challenges and aspirations does your area have in the next year and in the longer term?

Once you are comfortable with this networking then network with as many people ranked as Medium as you can. If you think you do not have enough time to do that then really challenge that thought: Would this be time well spent in the long term and are you just allowing yourself to be distracted by doing things that seem urgent but are really less important?

2. What opportunities do you already have?

In daily working life we often have many opportunities to network that we don't take advantage of. You can turn them into networking opportunities by:

- Meet with someone rather than sending them an email if it's important or a long email would be required. Even a phone call would be better than an email.
- Get advice from three people rather than just one person: Email or call if it is quick and meet up if it is a larger topic.
- When you change roles or start a new piece of work or project, go and talk to people about their views on it. What hopes, concerns and challenges do they have and how can you help them or they help you?
- You think someone might be useful to ask but don't do it: Do it. Email if it is quick or meet with them to have a fuller discussion.
- You think someone might like to know about something or could be interested in something, but don't talk to them about it; Talk to them about it. Email it, take it to them or meet with them to discuss.
- You are making a decision or doing a presentation, consult with people and get their views on it. What do they like about it and what concerns do they have about

it? What needs to be different for them to support the decision or enjoy the presentation?

- You have a problem or challenge. Instead of struggling through it on your own, talk to experienced managers about it and get their advice. How would they handle it? What are their thoughts on it? What advice would they give you?
- Get feedback on your team's performance from Customers and Suppliers. Meeting with people and asking them these three simple questions will give you and your team a wealth of feedback: What are we doing well? What do we need to do less of or differently? What do we need to start doing?
- Accept requests to network with you more often even if you are not sure what you will get from the conversation. People who network well are also very open to networking invitations.
- Get involved in groups who are doing company-wide initiatives or projects to get connected with a broader cross section of managers in the company. Most companies encourage or expect managers to be involved in company-wide activities above and beyond their own role. This can be an opportunity to meet others and network with them outside of those meetings. These people can also help you keep your thinking and perspectives fresh as they are not part of your natural work area. They will ask questions from a different angle that can challenge your thinking in a valuable way.

Therefore, you have many opportunities for informal networking with others or for more purposeful networking with your High and Medium ranked stakeholders.

3. Create a simple plan

A spreadsheet is a useful way to keep track of how often you engage with your High and Medium ranked people from Step 1. It can be as simple as:

Name/ Business area	Reason for maintaining the relationship	How & Date E.g. Meeting, phone call, etc.	Notes

This allows you to easily check when you last networked with a person and when you need to make an effort to meet with them again soon.

4. The networking meeting

When you are going to meet with someone, these are useful stages to go through.

- When you ask for a meeting, tell the person the reason you want to meet with them: Advice about, information on, helping you to think through something, catch up since our last meeting, etc.
- Prepare for the conversation by thinking about what questions you want to ask them. In this way you create a simple agenda and it means that you come away from the meeting with something useful. You do not need many questions to fill an hour's meeting, maybe three to five.
- Take notes during the meeting but do not take so many that you disrupt the flow of conversation or do not appear to be listening. Immediately afterwards write up any notes you were not able to take during the meeting.
- If appropriate, a week to two weeks later let the person know what benefit you got from their advice or what you did differently because of their advice. This lets the person know that you appreciated their time and that their thoughts added value. Also, thank them for meeting which can be as simple as:

"Thank you for your time last week. I made the changes to the presentation as you suggested. It was very well received at the meeting and we can now go ahead with the project which I didn't expect to happen."

5. Reviewing

Every four months review your networking and check that the Low, Medium and High rankings are still appropriate. Add in any new people and rank them. Update your spreadsheet accordingly.

Also think about how your networking has been going:

Reviewing:

1. What worked?
2. What didn't go as you wanted it to?
    a. What can you learn from this?
4. Overall, what have you learned about yourself?
5. What do you need to do differently going forwards?

---

52. External Networking to Improve Your Team's Work

What are the benefits of doing this?

It is easy to be internally focussed but the danger of that is that you become stale and narrow in your thinking. Networking externally can help bring in fresh ideas and keep your thinking up to date as well as keeping you open to new ideas and ways of working. External networks can also challenge your thinking and how you do things as they will have different approaches and experiences. This can stop you from getting complacent about your work and keep you thinking differently about future possibilities.

An external network has a wealth of ideas, knowledge and learning to tap into and really enables you to have a balanced view on your role and the decisions you make. It is also a pool of unknown opportunities that can be very useful to understand and have access to if you need them. I think external networking is a key aspect of career resilience as it keeps you fresh and open to change whilst at the same time connecting you to other possible career options and an understanding of your worth externally.

Possible pitfalls and concerns to consider

- Takes too much time / I have more important things to do: In the short term it appears to take time but as a way of life, networking brings in fresh ideas and innovative solutions to problems thus solving more problems quicker.
- It is manipulative/ Wasting other people's time/ They will not be able to help: If you are asking for advice or information then people love to help especially if you also let them know how you benefitted from it. As adults, let them decide if they want to spend some of their valuable time helping you and whether they feel they can help you, rather than you deciding for them. Think about how you would respond if someone asked you for some advice on a topic you knew a lot about?
- Don't know what to say: This is a good point and I am not suggesting that you systematically force yourself to meet with people. On the other hand, you will have a lot of opportunities and reasons to speak with other people and then you naturally have questions to ask.
- Don't know anyone: This could be true therefore you need to think about networking overtime and building your network over time by using your existing network to open up the ability to meet new people.

- Not preparing for the meeting: If you don't prepare for the networking meeting then you are probably wasting the other person's time and your own. Think of networking as a purposeful conversation rather than just a chat. By preparing you will come out of the meeting with something useful and this is the power of networking.
- At the other end of the spectrum, if the target person is someone who you do not know well there can be an element of shyness or concern about the result of an approach. This can be dealt with in many ways; perhaps connecting through someone else who is on better terms with them or by doing your homework on the person which ensures your approach makes sense.

Other relevant chapters
- Chapter 11   Questions That Invite Others to Contribute
- Chapter 15   Listening With Your Eyes, Ears and Intuition
- Chapter 27   Building Rapport

How

Covers two aspects of external networking and the steps that make it valuable

Networking to help with a problem or project

1. What is the advice or information that you want?
2. Who could help you?
3. Prepare before you call each person.
4. Call and get the meeting.
5. Prepare for the meeting as you need to run it.
6. The meeting and taking notes
7. Afterwards
8. Maintaining your external network

Professional networking to keep yourself up to date and relevant

1. What opportunities are there?
2. Research the options
3. Prepare and attend
4. Afterwards

I consistently find people understand networking and the benefits it creates and still do not do it. There are many common concerns over networking and interestingly enough few turn out to be true. A lot of the time it is the assumptions that we make before we give it a go that cause us anxiety and get us off to a poor start. Think about the last time that someone asked you for some help and advice, how did you respond? Probably very generously and the person you helped was probably very grateful. Remember it is only about exploring ideas and possible options to expand and help your own thinking.

Often concerns or perceptions are created in our minds by making assumptions that we may not have evidence for. We need to realise that we are doing this and stop ourselves. Write down the thoughts and the assumptions you are making. Then come up with other useful scenarios that challenge this thinking and help you move forwards. Also start with people you feel more comfortable with and then expand your network as you grow more confident and are enjoying it.

Networking to help with a problem or project

1. What is the advice or information that you want?

Write down the questions that you have and would like to find the answers to or to find out more about. This forms the basis of your networking and provides a ready-made structure (agenda) for any meetings. It also means that you now have something that you do want to talk about or know more about.

2. Who could help you?

Write down all the people that you can think of that might be able to help you and write down the names of people who you know that might know someone who can help you. The reason for writing all the names down is that one name triggers the memory of someone else and then someone else. It maybe that those later people are more useful to speak with rather than the person you initially thought of. Now you have a list of possible people to speak to.

Next, decide up to 4 or 5 people you will speak to given the questions you want to ask. Meeting a number of people will give you more rounded and informed answers to your questions.

- If you know the person, then you can contact them directly.
- If you don't know the person but have a mutual contact, then ask the mutual contact if they will introduce you to them.

- Asking someone you don't know to help you is less likely to work. So try to find out if you know someone who knows them. If not, then you can contact them although do not be disappointed if they do not wish to meet with you or do not respond to your initial contact. Trying two or three times may get a result as you have shown an amount of effort in contacting them. If it is through an organisation or association, then that may get a better result.

3. Prepare before you call each person

Think about the help you would like and the outcome you wish to get from the call, ideally to get a meeting. Then think about how to handle possible issues around getting the meeting and some fallback options. If they cannot make a meeting, then a video conference call is quite good and is better than just a phone conversation as networking is about building relationships. You may need to do a bit of research about the person and their company or sector, even at this stage.

4. Call and get the meeting

Always try to speak to someone on the phone to get a meeting as it has a better success rate than emails. It shows that you have put effort into connecting with them. Prepare for the call using this structure:

- Orientate them as to who you are and how you know them or the person who recommended you.
- The key element of the call is about what advice or information would you like to get from them?
- Conclude well by asking if you can meet them.

Be polite and firm about what you want rather than passive. Also be careful if you are nervous as you may say things like 'if, maybe not, I know you don't really have the time but...'. Practicing what you are going to say, especially for the start of the call, really helps. Remember to be graceful if you get a 'no' and practice how you will handle that.

After the call reflect on what you learned: What worked and what you would do differently next time?

5. Prepare for the meeting as you need to run it

Your list of questions from Step 1 gives you the meeting agenda, so prepare any background information and your list of questions. This shows them that you are taking the meeting seriously and then they will be happy to give you their time.

6. The meeting and taking notes

Take notes during the meeting although don't let this get in the way of you being able to build a good connection with them. It is very annoying talking to someone who is not looking at you as they have their eyes down writing notes. Partly the meeting is about building a relationship with the person so that you can network with them again. Once the meeting has finished, write down any more notes as soon as possible as there are bound to be lots of things that you were not able to write down.

7. Afterwards

Reflect on what you have learned about how to handle those meetings: What worked and what would you do differently next time?

> Reviewing:
> 1. What worked?
> 2. What didn't go as you wanted it to?
>   a. What can you learn from this?
> 4. Overall, what have you learned about yourself?
> 5. What do you need to do differently going forwards?

If you have promised to send them information, then do that promptly after the meeting and thank them for their time. Otherwise, one to two weeks later send a personal thank you letter or email. The reason for the delay is twofold. Firstly, it puts your name back into their mind so they are more likely to remember you for longer. In addition, it allows you to have done something with their advice. It is much more satisfying for them if you tell them what you did with their advice and how it helped you. It would be worth doing this if you sent an earlier email and have not been able to tell them how they helped you.

Also remember to leave the door open so that you can go back to them again. An easy way to do this is to end your email with a comment such as "I will let you know how it goes" or "I will let you know what outcome we eventually get".

8. Maintaining your external network

It may be that some of the people you meet become part of your external network and it is valuable to meet with them once or twice across the year Also it is easy to stay connected with someone if you use the opportunities you genuinely have. These can be as simple as calling or emailing them to ask their advice about something, sending them a relevant article or internet link, arranging to meet them at a conference or sending them useful course details. Two or three times a year is enough. In addition, you might connect them to people that they would find useful and of course, you might network with someone they ask you to help.

Another simple way to create an external network is to keep in touch with the people you worked with through the years. Many are now in other interesting roles or companies and this is a very useful set of contacts. This is also a two-way process, with that community asking for your help from time to time.

Adding the external contacts to your internal networking spreadsheet is an easy way to manage that. Once a year, review your external contacts and check how often you did actually meet with them: How valuable was it or what is it that stopped you from meeting them? From this review, think about the actions that you are going to take.

Professional networking to keep yourself up to date and relevant

1. What opportunities are there?

Think about different ways in which you can professionally network. These may include:

- Networking groups
- Small group gatherings of like-minded people
- Committees or working groups
- Seminars, conferences or presentations
- Institute or Association events

Also, ask other people what they do.

2. Research the options

Before you commit too much time or money to particular activities, see if anyone can give you information about them as well as researching them on the internet. In this way, you can avoid wasting your time with poor quality events and this is also a good networking conversation in its self.

3. Prepare and attend

As with all networking, think about what outcome you want from the networking event and what preparation you need to do. This could include:

- Researching about the people and who you want to connect with
- Writing down your questions about what you would like to find out
- Reading past meeting notes or other previous material
- When people ask you why you are attending, what is your reply going to be?
- Take notes

4. Afterwards

Reflect on what you have learned about how to handle those events: What worked and what would you do differently next time? If you have promised to send someone information, then do that promptly after the event.

Finally, think about who would you like to connect to further and how you will do that. Perhaps through a 1:1 meeting with them, maybe catch up before the next event or at another event.

Remember also to share your findings with others at work perhaps as a presentation, an update in a meeting or as a report. If you have one of your team going to a networking event them make them do this as it stops it being a jolly and makes them think about their reasons for going.

> Reviewing:
> 1. What worked?
> 2. What didn't go as you wanted it to?
>   a. What can you learn from this?
> 4. Overall, what have you learned about yourself?
> 5. What do you need to do differently going forwards?

References

Bridges, W. (2016) *Managing transitions.* 4th edition edn. Boston, MA: Da Capo Lifelong Books, A Member of the Perseus Books Group.

Brown, P.C., Roediger, H.L. and McDaniel, M.A. (2014) *Make it stick.* Harvard University Press.

Buckingham, M. and Coffman, C. (2014) *First, break all the rules: What the world's greatest managers do differently.* Simon and Schuster.

Burton, K. and Ready, R. (2010) *Neuro-linguistic programming for dummies.* John Wiley & Sons.

Covey, S.M. (2006) *The speed of trust: The one thing that changes everything.* Simon and Schuster.

Dryden, W. (1996) *Overcoming Anger: When anger helps and when it hurts.* London, England: Sheldon Press.

Joines, V. and Stewart, I. (2002) *Personality adaptations.* 1. publ. edn. Nottingham [u.a.]: Lifespace Publ.

Knight, S. (2010) *NLP at Work: The essence of excellence.* Nicholas Brealey Publishing.

Kotter, J.P. (2012) *Leading change.* Boston, Mass: Harvard Business Review Press.

Laborde, G.Z. (1983) *Influencing with integrity: Management skills for communication and negotiation.* Syntony Publishing.

Lencioni, P. (2002) *The five dysfunctions of a team.* 1. ed. edn. San Francisco, Calif: Jossey-Bass.

Lyall, D. (2008) 'Rich Questions in Coaching', *Training Journal,* Jun. pp. 60-63.

Macknik, S.L., Blakeslee, S. and Martinez-Conde, S. (2010) *Sleights of mind.* 1. ed. edn. New York, NY: Holt.

Seligman, M.E. (2004) *Authentic happiness: Using the new positive psychology to realize your potential for lasting fulfilment.* Simon and Schuster.

Senge, P.M. (1994) *The fifth discipline fieldbook: strategies and tools for building a learning organization.* London: Nicholas Brealey.

Index

Accountable, accountability
   Assigning 52
   Holding others to 189, 194-7
   Mindset of 49
Achievement motivation, McClelland 33
Added value 47
Affiliation motivation, McClelland 33
Analogies 124-6
Anchoring 141-5
Anger, overcoming 172
Assumptions 12, 169-70
Attention 83, 91, 104, 107, 162, 192, 242, 297, 315
Auditory, thinking preference 155
Authentic 105, 116

Behavioural issues 292
Beliefs 12, 25, 77, 169, 182, 288
Blame 59, 60, 68, 72, 84, 109, 195, 221, 226, 310, 319
Board layout, improving work activities 313
Breathing, matching 160
Brilliant- Skeptic 31
But 117

Cause & effect 84-6
Celebrate 192, 232, 240-1, 249-50, 255, 311, 320, 323

Change curve, Kubler-Ross 301, 305-7
Charming-Manipulator 32
Chunk size 160
Clarifying 74-5, 85, 219-20, 254-6, 292
Community, sense of 39
Composure 137-51
Conclusions 167-70
Confidence 57, 71, 120, 131, 141, 151, 192-3
Consequences 25, 41, 51, 57, 60, 110, 189-94, 196-7, 290, 292, 330-1
Conversations 11, 26, 40, 44, 53, 56, 64-7, 74-6, 77, 81, 99, 103-6, 107-11, 114-6, 124, 149, 153, 156, 164, 170, 182, 287-98, 337
Creative-Daydreamer 31
   Criticising, criticism 11, 32, 65, 71, 73, 124, 127, 134, 189
Curious, curiosity 10, 11, 24, 28, 73, 84, 109, 168

Decision-making 192-4
Delegating 189-92
Deletions 79-81
Difficult/ unexpected news 294
Distortions 84-7
Doubt, reducing 172-4
Drivers (motivation) 13-14, 25, 29, 33, 268

Index

Emails 199-200

Emotions, handling 296

Endings, Transition Model 301

Engage, engaging 107, 110, 124, 155, 176, 201

Enthusiastic- Overreactor 30

Evidence 115, 263, 273, 278-80, 289-90

Expectations 20, 26, 72, 128, 263, 291, 315

Exploring 75, 108-11

Eye contact 99-101

Feedback
    Giving 127-36
    Interviews for team appraisals 263

Filters 12, 79-87

Five steps to change 301, 303-4

Gap, establish, explore, eliminate 291-2

Generalisations 82-4

Humour 64, 66

Improving work activities 318-23

Influence, conversation design 167-71

Influencing 13, 24, 28, 77, 120, 147, 154, 333

Inspire, inspiring 55, 97, 181

Intention 5, 15, 18, 21, 22, 60, 73, 79, 112, 114-6, 127, 331

Invites 204, 207

Irritability 148

Judgment, getting past 11-23

Kinaesthetic / feelings, thinking preference 155

Ladder of inference, Chris Argyris 168

Language, matching 154-7

Lenses, six 12-17

Match and mirror 157-9

McClelland 32-4

Meaningful work 39, 231, 256

Meetings
    Improvements board 314
    Meeting agenda 205
    Preparation template 207-8
    Purpose of 203
    Structure templates 218, 219
    Structures 213-4, 222-3, 236, 239, 240, 245, 248, 250, 315
    Team, feedback 216
    Timings 205

Mentor 182-4

Messages, intended or unintended 103, 113-6, 186, 196

Metaphors 125

Metaprogrammes 34
    Away from – Towards 34
    Change – Stability 36
    Internally-externally referenced 35
    Options – Procedures 36

Mind reading 84-6

Moaning 65, 124, 307, 310, 319

Motivate, motivating 34-7, 113, 129, 178, 193, 299

Negativity 64-7
Networking
    Internal 333-7
    External 338-43
    Professional 343-4
Neutral Zone, Transition Model 302
New Beginnings, Transition Model 302

Participants 204
Performance issues 290
Personal development plans
    Create 230, 274-83
    Example of 284
    Review 231, 285-6
Personality Adaptations 29-32
Perspective 11-23, 24, 73, 107-11, 120, 146-8, 164-6
Playful-Resistor 30
Positive listings 140
Power motivation, McClelland 33
Praise 129-30
Presuppositions 12-17
Pride, proud 44, 147, 231, 256
Priorities 25, 35, 210, 242
Probing, questions 75, 171, 292, 293
Purpose
    Of meeting 203
    Work 42

Questions 69-97
    For a team analysis 254
    Unavoidable 95
    Unexpected 93
    Unfamiliar 92

Rapport, building 153-63
Rational analysis 139
Reactions 58-63
Reframe; Context, Content 120-3
Relationships 10, 11, 24, 28, 102, 117, 152, 163, 164, 172, 181, 268, 324-44
Reputation 258
Responsible-Workaholic 31
    Rich questions 90-7
Robust, conversations, plans, people 34, 49, 55, 71, 108, 115, 180, 191, 268
Rumours 64, 66, 185

Self-talk 151
Shifting responsibility 84-6
Should 39, 82, 148, 173
Silences, holding 99-101
Social Motives 32
    Achievement 33
    Affiliation 33
    Power 33
Stakeholders 328, 334
Stop, start, continue 253-4
Stories 124-6
Stronger (people feeling), strong (relationship) 31, 32, 55, 60, 73, 152, 180, 195, 330, 333

Style, my 181

Team performance, review 262
Team Systems Model 325, 327
Time, for your people 185-8
Transition Model, William Bridges 300, 301-3

Values 14, 25, 27, 36, 77, 102, 182, 218-9
Visual, thinking preference 155
Visually managing 308-17
Visualising, visualisation 139, 141, 150

Why? 118
Work purpose 39

CPSIA information can be obtained
at www.ICGtesting.com
Printed in the USA
LVHW061342270122
709322LV00015B/242